SEARCHING
FOR
SURNAMES

*A practical guide to their
meanings and origins*
John Titford

COUNTRYSIDE BOOKS
NEWBURY BERKSHIRE

First published 2002
© John Titford 2002

COUNTRYSIDE BOOKS
3 Catherine Road
Newbury, Berkshire

To view our complete range of books,
please visit us at
www.countrysidebooks.co.uk

ISBN 1 85306 765 2

Cover design by
Nautilus Design (UK) Ltd.

Typeset by Technical Typesetters, Newton-le-Willows
Produced through MRM Associates Ltd., Reading
Printed by J. W. Arrowsmith Ltd., Bristol

Contents

Acknowledgements

A comprehensive set of acknowledgements for a book such as this could run to several pages. Scores if not hundreds of individuals have helped me in one way or another over the years, whether they have known it or not. Some have encouraged me, offered sensible criticisms or shared their knowledge or their theories with me. The following list of names, then, is highly selective.

First and foremost I must thank George Redmonds of Lepton near Huddersfield for his friendship and for his unstinting encouragement. George's knowledge of surnames is breathtaking in its depth and breadth, the result of a lifetime's enthusiastic study and close attention to detail. Books on surname study written by George and by his friend David Hey have been a real inspiration to me and to others, and we owe them a great debt of gratitude.

Other friends and correspondents who deserve a specific mention here include: the Archivist and staff of Cambridgeshire Record Office, Cambridge; Richard Baker of the Institute of Heraldic and Genealogical Studies, Canterbury; Michael Gandy of Southgate, North London; Hilary Good of Prudhoe, Northumberland; Duncan Harrington of Lyminge, Kent; Cecil Humphery-Smith, Principal of the Institute of Heraldic and Genealogical Studies; Rev David and Mrs Anthea Jackson; Simon Kirby of Thomas Crapper & Co., Stratford-upon-Avon; Helen Reilly of Treluswell, St Gluvius, Cornwall; Elizabeth Simpson of Tollerton, Nottingham; Nick Vine Hall of Melbourne, Australia and Keith Wilson of Tatworth, South Chard, Somerset.

My wife Heather and I have enjoyed discussing various aspects of surname interpretation together while this book was being written, and I owe her my deepest gratitude for all the support and encouragement she has given me.

Illustrations

I am grateful to the following for providing me with illustrative material and/or permission to reproduce copyright material:

Intellectual Reserve, Inc; Simon Kirby of Thomas Crapper & Co; Andrew Knighton of Ilkeston, Derbyshire; the Public Record Office; Roy Stockdill of Watford, Herts; Eddie Stobart Ltd.

Some material in this publication is reprinted by permission of The Church of Jesus Christ of Latter-day-Saints. In granting permission for the use of copyrighted material, the Church does not imply endorsement or authorization of this publication.

All photographs featured in the book and various photographs on its cover are by the author.

PART ONE:
Studying Surnames

CHAPTER 1

First Things First

They're doing some brisk business down at Ye Olde Surname Shoppe in Somewheresville Shopping Mall:

Bloggs family: the meaning of your family surname! Your family coat-of-arms! Emblazon it on your favourite pair of Nike trainers or on your pet parrot!

The highly-acclaimed American film director John Ford, famous for his spirited cowboy films and for creating the myth that the West was won amidst the buttes and cactuses of Monument Valley in Arizona and Utah, once said that if there was a conflict between the legend and the fact, he would always 'print the legend'. Little has changed: legends about surnames and armorials are daily being printed out by computers in heraldic bucket shops throughout the English-speaking world. All this would be entertaining and harmless enough, were it not for the fact that money changes hands and that some fundamental untruths are being implied, if not stated openly. Without breaking the law as such, purveyors of surname and armorial legends so often pander to the innate snobbery of many of their customers, who would rather believe the legend than be bothered with anything so tedious as proven facts.

Two major myths usually lie at the core of this kind of commercial wish-fulfilment. The first is that there is any such thing as 'the **Bloggs** family' as a whole. All Bloggs may be related, but they may not: the Lincolnshire Bloggs could have acquired their surname quite independently of the Somerset Bloggs, and thus there will be no family connection between them, despite the fact that they bear the same surname.

The second myth is that it is possible to refer meaningfully to a 'family coat-of-arms'. There is no such thing. Heraldic practice and law vary in different countries, but in England, for example, it is usually the case that arms are officially granted to one individual, passing thereafter by right to succeeding generations in a prescribed manner. Armorial bearings, then, rightfully belong to a series of related individuals, not to any family as a whole. You're in no way entitled to a particular Bloggs coat-of-arms just because your name happens to be Bloggs.

Having cleared the ground, then, let's see what we can plant in it.

IS THIS BOOK FOR YOU?

Have you located surnames which interest you in the index to this book and so been able to find out something more about them? Good. This book is clearly for you.

Are there surnames which are a mystery to you which do *not* appear in the index? Even better. I hope that you may find something of lasting value here which will be of use to you not just now, but also in the future.

This is not a surname dictionary as such, though there are several of these around, of varying degrees of reliability. My intention here has been different: I have tried to provide a working guide to surname identification by outlining some historical principles, by trying to dispel some commonly-held myths and by suggesting that it can be a useful ploy not only to examine a surname as a whole, but also to pay some attention to its component parts.

Different readers will no doubt take different approaches here:

- If you are interested in the meaning of a given surname, you might like to read the relevant sections of this book first and try to determine its meaning before having recourse to a surname dictionary to see whether it is listed and explained, and if so, whether or not you have hit the mark.

- If a surname which interests you fails to appear in any readily-available surname dictionary, you're on your own, in which case something or other which I have to say here just might offer a clue which will help you make a breakthrough.

- You might find the subject of surname study fascinating in its own right, as I and many other people do. If that is the case, you could get started straightaway on what could be a life-long interest which will cost you very little and will give you countless hours of pleasure and no little amount of intellectual challenge.

CHAPTER 2

What Are Surnames?

This book will take the British Isles as its focus, though I'll have a word or two to say about names and naming patterns from elsewhere in the English-speaking world and beyond as we proceed, since not only is no man an island, but, to modify the expression somewhat, the British Isles themselves are not merely a group of islands when it comes to language and surnames. We should take this concept on board right at the start, and realise that one of the first challenges we may face in trying to make sense of a surname currently used in the British Isles is to determine which language may have given rise to it in the first place. It may be derived from Old English, from Old Norse, from Middle English or Modern English; it may be Norman French or French in origin, Dutch, German, Italian, Spanish, Hebrew, Greek, Chinese, or from the Indian sub-continent.

Surnames brought to Britain by immigrants from all over the world – be they Sephardic or Ashkenazic Jews, Muslims, Hindus or Sikhs, or those from Africa, China or south-east Asia – might have kept their original form, while others have been anglicised in some way or another. Some immigrants from America or from former colonial territories have brought back to Britain surnames which originated in the British Isles in the first place, and many men, women and children from the West Indies, most of whose family roots lie originally in Africa, will be using British surnames which had been imposed upon their slave ancestors by colonial planters or overseers in charge of sugar and other plantations in the Caribbean.

Britain, then, has been the Clapham Junction of peoples, language and names over many centuries, and we can't afford to be too insular in our thinking. British public officials who come into contact with individuals from ethnic minorities at the present day are rightly exhorted to learn all they can about naming practices which apply in other cultures, and to avoid giving gratuitous offence in such matters.

They will soon learn, for example, that it is not always safe to assume that a person's last name is necessarily an inherited family 'surname' as such, and we wouldn't need to travel beyond Europe itself to find naming practices which do not accord with the British way of doing things.

Leonard R.N. Ashley, in his book *What's in a name?* (Baltimore, USA, 1989), remarks upon the fact that in Iceland, where there are very few surnames, telephone subscribers are listed by their first-names in directories. He goes on to speak of the Hungarians and Chinese, who put their 'last name' first, and of the Spanish custom whereby an individual places his or her maternal family name after that of the father. I'm well aware of this from my own experience: an American friend of mine, Harvey **Good**, whose Nicaraguan-born mother has a maiden name of **Rosales**, refers to himself as *Harvey Good* **Rosales** whenever he finds himself in a Spanish-speaking country. This Hispanic system can become very complex, and can all-too-easily be misunderstood by those not in the know. Ashley quotes the example of a former Secretary-General of the Organisation of American States, who had this to say in 1979: *Galo is my Christian name; Plaza is my [father's] family name; Lasso is my mother's family name. Some call me Mr Plaza, others Mr Lasso. In fact, while I was ambassador for Ecuador in the United Nations, I was called Ambassador Plaza, and people thought I was a hotel.*

In the early days of the Roman Empire, men of some social standing usually had three names of the *Marcus Tullius Cicero* variety. The first of these was a personal name (the eldest son usually inheriting that of his father); the second was a kinship name, leaving the third to be either a nickname/byname of some sort, or a more precise kinship marker. The kinship name was hereditary in the male line, though for most women a feminine version of this was the only name by which they were known.

Russians, too, have traditionally had three names – a personal name, followed by one which is patronymic (ie, the father's name with the suffix *-vich* added for sons and *-vna* for daughters) and then a family surname. When a Russian woman marries, she will normally add a feminine ending to the new surname she has acquired from her husband, though it is possible to see copies of Tolstoy's novel *Anna Karenina* (employing a feminine '*-a*' suffix) which have chosen to use the alternative title of *Anna Karenin* (without the suffix). Characters in novels by **Tolstoy** [*fat man*] and others will commonly refer to each other by both a first and a patronymic name, and Victor **Komarovsky** in *Dr Zhivago* by Boris **Pasternak** [nickname from the word for a *parsnip*], hoping to endear himself to a young lady, says: *Don't call me 'Mr Komarovsky', my dear – call me 'Victor Ippolitovich'.* Not such a romantic-sounding mouthful, we may think?

HOW ARE SURNAMES ACQUIRED?

Surnames acquired in an orthodox way

Surnames as used in Britain can be thought of as inherited last names. The usual or *orthodox* custom is that these will be passed on directly from father to son throughout the generations, but others take more circuitous routes, as we'll see.

Various regions of the British Isles adopted surnames at different periods in history: the Irish were quick off the mark, while many living in the Highlands of Scotland or in Wales only opted for surnames, or had them forced upon them, in very recent times.

We find a few individuals in England bearing a second-name shortly after the Norman Conquest; by the mid 13th century they were being adopted by the knightly class and increasingly by landowners and freemen living in towns, and some decades later we find evidence in most areas of the country that the practice was beginning to spread. This process as a whole has been described very aptly by the surname scholar David Postles as one of *gravity feed*.

Of course, *second-names* are not always the same as *surnames*. At a time when a town or village was filling up with men bearing the first-name *Richard*, some of these could be referred to by pet-forms or diminutives such as *Dick, Dickon, Hick, Hitchcock* and the rest, but in time it was clearly going to make sense to use a second name as an extra distinguishing feature, giving us *Richard Williams, Richard Selby, Richard Black*, and so on. Second-names of this type began to be adopted in mediaeval towns with a large or particularly mobile population some time before the practice spread to rural areas. Initially such second-names – which were as likely to be chosen by a man's contemporaries as decided upon by himself – would constitute what we refer to as *bynames*, and these could be unstable, staying with a man only during his lifetime. If a last-name was unstable, of course, an individual might change it as he moved around the country – so the 14th-century poet Geoffrey **Chaucer** was also known as Geoffrey **Malin** and Geoffrey **de London**. It was not unknown for a person to be accorded not just one byname, but two: the first might describe his occupation, leaving the second to define his place of origin.

Only when bynames were passed on to the next generation can we refer to them as fully-fledged hereditary *surnames* – meaning a *super* (*extra*) name, or from a *sire*-name, depending on your view. So if you come across a man who is accorded a second-name in early documents, don't assume without proof that his children would inherit such a name as their own.

It is the very existence of hereditary surnames that allows family historians to trace pedigrees back through several centuries (with a bit of luck...), and the surname you bear may tell you at least something about some far-distant mediaeval ancestor in the male-line – that he had come from Flanders, that he had red hair, that he was a smith by trade, that his father's name was William – and so on.

If you are to be successful in establishing the origin and meaning of surnames which interest you, it is essential that you take a flexible view as to form and spelling. If it's your own name you are investigating, you simply cannot afford to be too precious about it: for the purposes of surname study, it's simply a specimen to be analyzed in a detached and disciplined fashion, in a way that is as free from any kind of emotional attachment as you can make it. Most surnames have varied significantly over the centuries, being affected by local dialect, intonation, the inability of parish clerks to spell consistently or to write legibly, and illiteracy or speech impediments on the part of our ancestors.

In earlier times various spellings of a surname would have been used almost indiscriminately, according to whim, uncertainty, local usage and pronunciation – or even downright cussedness – and it was not until the 19th century and the advent of compulsory education that some kind of real stability came to surnames, establishing them in the way that we spell them today. Spelling variations of what is essentially the same surname can offer vital clues as to origin or meaning, but whereas genealogists are generally well advised not to get too hung up on such things, there are times when different family branches can be distinguished one from the other according to whether they spell their surname as **Fennymore** or **Vennimore**, or as **Alford**, **Elford**, **Halford** or **Helford**.

Elizabeth and Phil Simpson of Tollerton near Nottingham have long been active in the family history world, and Elizabeth tells me she has never yet seen her mother's maiden surname of **Allmey** featured in any book on surnames. Well, Elizabeth, here it is – not that I can offer any definitive conclusion as to its meaning, alas, though I'll try my best. The Allmeys in question were a Liverpool family whose roots can be traced back through Cheshire to a pair of adjoining settlements in Leicestershire called Kibworth Beauchamp and Kibworth Harcourt, where Elizabeth's earliest known Allmey ancestor, Thomas, was living in the late 17th century. The Allmeys were very much a Leicestershire family, and the family surname can be found in the small village of South Kilworth, near Lutterworth, from at least as early as the 16th century. Known variants are legion (**Allmey**, **Almey**, **Allmy**, **Almy**, **Allmye**, **Almye**, **Allmay**, **Almay**, **Almae**, **Alme**, **Almie**, **Aulme**, **Aulmy**, **Aumey**, **Awemy**, **Awmy** and **Awlmy**), and we might safely assume that the families which used the *aul* or *awl* spelling (if not others, too) would have pronounced the first element in the surname to rhyme with *pall* rather than with *pal*. Elizabeth tells me that her own family favoured the pronunciation *Awl-may*, whereas in Leicestershire it was *Al-mee*. Even more significantly, she also says that, given the present state of her research, she can find an ancestral connection with all the Allmeys (two '*l*'s), but with none of the Almeys (one '*l*'). It would seem highly likely on the face of it that Allmeys and Almeys are related and have common roots in Leicestershire, but in this instance a genealogist has found that a fairly minor spelling variation which may betoken very little in terms of the meaning of a surname does prove useful when it comes to making a distinction between different branches of the family.

As to the meaning of the Allmey surname, there are no easy answers. Given the fact that there are individuals called Agnes **Ameley** and Galfrido **Alwey** in the 1379 Poll Tax returns for Leicestershire, we might be tempted to opt for a place-name origin. If I had to place a bet on it, however, I'd suggest that Allmey could well be a variant on one of two surnames which themselves are derived from Middle English personal names: either **Aylmer** (from *Ailmar*) or **Alvey** (from *Alfwy*), a Nottinghamshire surname which occasionally strayed over the border into Leicestershire. This is in the nature of surname study – that sometimes a balance of probabilities is the best outcome we can hope for.

Some evidence of the kind of inconsistent spelling of surnames that was once so prevalent has survived to the present day. A dictionary may give us an unequivocal spelling for a word like *smith*, but when it comes to surnames we may be transported back to a time when a number of forms of the word were equally valid, and find people at the present day who are called **Smyth, Smythe** – or even **Smijth**. It has always intrigued and mystified me that a person who makes clothes is referred to as a *tailor*, but that the vast majority of people bearing a related surname spell it with a letter '*y*' instead of an '*i*': **Taylor**. *Taylor* and *tailor* would simply have been alternative spellings of the same word at one time, but it's almost as if someone clapped his hands at some point (probably in the 19th century) and barked out instructions to men and women of this surname that henceforth, on pain of death, they must all use the '*y*' spelling... We could say that in matters of spelling, at least, the music has stopped, as it were, and we have to accept what we're left with gracefully, in a world that no longer appreciates or allows further changes to be made. Once the word *tailor* is well-established in dictionaries and a passport announces the fact that an individual's surname is spelt Taylor, then both the word and the surname have become set in concrete for all time.

When it comes to surnames which have changed their shape or spelling significantly over the years – and very many have done just that – it's worth mentioning right at the start a process which is commonly called *folk etymology*. It works like this: if an individual or a family decided to make their home in a new location at home or abroad, they may well have found that their surname caused problems to their new neighbours, who might then have re-shaped the name to suit their own purposes, forcing it to conform with a word in everyday use, a local

Canting arms. The surname of the *Welbore* family of Cambridgeshire would seem to have its origins in the Yorkshire name **Wyldebor** [wild boar]. Thus it is that the **Welbore** coat-of-arms proudly features a fess (shown as a horizontal strip) between three pigs. William Clafton, the artist who drew the arms shown above for his own manuscript version of the *Heraldic Visitation of the County of Cambridge (1575 and 1619)* in 1887, has seen fit to reduce the number of pigs to two, the device being repeated in the first and fourth quarters.

place-name or a surname or personal name with which they are already familiar. Later in this book I will contend that this may be precisely what happened to a man who arrived in Maryland, USA, in the late 17th century bearing the surname **Pennicott**, or something very like it. Almost at once, it would seem, the Marylanders decided that his surname would henceforth be **Petticoat** since that, after all, was already a word in common use and could readily be attached to the hapless Mr Pennicott, whose protests, if he made any, went unheeded. Sometimes ownership of a surname would seem to belong to almost anyone except the poor soul who bears it.

The world of heraldry has made its own contribution to this process of folk etymology, though in a rather different way. A harmless bit of fun much favoured by armigerous individuals and by the heralds themselves over the centuries has been the use of *canting arms*, whereby a heraldic device is chosen because it constitutes a neat pun on the surname of the bearer.

Examples of this practice are legion, and we can choose one almost at random from the Heralds' Visitation of the county of Cambridgeshire for 1619, which features a pedigree of a family called **Welbore**, together with armorial bearings which include *three boars argent*. The Cambridgeshire Welbores are said to have come originally from Yorkshire, and their surname probably represents a corruption of **Wyldebor** [wild boar] and its variants, which are known to have been established in that county from as early as the fourteenth century. So, armorial boars it is.

If we stay within Cambridgeshire and consider the arms borne by a family called **Alcock**, a significantly different picture emerges, however. Visitors to Jesus College, Cambridge, might be quick to spot the arms of the founder, John Alcock, Bishop of Ely, displayed on various buildings and gateways. The surname Alcock consists of a shortened form of one of a number of personal names such as *Alan*, or *Alexander*, followed by the diminutive suffix *-cock*. It is clear, then, that such a name has nothing to do with *cockerels*, yet the worthy Bishop's arms have opted for a harmless play on words, proudly displaying *three cocks' heads razed sable* as the dominant heraldic device.

In cases like this, the heraldic authorities have connived at the folk process which associates a surname with a familiar word, object or creature, regardless of its true etymology. Don't be tempted, therefore, to assume that a name like Alcock has any connection with *cockerels*, just because these appear on a related coat-of-arms.

The process of folk etymology can readily affect place-names as well as surnames. A.D. Mills, in *The place-names of the Isle of Wight* (1996), puts it like this:

*Familiar words which are quite unhistorical but which make a
kind of sense, have replaced unfamiliar or obscure words, or
words which have undergone phonetic change.*

Examples from the Isle of Wight itself include *Dolcoppice*, originally
named after a man called *William Dolecope*, but which acquired the
element *coppice* because this was a known and trusted word in its own
right, and *Bathingbourne*, a corruption of *Beaddingaburna* (*Beadda's
stream*).

Now, I think, would be a good time to risk overwhelming you, and
even dispiriting you, by offering a series of variant spellings of just one
surname – that of **Fennymore**. The family in question probably has its
origins in the Oxfordshire village of *Finmere*, though **Phillimore** and
other variants using a letter '*l*' in place of an '*n*' are not uncommon.
There are several definable branches, and famous bearers of the
surname include the former American President Millard **Fillmore** and
the well-known English genealogist, William P.W. Phillimore, whose
book on the **Fynmore**, **Finnimore**, **Phillimore**, **Fillmore** and **Filmer**, etc
family, published in 1886, includes the following list of known
alternatives, arranged into related groups:

> **Fenemore, Fenimore, Fenimoore, Fennamore, Fennemore,
> Fennimore, Fenymore, Fenneymore, Fennymore, Fennymor,
> Fennemer, Fennemere, Fennimor, Fennymare, Phenemore,
> Phenimore, Phennemere.**

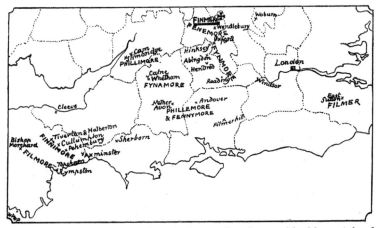

Phillimores from Finmere (Oxon). A map first featured in *Memorials of
the family of Fynmore* by W.P.W.Phillimore (1886), showing the
distribution of variants on the *Fynmore* surname throughout Southern
England.

Finamore, Finamour, Finnamore, Finemor, Finemore, Finnemore, Finneymore, Finnemor, Finimore, Finnimore, Finnymore, Fynamore, Fynamour, Fynamoure, Finemour, Fynemore, Fynnemore, Fynemor, Fynemour, Fynimore, Fynymore, Fynamore, Fynamour, Fynamur, Fynnamoore, Fynnamore, Fynnemore, Fynnemoore, Fynnimore, Fynnymore, Fynymour, Finemer, Finemere, Fynemere, Phinemore, Phinnemore, Phinimore, Phinnimore, Phynimore, Phynnimore.

Venemore, Venimore, Vennemore, Vennimore.

Fillamor, Fillamore, Fillimore, Filyemore, Fyllimore, Fylymore, Philamore, Phillamore, Philemore, Phullemore, Philimore, Phillimore, Philemoor, Phillemoor, Philimoor, Phillomoar, Phullimar, Philomer.

Pillimore, Billamore, Billimore.

Finmare, Fynmer, Fynmere, Fenmore, Finmore, Finnmore, Fynmore, Phinmore, Phynnmore, Finmoore, Finnmoore.

Venmore, Binmore, Benmore, Pinmoore.

Filmore, Filmour, Fillmore, Fillmoore, Filmor, Philmore, Phillmore, Filmer, Fillmer, Fylmer, Fylmere, Philmer, Felmer.

Pilmore, Pillmore, Pilmoor, Pilmour, Pilimoore, Pilmor, Pilmer.

Belmer, Belmore, Bellmore, Belemore, Bellamore.

The intention here, believe me, is not to intimidate you and to warn off the faint-hearted, but to give a flavour of the kind of challenges that may lie in store, and to underline the necessity of taking a flexible and imaginative approach. You can never be quite sure which surnames might or might not have behaved rather like chameleons over the centuries.

Surnames acquired in an unorthodox way

Even within English-speaking communities there are some less orthodox ways in which a person may acquire a surname than the straight father-to-son practice which is the generally accepted norm, though these are very much the exception rather than the rule.

John Pollexfen Bastard.

Fewer Bastards nowadays than there once were. The surname *Bastard* was once more commonly found than it is today. When the term 'bastard' had become a general term of abuse, many families bearing such a name abandoned it in favour of safer alternatives.

Surnames acquired at birth

In cases where a mother is unmarried, or where a child has been abandoned with no clue as to its identity, the customary practice of passing on a father's surname to his offspring will usually not apply.

● *Illegitimacy*

Illegitimate offspring usually bear their mother's surname, though if a child is called something like Ellen **Parker Wilson**, the Parker element could well be a means of perpetuating the known or presumed father's own surname. If the parents of an illegitimate child or children subsequently get married, their offspring could then be given the father's surname instead of the mother's, so a daughter formerly known as Ellen Wilson or Ellen Parker Wilson could become Ellen Parker, named after her father in the usual way.

● *Foundlings*

Not all surnames first saw the light of day as long ago as mediaeval times, and amongst names of more recent origin we can include those given to foundlings.

The story is all-too-familiar: an unmarried mother with a tiny infant whom she has no hope of supporting wraps the precious bundle in a shawl, lays it carefully on the steps of a church and scuttles off into the night. A passer-by stumbles across the tiny baby and presents it to the churchwardens or overseers of the parish, who will then have to pay for its upkeep out of the rates until it is old enough to be apprenticed – if it lives that long.

Sooner rather than later, the hapless child would have to be given a name – a byname rather than a surname, of course, the identity of both mother and father being generally unknown, though a foundling surviving into adulthood could then pass such a name on to any legitimate or illegitimate offspring.

Foundlings might be given a catch-all byname such as **Found**, or be known by the day of the week on which they were discovered. An even commoner practice was to use the name of the street or the parish in which they had been abandoned – though more imaginative strategies were not unknown.

A woman child, of the age of one year and a half or thereabouts, being found in her swadlinge clothes, layed at the Ladye Coopers gate, baptized by the name of Mary Troovie, 10th October 1614. (Parish register, Kensington, Middlesex). This child had thus acquired a French-sounding name (from *trouvé*, meaning *found*), though there was nothing French about her, as far as we know.

Subpena, a man childe found at the Subpena Office in Chancery Lane. Baptised 11 July 1629. (Parish register of St Dunstan in the West, London).

By far the most usual practice, however, is represented by the following examples:

> *Mary* **Throgmorton**, Sarah **Threadneedle**, Jephtah **Minories** (named after the London streets in which they had been found).

Moses **Bartholomew**, Heydon **Trinitie** (named after the
London parishes of *St Bartholomew Exchange* and *Holy
Trinity Minories*). In 1710 the said Heydon **Trinitie** cost the
parish which had adopted him two shillings, spent *on his
Master and all officers when he was Deteckted in Pheaving*.
No gratitude, some foundlings…

It's not only in Britain or in Protestant countries that unwanted babies
are left to the tender mercies of the weather or of the parish authorities:
in *The means of naming* (1998) Stephen Wilson makes the point that a
foundling name like **Esposito** (literally *exposed*) is the sixth most
popular surname in Italy.

Surnames acquired in adulthood

Illegitimate children and foundlings have little enough control over the
second-names conferred upon them at birth, but a not inconsiderable
number of people choose to change their inherited surname once they
reach adulthood.

● *Changing a name as a condition of inheritance*

It is not difficult to find examples of titled or landed families who have
carried the same surname for many generations. Very often this
apparent continuity has been achieved by the transmission of the name
in unorthodox ways in order to ensure its survival, just as quartered
coats of arms are used by certain families to perpetuate one or more
female ancestral lines. When an individual with no living issue has a title
and/or a significant amount of property to pass on to future generations,
it may well be a condition of his or her will – or an ardent expectation, at
least – that the principal legatee should take on the testator's surname
along with the rest of the inheritance. Well-known instances of this
process at work are provided by the case of Florence **Nightingale**'s
father, William Edward **Shore**, who abandoned his own surname and
became Nightingale in 1815 on inheriting the Derbyshire estates of his
mother's uncle, Peter Nightingale, and that of Jane **Austen**'s brother
Edward, who took the surname of **Knight** by Royal Licence in 1812
when he inherited an estate from his father's cousin, Thomas Knight.

● *Choosing a pleasanter name*

Not everyone likes his or her surname, and several ancient names have
all but died out because their bearers have chosen to be known by a
more acceptable alternative.

Such has been the case with the old Cambridgeshire name of **Gotobed** (used originally of a lazy person), which may be found on many a tombstone in that county, but is a great scarcity in modern telephone directories. If the meaning and origin of a given surname have become obscured over time, however, its bearers may feel safe enough in continuing to use it. The eminent American family of **Kennedy**, for example, can probably rest assured that few people will know that the original Celtic meaning of their name is *ugly head*.

Names have more power than we might at first realise. We may say that a successful person has *made a name* for himself or herself, or speak of the *illustrious name* borne by some families which enjoy particular status and power. Names are an essential part of our image whether we like it or not, and as such can clearly affect social relationships, making other people keen to know us or eager to avoid us. I have a young god-daughter called *Holly* **Popple**; this seems to me to be a delightful name, and I can well imagine that her contemporaries at school have been only too keen to get to know her as a result. People with a high public profile, especially those in the world of entertainment, know very well that an attractive name can boost their chances of success in an image-conscious world, and many have invented a fancy stage-name or screen-name for themselves as a result. *Cary Grant* is a more memorable name than Archibald **Leach**, and an actress called *Marilyn Monroe* promises to be more fun than one named Norma Jean **Baker**. The American film and music industries are awash with examples of stars who have been only too keen to abandon a foreign-sounding name in order to give the impression that they belong to the Anglo-Saxon mainstream: *Jack Benny* was originally Benjamin **Kubelsky** [Polish, from the village of *Kubeldzie*]; *Eddie Cantor* was Edward Israel **Isskowitz** [from the given name, *Isaac*], *Bob Dylan* was Robert Allen **Zimmerman** [German, *carpenter*] and *Woody Allen* was born Allen Stewart **Konigsberg** [German town name]. In England, Jan Ludvik **Hoch** chose to be known as *Robert Maxwell*; Lew **Winogradsky** achieved great success in the media world as *Lew Grade*, while his brother opted for a more radical change of name and became *Bernard Delfont*.

Interestingly enough, a reverse process can sometimes set in: the best-selling American author, *Irving Wallace* (1916-1990), born in Chicago to Russian immigrant parents, had a son who decided to re-adopt his father's original surname with new-found pride, and calls himself David **Wallechinsky** [Russian, Velichanskij, from the village of *Velika*].

Anecdotal evidence suggests that many public figures and others who have taken on a new surname become genuinely attached to it and it to them, even to the point where it is passed on to the next generation and acts thereafter as a genuinely hereditary name. A particularly fascinating example of this process at work can be observed in the case of the American film actress *Jamie Lee Curtis*. Both her parents

An adventurous life. In adult life a gifted West African boy named *Adjai* became *Bishop Samuel Adjai Crowther*. [From *The Church Missionary Gleaner*, volume one (1874)].

were well-known Hollywood film stars: the real name of her father, *Tony Curtis*, was Bernard **Schwartz**, and her mother, *Janet Leigh*, had originally been named Jannette **Morrison** when she was born in California in 1927. *Jamie Lee Curtis* thus inherited not one, but two, screen surnames from her father and mother.

● *Change of religion, change of name*

A man or woman who undergoes a religious conversion as an adult may well feel that the time has come to adopt a new name to reflect a change of persona. *Saul of Tarsus*, onetime persecutor of Christians, famously underwent a dramatic conversion on the road to Damascus and achieved lasting fame under his new name of *Paul*. *Cassius Marcellus Clay*, born in Louisville, Kentucky, achieved a different kind of fame as a heavyweight boxer of world renown, and changed his name to *Mohammed Ali* once he had become a Muslim. Another convert to Islam was *Steven Demetre Georgiou*, born in 1948 to a Greek Cypriot father and a Swedish mother, who made a success as a singer under the name *Cat Stevens*, but eventually chose to be known as *Yusuf Islam*.

The life of *Samuel Adjai Crowther* (c.1809-1891) reads like something out of an adventure novel. Born with the name *Adjai* in the early 19th century at Oshogun in the Yoruba country of West Africa, he was sold into slavery whilst still in his teens, and was put on board a ship bound for America, only to be rescued by a British cruiser and taken to Sierra Leone, where he was converted to Christianity and baptised on 11 December 1825, taking the name of a Church of England minister, *Samuel Crowther*. His exceptional abilities as an evangelist, translator and administrator eventually brought him to the attention of the Church Missionary Society and of the Anglican establishment, and in 1864 he became the first native African to be consecrated a Bishop, with jurisdiction over the Niger Territory. By his wife Asano Susan, the Bishop had several children, all of whom inherited his adopted **Crowther** surname, and his son Dandeson Coates Crowther became Archdeacon of the Niger Delta. A *crowther* was originally a man who played the *crowd*, a mediaeval stringed instrument; related surnames include **Crowther**, **Crowder** and **Crother**.

So much for adults who choose to change their surname; I need hardly add that changed names and aliases have also long been favoured by the criminal fraternity, keen to escape detection. In Britain, at least, changing a surname is an easy enough matter. You don't need anything elaborate like a Deed Poll, though these are available for those who wish to pay for them; you simply inform your family, your friends, the tax man and the bank manager that instead of being *Fred Blooper*, you are now *Fred Nerk* – and you get on with your life bearing this new identity. Oddly enough, it is your baptismal name (if you have one) which you cannot change, except with great difficulty. Your surname, after all, is simply an added name and, surprisingly enough, you can change it at will.

Surname aliases

When researching ancestral surnames in parish registers and in other records, you might come across two surnames yoked together in this way: **Smith**, *alias* **Jones** or **Jones**, *alias* **Smith**. Quite often one of these alternatives will be abandoned entirely, or the two surnames may be fused permanently into a double-barrelled surname: **Smith-Jones**.

These aliases, often shown as *als* or *otherwise*, can have arisen due to a variety of circumstances. If a mother remarried, her children might take the surname of their new step-father, with their original surname as an alias – or *vice-versa*. Illegitimacy often gave rise to the use of two surnames; a child might bear the maiden surname of the mother and also the surname of the father. When a couple were not married, the common-law wife may be entered in records under her maiden name, with the surname of her partner as an alias. Any children born to the couple might bear this same double surname. Some tenants who held copyhold land in more than one manor would be known by a different form of an alias in each, so a man might be referred to as *James* **Knighton**, *alias* **Emery** in one manor, but *James* **Emery**, *alias* **Knighton** in the other. Sometimes the term *alias* is used when there are two or more possible spellings of the same surname (*Matthew* **Cook**, *alias* **Coke**), and aliases of this sort can provide vital evidence that specific variants of a name were actually used in the real world.

You'll find that I have dealt in more detail with the subject of surname changes and aliases, together with nicknames and other related topics, in *Succeeding in family history* (2001), pages 7 to 49.

CHAPTER 3

Some History

I suppose I ought to say, without wishing to intimidate anyone, that surname study can be more complex than it may at first appear, and for one very good reason. The fact is that until very recent times many names have been dynamic – that is, they have changed and developed, just as the language which gave rise to them has not stood still but has also grown and moved on.

As we take our first steps into the 21st century, with officialdom breathing down our necks and Big Brother watching us at every turn, we've grown used to the fact that surnames and place-names – not to mention the millions of words that make up the English language as a whole – are essentially stable entities and, for that matter, are spelt in a way which never changes from year to year. If this were not the case, then we'd find it a nightmare to try to use telephone directories, gazetteers and dictionaries; the tax man wouldn't be able to keep tabs on us, ID cards or passports would lose their value as identifiers, and we'd have a hard job convincing the insurance company that we were genuine policy holders when it came to making a claim.

We tend to take this degree of stability in the written and printed word for granted, to assume that matters were ever thus. Not so. A degree of linguistic consistency has increasingly been an essential element in the smooth running of advanced Western democracies with their generally literate populations, but it has only been in comparatively recent times that an individual could be expected to give an accurate response to a question such as *How do you spell your last name?* or *What is the correct spelling of your full postal address?*

Yet even at the present day, language is at best only a semi-domesticated beast. Ultimately it belongs not to government officials or to pompous arbiters of correct usage such as the *Académie Française*, but to the people who use it as an everyday means of communication, who write or type it – and, above all, who speak it, since ultimately the spoken word (which is where language first began) still has primacy over the written forms which seek to represent it. Beneath the calm exterior of state control lies a heaving mass of language *as she is spoke*.

A CHANGING LANGUAGE

If we wish to make sense of the idea that language is a dynamic medium, then initially we need look no further than our own times. In what ways has language moved and changed before our very eyes and ears, during the lifetime of people alive today?

Words and expressions have come and gone

Words like *chump*, *bounder* and *cad*, new and fashionable in their day, have long since passed out of everyday use, but we've welcomed, or learned to live with, countless new coinings, imports or modified meanings. *Cyberspace*, *digital*, *nimby* (not in my back yard), and *dinks* (double-income, no kids) are all new words.

Not just words, but entire phrases enter the language as if from nowhere – and some make an undignified exit after a brief spell in the limelight. Such was the case with that most redundant and clumsy of expressions, *at this moment in time*; just as the American grey squirrel almost drove out the British red variety, so *at this moment in time*, an American import, once seemed to threaten the very existence of its more modest British equivalent, *at the moment*.

I wouldn't want you to think that I reject all new language usage or vocabulary out of hand, or that I don't appreciate the best of the linguistic novelties that Britain has imported from across the Atlantic. *At the end of the day* (to coin a phrase...), it is America which has given us such gems as *couch potato, fuddy-duddy, nutty as a fruit cake, pass the buck, going cold turkey* and *gate crasher*. Add to all this the language of rap and of the drug culture, throw in some underworld material including a smattering of home-grown British rhyming slang, and you've got a heady linguistic mix which can be a sheer delight.

Existing words and expressions have acquired new meanings

Speakers of the language not only have to come to terms with neologisms (freshly-coined words), but also have to be sensitive to the fact that a number of familiar words and expressions have acquired one or more new meanings.

A classic instance of this process at work in recent years is provided by the word *gay*, now universally recognised as a term meaning *homosexual* and so leaving the original sense of *happy, jolly, cheerful* to linger in the mid-distance as a kind of sub-meaning. The word *gay*, orginally an adjective only, can now also be used as a noun; behaving as nouns do, then, it can take on plural form *gays*, giving us a word that would have been incomprehensible to speakers of English a few decades ago.

And what of the verb *to grow*? You could always *grow tomatoes*, but only in the last few years or so have you been able to *grow a business*. I take it that this means to *expand a business*; if so, it would seem to be a redundant addition to the language. There was a time, too, when you would *address an envelope*, but now you can *address an issue* (and *take it on board*), especially if you're a politician who intends to take no action, but wants to be seen to be doing something.

Dictionaries, of course, come after the event, not before it, and are always playing catch-up as the language evolves, twists and turns, takes on words and new expressions, gives new meaning to old words, uses adjectives as nouns and nouns as verbs, trying to reflect the language as it is used in everyday communication. And although many new words or linguistic usages are now born in cyberspace and spread like wildfire through written media such as e-mails, it is in the mouths of speakers of the language that linguistic fashions including slang, jargon, colloquialisms and trendy catch-phrases are primarily born, developed and then retained or rejected.

Fashions in pronunciation change

People can get very hot under the collar when it comes to the pronunciation of the English language, berating their fellow-speakers for saying *controversy* instead of **controversy**, or lamenting the fact that a literate population now tries to pronounce words as they are spelt, regardless of older conventions. So the letter '*t*' is now commonly given its full force in the word *often*, much to the horror of traditionalists, while what was once *Saturdee* has become *Saturday*, *forred* is now *forehead* and *weskitt* is *waistcoat*. I once asked a group of Tunisian students who were paying a visit to Derby to tell me which pronunciations used in the Midlands differed from those taught them at school back home; saying nothing about regional pronunciation as such, they all focused instead on the fact that Derby people said *often*, pronouncing the letter '*t*', where they had been taught to say *offen*. Now *often* is a classic example of what is known as a *spelling pronunciation*, whereby certain speakers who are able to read the language begin to bring their pronunciation in line with what the spelling seems to suggest, rather than continuing with a traditional pronunciation which had orginally been developed amongst a generally illiterate society. All of this, of course, can have implications for the way in which surnames are pronounced in an age of universal literacy.

Fashions in pronunciation, like those in vocabulary, do change before our very ears. If you listen carefully, you'll hear that what had once been the usual pronunciation of the word *good* is giving way, in the mouths of trendy young things, to something approaching a Scottish, tight-lipped version of the word, so that something or other can be described as being *really, really* **guid**. Even more dramatic headway is being made, thanks partly to the influence of the media, by *Estuary English*, a style of pronunciation which has its origins in the eastern fringes of London around the Thames Estuary, and is much beloved of *Essex Man* and *Essex Woman*. To speak *Estuarese* you need to sound something like a slightly upmarket Cockney, to say *fink* instead of **think** and to lard your speech liberally with glottal stops – that is, to close off the sound as you speak, rather than pronounce a full letter 't', rendering *tomato* as *toma'o* and saying *wha' a lo' o' li'lle bo'les* instead of *what a lot of little bottles*. Is this, then, where the future lies?

Changes in pronunciation over many centuries can account for the fact that a certain number of British surnames seem not to be pronounced in the way in which they are spelt. The English language is generally a model of efficiency and simplicity in matters of grammar, but the relationship between the way in which words are spelt and the way in which they are pronounced can appear on occasions to be somewhat arbitrary if not downright bizarre. Sometimes there is a good reason for this – as with the word *knight*, which acquired its spelling at a time when it would have been pronounced *kernicht* rather than *nite* – but on other occasions we just have to grin and bear it, especially where place-names and surnames are concerned. It may not even have dawned on us that the usual pronunciation of *Leicester* does not match the spelling, until we hear a non-native speaker come up with a spoken version such as *Lye-sess-ter*. Many an unwary traveller in Gloucestershire must have wondered where *Sissester* might be, before realising that it was a local pronunciation of *Cirencester*, and the Duke of Rutland's principal country seat in Leicestershire, though it is spelt *Belvoir* Castle, is pronounced *Beevor*. Not so far away, the inhabitants of *Southwell* in Nottinghamshire still seem divided as to whether they live in *South-well* or *Suthall*, and the local Round Table group which meets in the town refers to itself, only half-jokingly, as *South-well and Suthall and District*.

Sometimes surnames are user-friendly enough to cast aside the formal spelling of the place-name which gave rise to them, in favour of one which truly reflects the pronunciation, giving us **Wooster** (*Worcester*), **Bister** (*Bicester*), **Ensor** (*Edensor* in Derbyshire), **Pomfret** (*Pontefract*), **Norridge** (*Norwich*) and **Bro(m)mage** or **Bromidge** (*Bromwich*).

Beauchamp's Pills. *Beecham* is a user-friendly variant on the surname *Beauchamp*, and reflects the usual pronunciation of that name.

By contrast, certain families who like to keep themselves at arm's length from *hoi polloi* can make life more difficult, rather than simpler, by insisting that their surname be pronounced in a way that you would hardly guess at from the way in which it is spelt. This is especially true of surnames with a French origin: **Fiennes** is pronounced *Fines*, **Grosvenor** is *Grovenor*, **Beauchamp** is *Beecham* and **Villiers** is *Villers*. The **Waldegrave**s might suggest, politely, that you should refer to them as *Waldgrave*; the **Cholmondeley**s prefer the pronunciation *Chumly*, the **St John**'s are *Sinjun* and the double-barrelled **Leveson-Gower**s are *Looson Gore*. And I suppose that if you had the longest surname in the English-speaking world, **Featherstonehaugh**, then you, too, would be happy to see it shortened in everyday speech to *Fanshaw*.

Booby-traps also lie in wait North of the border. Many years ago, young and impressionable, I purchased some books in a John Menzies shop on Princes Street, Edinburgh; when I asked whether I should make out a cheque to *John Menzies*, I got the very sniffy reply that the acceptable pronounciation was *Mingis*, if you please.... If I were ever to bump into that intimidatory shop assistant again, I'd now have great delight in pointing out the fact that the name **Menzies**, however it is pronounced, is a corruption of the French place-name *Mesnières*. In a similar way, and with equally unimpeachable historical precedent, the surname **Dalziel** is pronounced *Deeyell*, while **Auchinleck** is *Afflek*. Once we have those sorted out, we'll need to pay some attention to **Marjoribanks** [adopted in the 16th century, it is said, by the family of **Johnston** when they acquired lands of this name in Renfrew which had once belonged to Robert the Bruce's daughter *Marjorie*], which is commonly pronounced *Marchbanks*. And that's just the beginning...

Dialects and accents

It has only been in comparatively recent times that London-based officialdom has learned to tolerate, if not to appreciate, the plethora of non-standard dialects and accents which exist throughout the British Isles.

While the standard English language is changing and its store of regularly-used words is both growing and contracting all at the same time, various dialects continue to flourish, be they particular to a country, a region, a town or village – or even to one family or to one individual, whose own unique turn of phrase would constitute what is known as his or her *idiolect*. Many regional dialects used throughout Britain have a pedigree which is every bit as worthy as that of the standard language itself, and it is very often the case that dialect speakers are simply using older forms of the language which have been left behind in a kind of time-warp. So the second-person singular pronoun *thou*, which was once part of the mainstream but has long-since been abandoned in both written and spoken Standard English, is still alive and well in the mouths of dialect speakers, especially in the Midlands and the North, complete with its associated forms of *thee*, *thy* and *thine*. Whether you use and understand dialect words such as *lake* (play), *netty* (lavatory), *jitty* (narrow passageway) or *nesh* (susceptible to the cold) will depend upon where you were born or have lived for any length of time, and although Standard English may insist on a reflexive form like *myself*, it could whistle in the wind in the face of regional variations such as *mesen* or *mysel'*.

Attempts to standardise the vocabulary and grammar of the written and spoken language, to establish what we refer to as Standard English, date from the 14th century, when what was initially just one among several dialects of English centred on the influential power-base of London, Oxford and Cambridge began to acquire particular prestige. The success achieved by Standard English in the centuries which followed has been considerable but by no means complete; it has been said that only 12% of the population were speaking Standard English at the close of the 20th century, though many more were able to write it in some fashion or other. The standardisers were eventually at work, too, in matters of accent, with the result that particular prestige has long been accorded to what is known as *Received Pronunciation* – formerly thought of as *Oxford* or *BBC* English, which has a strong south-of-England and social class bias. Even fewer speakers in modern times speak with an RP accent, as it is known, than speak Standard English – a mere 3% at the latest count. *Dialect*, incidentally, refers to non-standard features of vocabulary or grammar, while *accent* is a matter of how you pronounce the words you speak – whether they be Standard English or local dialect words. Accents, like dialects, can vary according to locality, occupation, class, age and gender.

Just as words which once belonged to the main stock of the language have been left behind to the point where they are regarded as quaint regional colloquialisms, so some features of accent which were once unequivocally RP will now clearly identify speakers as coming from somewhere outside London and the south-east.

In 1791 John Walker, a writer with a special interest in language in general and pronunciation in particular, first published his *Pronouncing dictionary*, which sold millions of copies over the years and was still in print as late as 1904! Walker is nothing if not prescriptive and intolerant; in his mind there was one acceptable manner in which to pronounce each word in the English language, local dialect notwithstanding, and his book indicates by the simplest of phonetic systems what that pronunciation should be. Present-day readers from the south of England may be surprised to discover that even mid-19th-century editions of Walker still carried his instruction that the word *grass* should be pronounced with a short '*a*' (to rhyme with *lass*). As it happens, a short '*a*' sound in a word like *grass* and a full '*u*' sound in *summer* or *love* were once the norm rather than the exception throughout England, though they are now used almost exclusively by speakers from the Midlands or the North. In the 14th century the poet Geoffrey Chaucer, London-based as he was, would have used a short '*a*' and a full '*u*' in this way, and speakers of RP have only replaced the short '*a*' sound by an '*ah*' sound (as in *grahss*) in the last two centuries or so. Despite variations in the pronunciation of these '*a*' and '*u*' sounds, present-day speakers of English from different regions of the country clearly have no problem in understanding each other. I've taken part in conversations in Derbyshire where the surname of a man called John **Last** [a cobbler, or a maker of cobblers' *lasts*] is pronounced with a short '*a*' by local speakers but with a long '*a*' (*Lahst*) by those who hail from the south of England.

Walker's *Dictionary*, then, is great fun to browse through. Here you will find that he pronounced the word *herb* as *erb*, and that *balcony* was closer to its Italian origins, with the stress on the second syllable: *balcohnee*. These days most Americans still say *erb*, a pronunciation which has long since been abandoned by their British cousins. *I plant* **erbs** *in the* ***fall*** sounds oh-so-American to English ears, yet the pronunciation *erb* (herb) and the word *fall* (autumn) are original features of the language which the English have rejected, leaving Americans, in this instance, to speak in a more traditional way.

Despite the attempts of generations of educators and officials, a rich variety of dialects and accents exists throughout Britain even at the present day, most of which are regional in nature. The fact that we are surrounded every day by a standard written and printed variety of English, and that television and radio have presented us until very recent times with an unabated diet of standard southern-based English, pronounced with an RP accent, has served to mask the fact that English as it is spoken in the 21st century is infinitely more varied in terms of its vocabulary, grammar and pronunciation than we might have thought. If we imagine a time in the late 13th or 14th centuries when many surnames were first being adopted, when there was no standard version of the language to aspire to, and when local dialects and accents would have been far more distinctive – not to say incomprehensible to outsiders – than they are today, then we can begin to see how naïve it would be of us to expect to find even the degree of linguistic consistency we expect in our modern world when we are dealing with names which first saw the light of day during the Middle Ages.

English is fundamentally a Germanic language which was brought to a land which they themselves would refer to as *England* by Angle, Saxon,

Jute and Frisian invaders from the fourth century AD onwards, and which drove out the original Celtic languages almost completely in the process, or forced them to the geographical and cultural fringes of Britain. Viking invaders from the 9th and 10th centuries spoke what we now refer to as Old Norse, a language which could meld very readily with Old English, but the arrival of a further group of Vikings from Normandy in 1066 posed a more serious linguistic challenge. The Normans used a variety of French which, together with written Latin, could in theory have eradicated the English language entirely during the next few centuries. Nothing of the sort happened: English promptly went underground, simplified its grammar, borrowed as many French words as it found useful, and ultimately emerged during the 14th century, robust and healthy, a new hybrid which we refer to as *Middle English*, which could hold its head high as an official and literary language as well as a vernacular one.

So at the time when many surnames were first beginning to appear, the English language which gave rise to them was still learning to come to an accommodation with Norman French, and was under infinitely less centralised control than it is today. This is something to think about if ever we are tempted to expect surnames to be constant and consistent throughout time and place. Some are, but many are not.

I hope to have made the point here – at some length, admittedly – that written and spoken language has changed over the centuries, and is likely to continue to do so. Surnames are a part of that language; most were born in an era of linguistic flux, have lived through changes in fashion and usage over the centuries, yet are still with us today. Some arose from the standard language, others have their roots in dialect usage; some are based upon occupations, place-names or descriptive terms for the human body or spirit which have long-since vanished; many would be pronounced differently in various parts of the country and might or might not travel well; some have died away, others have been significantly altered, elements being added or subtracted. Above all, most are survivors in one form or another, and could be thought of as a national treasure in their way, one which we would do well to appreciate.

Incidentally, perhaps it goes without saying, or perhaps it doesn't, that a significant number of surnames can have more than one possible origin. Eve McLaughlin makes the point firmly and with a touch of humour by using the surname of **Cock** as an example: *A Cock could be a cook, a watchman (getting up early), a hill dweller, an arrogant person (strutting like a cock), rather randy, a small boatman, a diminutive of Isaac, or just a young lad.* Be warned...

CHAPTER 4

Collecting and Analysing Surnames

You might choose to expand your interest in surnames to the point where you become fascinated by any unusual specimens that you come across; if so, you'll find that you can collect these almost anywhere – in the home, in the street, on the open road, listening to the radio, watching television, reading modern or historical works of fact or fiction – and so on. Jot down ones which you find intriguing or challenging, give them some thought, apply some basic principles, and see what you end up with. Your success rate should improve as time goes by and you gain experience.

A surprising number of people find it possible to carry a surname with them every day of their lives without once stopping to think what it might mean. This being the case, you might like to amaze and entertain your friends by offering them some ready-made explanations. Do be careful, though: some apparently innocuous names have embarrassing origins which you might like to keep hidden for fear of offending the faint-hearted, though others might be relieved to find that the surname **Belcher,** for example, need not necessarily have anything to do with the indelicate expulsion of wind through the mouth.

Just how inexpensive a pastime can this be? You might notice that I'm fighting shy of seeming to trivialise the matter in hand by using the word *hobby* here, but you know what I mean. You can make it almost as cheap as you like, and even if you decide to delve deeper, a good deal can be achieved initially without leaving what the advertisers insist on calling *the comfort of your own home* and what I would think of as your armchair or the firm, virtuous seat you use when you're staring at the computer.

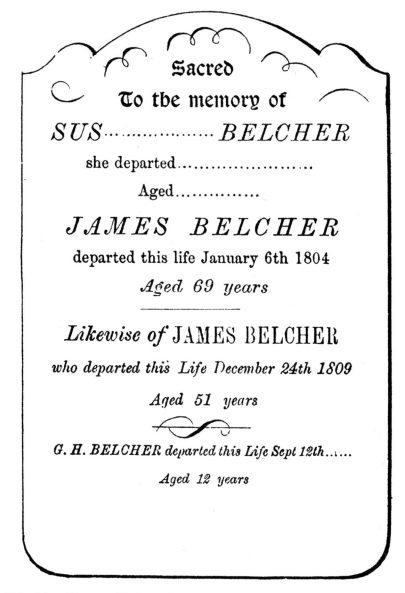

Sacred

To the memory of

SUS ·················· *BELCHER*

she departed······················

Aged··············

JAMES BELCHER

departed this life January 6th 1804

Aged 69 years

Likewise of JAMES BELCHER

who departed this Life December 24th 1809

Aged 51 years

G. H. BELCHER departed this Life Sept 12th········

Aged 12 years

Fair of face. The most likely explanation for the origin of the surname *Belcher* is that it is a corruption of the French *bel chere* (fair face). [From *Memorials of the Old Meeting House and burial ground, Birmingham* by Catherine Hutton Beale, 1882].

USEFUL RESOURCES: BOOKS

The first essential, once you've decided that you'd like to take matters a little further, is to buy or borrow one of the more reputable surname dictionaries which are readily available. All works of this sort are necessarily selective, and none has all the answers, so my advice would be to try and obtain copies of at least two or three of the classic books which I am now going to list:

C.W. Bardsley's *Dictionary of English and Welsh surnames* was first published in 1901 but has been reprinted many times since. For several years I was content to use Bardsley and little else; he is thorough and thoughtful in his own way, and his book is still extremely useful, but surname study has moved on and conquered new heights since his work first saw the light of day, and he can now seem rather old-fashioned both in his choice of names and in some of his explanations.

P.H. Reaney's *Dictionary of British surnames* first appeared in 1958; later editions with corrections and additions by R.M.Wilson bear the more strictly accurate title of *A dictionary of English surnames*, and you can now purchase one of these in paperback at a very affordable price. Reaney was a dedicated scholar of the subject, and he offers a number of very helpful examples of surnames being used in early written records. Modern scholars have had reservations about some of his work, however, since he appears not to have taken sufficient account of the fact that many surnames died out when those who bore them fell victim to the Black Death, which ravaged the country during the 14th century, or to similar but less severe outbreaks of plague and other fatal diseases.

P. Hanks and F. Hodges' *A dictionary of surnames* (1988) is a substantial and scholarly work, and I am only too happy to acknowledge the fact that I have found it to be of immense value in compiling this present book. Its arrangement has something of the inspirational about it: surnames with the same or very similar meanings (like **Baker**, **Bacher** and **Baxter**) are grouped together for the purpose of explanation, and access to all the names included can be gained by way of an index at the back.

By the time Hanks and Hodges published their dictionary in 1988, surname studies had moved on a great deal since Bardsley and Reaney, so that many convincing new meanings and origins are included, and a number of old myths laid to rest. The compilers also had the good sense to enlist the help of a number of professional and amateur family historians as they moved towards publication, many of whom have registered their interest in one or more specific surnames with the *Guild of One-Name Studies [GOONS]* (Box G, 14 Charterhouse Buildings, Goswell Road, London EC1M 7BA), whose members are dedicated to helping each other in their researches. After all, a dedicated family historian who carries out an in-depth study into particular surnames will very often know more about them in detail than any number of scholars whose own focus cannot afford to be so narrow and precise.

Basil Cottle's *The Penguin dictionary of surnames* (1967). This does not purport to be as detailed as some of the above works, but it is easy to use and entertaining, and should be readily affordable in paperback.

A number of other surname dictionaries published in the 19th and 20th centuries are listed in the bibliography at the back of this book. There are separate works on names used in the Isle of Man, Cornwall, the United States of America and elsewhere, but special mention should be made here of the following:

The surnames of Wales by John and Sheila Rowlands (1996) is a useful and very well-informed work by a dedicated husband-and-wife team of family historians.

Welsh surnames by T.J. Morgan and Prys Morgan (1985). A scholarly introduction is followed by an alphabetical dictionary featuring a selection of Welsh surnames in detail.

The surnames of Scotland by G.F. Black (first published in 1946, and reprinted since) is a wonderfully informative book with a great deal of historical detail.

Irish names and surnames by Rev P. Woulfe (first published in 1923, reprinted since). Woulfe takes an unashamedly academic approach, and you'll need to develop a nodding acquaintance with Irish letter-forms in order to work your way through his alphabetical lists.

The surnames of Ireland by Edward MacLysaght (first published 1964) is more user-friendly than Woulfe, yet still very informative, and can be found in paperback at a reasonable price.

USEFUL RESOURCES: DATABASES ON CD-ROM

It's possible to make great strides in the study of surnames using the printed word alone, but I'd like to move on a stage further and make the assumption that you have a computer and can use it to perform fairly straightforward tasks. Not that you need to be a computer *nerd* as such – just that you won't be intimidated at the thought of accessing information stored on a CD-ROM or made available on the Internet.

I'll restrict myself here to mentioning a mere handful of CD-ROMs and one principal internet site which can be a real boon when it comes to studying surnames. You'll notice that most of these are produced by, and/or intended for, family historians, and I'll have something to say in a moment about the link between surname research and family history.

The following CD-ROMs are easy enough to obtain, and can all be purchased at a remarkably cheap price:

WM. MARWOOD,

EXECUTIONER,

CHURCH LANE,

HORNCASTLE,

LINCOLNSHIRE, ENGLAND.

James Berry,

EXECUTIONER.

8, BILTON PLACE.
BRADFORD. YORKS.

Telephone : FAI

Albert Pierrepoint,

Licensee :
Help the Poor Struggler

303 Manchester Road,
Hollinwood, Manchester.

UK Info Disk

This consists of a remarkable collection of information, taken from electoral rolls and from the BT directory enquiries database, which links the names of over 50 million individuals in the United Kingdom to an address and (where available) a telephone number. The basic version of the CD-ROM is offered at a cheap price, and has even been given away free as a cover disk with a computer magazine. The more advanced so-called *PRO* version is more expensive, and provides a number of all-singing, all-dancing search facilities and maps which you might feel you could live without at this stage.

UK Info Disk can have a number of uses, but what is of particular relevance to us here is that it will allow you to type in any surname and to see at a glance what its present-day distribution is across the United Kingdom. If you so choose you can compile distribution maps based upon the information provided; somewhere in such a map might lurk the place of origin, the epicentre if you like, of a surname which interests

Opposite page: **The hangman pays a call**.

William Marwood (1820-1883), a Horncastle cobbler and the inventor of the 'long drop' style of hanging, was paid a retainer of £20 per year, together with £10 (plus expenses) for each execution he carried out. He augmented his income by selling his hanging ropes and the personal effects and clothing of his victims as souvenirs. Significantly enough, although the surname *Marwood* can have a place-name origin, it was also a Norman nickname for someone who had the power to cast the 'evil eye'.

James Berry. Born in Heckmondwike, Yorkshire, in 1852, son of a woolstapler, James Berry was a police constable and a shoe salesman before replacing William Marwood as the official hangman in 1884. He hanged 134 people in an eight-year period, though he had the unfortunate habit of decapitating not a few of his victims by mistake. He underwent a religious conversion later in life, and died in 1913. As an English surname, *Berry* has its origins in the Old English word *Burh*, meaning 'a fortified place'.

Albert Pierrepoint. Born at Clayton in Yorkshire in 1905, Albert Pierrepoint came from a family of hangmen. He achieved his lifelong ambition of becoming the official executioner in 1940, and succeeded in getting the rate of pay raised from £10 to £15 for each successfully-completed job. There were other perks, too: Albert always said that he 'liked the travel', and he put paid to a number of Nazi War Criminals on the mainland of Europe during the 1940s. In 1946 he took over a pub in Manchester called, appropriately enough, 'Help the poor struggler'; finally retiring ten years later, he promptly led a campaign for the abolition of capital punishment. The surname *Pierrepoint* has its origins in any one of a number of French place-names.

you. Knowing where a surname originated can often be a vital clue in helping to determine its meaning, especially if it is derived from a place-name.

To obtain details of the latest issue of the *UK Info Disk* I'd recommend that you conduct a search on the Internet – or, more prosaically, you can keep your eyes open for a relevant advertisement attached to the entrances of a number of English motorway service station lavatories. I jest not!

1881 British census on CD-ROM

Unlike *UK Info Disk*, this set of CD-ROMs has been produced with the interests of family and local historians chiefly in mind. It was only a few years ago that a project was inaugurated by the British Genealogical Record Users' Committee and the Genealogical Society of Utah, whereby the whole of the decennial census taken in 1881 for England, Wales and Scotland would be transcribed and indexed. This mammoth task was brought to completion thanks to the sterling efforts of the Church of Jesus Christ of Latter-day Saints and of volunteers working under the guiding hand of the Federation of Family History Societies. The results have been made available on microfiche (county by county, with a national index), and then on a set of 25 CD-ROMs; do be aware, however, that the microfiche listing is strictly alphabetical in its arrangement, whereas the CD-ROM version groups some known surname variants together.

The LDS Church has also published a similar index on both microfiche and CD-ROM for the 1851 census, covering the counties of Devon, Norfolk and Warwickshire only.

Dedicated family and local historians have had a field-day with the 1881 census database ever since it was published, since it covers the country household-by-household and contains voluminous regional and national name-indexes. Herein lies its main value for surname studies: as with *UK Info Disk*, you can plot the distribution of surnames, here at the height of the Victorian period, and migratory patterns across the country are clearly evident when a person's stated place of birth is different from his or her place of abode in 1881.

The *1881 census on CD-ROM is* available at what I can only describe as a bargain price from: LDS Church Distribution Centre, 399 Garretts Green Lane, Birmingham B33 OUH.

National Burial Index

In 2001 the Federation of Family History Societies, ever active in the field of genealogical publishing, produced its *National Burial Index*, the result of several years' work by constituent societies and members up and down the country. The index is available on two CD-ROMs (burials 1538-1825 and 1826-2000), and features over five million names taken from parish, nonconformist, Roman Catholic and cemetery registers throughout England and Wales.

Now an index such as this, though its coverage is uneven so far, can act as a further guide to surname distribution, taking us back in time, in some instances, to the 16th century. It is hoped, incidentally, that many more entries will be made available in future editions of the index.

The National Burial Index on CD-ROM can be purchased at an exceptionally reasonable price by writing to: FFHS (Pubs) Ltd., Units 15-16, Chesham Industrial Centre, Oram Street, Bury, Lancashire BL9 6EN.

Another useful resource I should mention here is the **Genealogical Research Directory** (GRD), which is published on CD-ROM as well as in book form. Here you will find an alphabetical listing of surnames being researched throughout the world, keyed in to the names and addresses of individuals who are known to have a particular interest in each one. The GRD should tell you at a glance which locations are known to be associated with each surname at a given period in time, and may thus hold a few surprises in store.

USEFUL RESOURCES: DATABASES ON THE INTERNET

The Internet is astonishingly rich in information which is of use to anyone conducting research into family history or into the meaning and origins of surnames. There is a host of family history sites, some free of charge and some demanding fees; not only that, but you can use your favourite search engine (*Google, Dogpile,* or whatever) to obtain information on a given surname – especially if it is unusual and distinctive. Just type it in and prepare to be bombarded with information which you can then sift and sort. A web-site which describes itself as being *devoted to the resources available for the study of the distribution, incidence and statistical analysis of the surnames of Britain, mainly post 1837...,* though which does not generally include information on the history or etymology of individual surnames, may be found at: http://homepages.newnet.co.uk/dance/webpjd.

A number of interested parties, including academics from the University of Essex, the Institute of Heraldic and Genealogical Studies and elsewhere, are currently giving some thought to the compilation of a *Thesaurus of British surnames,* which will focus principally on spelling variations rather than on surname origins and meanings as such. It is intended that any database which is produced as a result should be made publicly available, and we might well hope that the Internet will eventually be used for this purpose.

The International Genealogical Index

Of all the currently available web-sites devoted to aspects of family history, none can compare with the *International Genealogical Index*. The IGI, as it is known, has been developed over many years by the Church of Jesus Christ of Latter-Day Saints (Mormons), who have a special interest in genealogical matters. The IGI consists of a series of single-line entries providing information about literally millions of individuals throughout the world. Britain is strongly represented; a certain amount of miscellaneous information from various sources is included, but the essential core of the British index is its collection of baptism and marriage entries taken from parish registers, mostly pre-dating the advent of national civil registration of births, marriages and deaths in 1837. Genealogists throughout the world have been using the IGI for many years; originally available on microfiche and organised county by county for most parts of the British Isles, it has recently been produced on a set of CD-ROMs, which may be consulted at a number of libraries and institutions, but is also now available free of charge on-line at www.familysearch.org. The arrangement is country-wide for the British Isles – a luxury indeed for those who wish to map and to plot surnames, and can now do so at one fell swoop. The earliest entries in the IGI date from the first half of the 16th century, so you can find yourself moving back nearer and nearer to the point of origin of most surnames – and can examine closely the changes in form and spelling of such names over time and place.

The IGI has its faults, which are well-known but which don't detract from its great value to family historians and surname-seekers alike. Some entries will have been mis-transcribed, some will have been made by inexperienced or unsuccessful researchers who have found little, but are essentially asking the same questions as you are asking yourself; many parishes will not have had their registers transcribed, or there may be gaps in the coverage (consult the *Parish and vital records listing* to determine how matters stand here); adult baptism will not be noted as such – and so on. Do remember, in short, that you might be able to learn a lot from what is included in the index, but should draw no firm conclusions about what is NOT there, and that – if you are carrying out serious and detailed pedigree work and not just a more generalised surname study – you should make arrangements to check the original record for every event which interests you.

So a caveat needs to be entered here, and it applies not just to the IGI but also to the CD-ROMs I have recommended and to family history sites on the Internet: I would exhort you to be sceptical about the claims made by some optimistic (or dishonest) individuals that they have traced their own ancestry back for countless generations using CD-ROMs or the Internet alone. Genealogists are fond of saying that computer-generated and other databases are only a *finding aid*, when all is said and done. That means that they can be invaluable in pointing you in the right direction, but should not be assumed to be totally accurate or complete in all cases. Most databases consist of nothing more than a series of entries which are copies of copies of copies of original records, each of which may or may not have been accurately made; only the original record itself will constitute anything approaching incontrovertible evidence, and you should endeavour to trace information back to its source whenever you possibly can.

One of the beauties of using the IGI on the Internet is that you can do so at very little cost, and in the process you can access a range of information that was never readily available to the intrepid compilers of surname dictionaries working earlier in the 20th century. There has been a process of democratisation at work here which now allows dedicated researchers outside the world of academia to make a real contribution to surname studies. If you choose to make an in-depth examination of a number of names in which you have a particular interest, it is quite likely that you will become the world expert on each. That is in many ways a very satisfying stage to have reached, though it can also be a lonely experience; if no one knows more than you do on a given subject, there is no one to whom you can readily turn for advice. You're on the cutting edge, *pushing the outside of the envelope* as they say, and you're on your own. Now you'll know what explorers, radical thinkers and researchers in arcane areas of knowledge have had to contend with for centuries.

CHAPTER 5

A Genealogical Approach
to Surname Study

Families and surnames are inextricably related; the study of one must involve a study of the other, and to gain a full understanding of any surname you'd be well advised to pay close attention to its behaviour and its distribution in a historical context, to give as much consideration to the families who have carried it down through the generations as to the name itself in isolation. In essence this means taking an approach which is not dissimilar to that employed by *genealogists* and *family historians*. In practice there is often very little difference in meaning between these two terms, but if we are forced to distinguish between them, we might say that *genealogists* tend to be concerned primarily with the precise nature of the family relationships which bind individuals together – with pedigree-work if you like – leaving *family historians* to be at least as interested in placing a family within its historical, social and geographical context.

We should take it as an article of faith that the further back in time we are able to take a surname, the greater the chance of our being able to determine more precisely where it might have originated and what it means. This is especially true, for example, of surnames based upon the name of a place, be it large or small, where a journey back in history should bring us ever closer to the place-name origin. Not only that, but even the most basic research programme which moves us back through the generations should throw up variant forms and spellings of a surname which might offer a clue as to its meaning.

Modern surname scholars such as George Redmonds have emphasised precisely this point, and his book *Surnames and genealogy: a new approach*, originally published by the New England Historic Genealogical Society in 1997, and again by the Federation of Family History Societies in 2002, is a seminal work which I cannot recommend too highly. George offers us a timely reminder that in the last analysis every surname is unique, in that it begins life by being attached to one individual at a specific moment in time. *The surname detective* by Colin Rogers (1995) and *Family names and family history* by David Hey (2000) also adopt a genealogical approach, and make entertaining and stimulating reading. David Hey's book is only the tip of a very large iceberg; his sterling work over many years for the University of Sheffield's Surname Project and his interest in Staffordshire surnames is reflected in a number of published works.

One of the major failings of older surname dictionaries is that they have tended to treat surnames out of context, as some kind of linguistic challenge unrelated to genealogical evidence. Some scholars have recently begun to redress the balance, and a series of *Radio Four* programmes on surnames presented by George Redmonds in 2001 was also able to incorporate the results of relevant DNA research by Professor Brian Sykes at the University of Oxford; his work, together with that of others in the field, has enabled the skills of the geneticist to complement and to augment the findings of surname scholars and genealogists, and this is truly a ground-breaking approach which opens up a number of new avenues for future research.

Brian Sykes carried out his own investigation to determine whether there might be a provable biological relationship between a number of living individuals who shared his own surname. Each provided a collection of cheek cells for analysis, and the 'Y' chromosomes – those which are inherited through the male line and so which, in principle, follow the surname – were compared. The results were truly impressive: around one-half of fifty male Sykeses had exactly the same 'Y' chromosome, suggesting that they share a common male-line ancestor. But what of the other participants? Their 'Y' chromosome patterns resembled those of the population at large, suggesting that, although they carried the Sykes surname, they may belong to a line descended from a different ancestor of this name, or there had been some 'non paternity' event in the past such as adoption, illegitimacy, or a change of name. Such research, then, can be very exciting – but is not for the squeamish!

Studies into mitochondrial ('MT') DNA, which is transmitted down the female line, are also gaining momentum and producing some exciting results. Old and new technologies are thus coming together, answering some existing questions but also posing a whole host of fresh ones. Already a number of 'One-name' family organisations have made use of what DNA comparison has to offer, and such an approach promises to make a major contribution to a major research programme such as the Great Migration Project, sponsored by the New England Historic Genealogical Society, which is attempting to trace the genealogies of the five thousand or so families that crossed the Atlantic in the 1630s. You may run, we may say, but you can't hide your DNA...

Other fresh approaches to the challenges posed by surname studies include the careful compilation of distribution maps which show the location of a given name at different historical periods, and which can often help to pinpoint its origin. The work carried out by Professor Kevin Schürer of the University of Essex and others for the Historical Censuses and Social Surveys Research Group is making great headway in this area of research.

For all the impressive work being carried out in major seats of learning at home and abroad, you don't need to be a university professor to begin to make your own contribution to the world of surname study. Amateur students of surnames and genealogy, like amateur astronomers, have their own important part to play in widening the skirts of knowledge. If you decide to adopt a genealogical approach to surnames – and it can be an enormously satisfying activity at almost any level – then the sooner you can become familiar with the relevant digital, printed and written material which is now widely available, and the more knotty problems you should stand a chance of solving. You may be familiar with basic genealogical techniques already, or you may not. If this is new territory to you, then let me – modestly – recommend that you read a basic but comprehensive illustrated guide such as *Tracing your family tree* by Jean Cole and John Titford (third edition, 2001). If at some stage you need a much larger, detailed and definitive work on the same subject, you will find nothing better than *Ancestral trails* by Mark Herber (1997). Both books are updated by their authors on a regular basis.

My genealogical friends would never forgive me if I were to give the impression that meaningful pedigrees could be compiled by lifting information almost at random from databases or printed books. Genealogical research needs to be far more disciplined than that, as you use original records to move painstakingly back in time, proving and confirming each generation as you go. With surname study it is different: detailed genealogical work would certainly never come amiss, but the books and digital sources I have listed above provide an excellent starting point for research, offering at least some information about the existence of thousands of surnames in certain places at certain times. Above all, perhaps, they can help you determine how surnames have changed in spelling or form over the years. The IGI, for example, yokes together what are presumed to be established variations of any one name in a consolidated listing; take this as a useful but not unimpeachable guide, but do come up with possible variants of your own and see if the IGI has featured any of these separately. Take the surname **Palethorpe**, for example, which has its origins in the

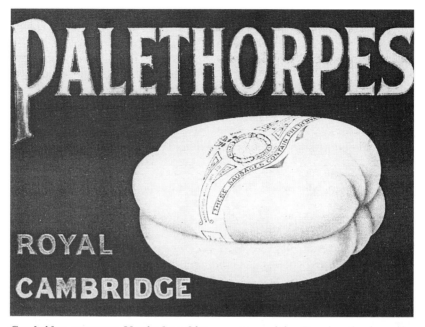

Cambridge sausages; Nottinghamshire surname origin. People who bear the surname *Palethorpe* have their far-off origin in a Nottinghamshire village now known as *Perlethorpe*.

Nottinghamshire village of *Perlethorpe*. An IGI search on **Palethorpe** will throw up an interesting set of variants, but there are no entries of an earlier date than the 17th century. Only if it had struck you that an alternative early spelling could be **Parlethorpe**, and you were to enter that as a separate search, would you unearth the earliest IGI references to the surname, dating back to the 1570s.

You'll find that a number of indexes, particularly in the USA, favour the *Soundex* system of grouping together name variants in a rational way; unexpected discoveries can sometimes result from such an approach.

When using the name index to a printed book, try to establish what principles have been adopted: are the surname varieties **Culpin**, **Culpan** and **Culpon** indexed separately, or are they brought together in one entry and cross-referenced accordingly? Indexes which do consolidate known variants can be of enormous value in alerting you to alternative spellings you hadn't previously considered, and over the years I have found many indexed calendars of wills and administrations to be particularly useful in this respect.

CHAPTER 6

Opening Quiz:

Test Yourself!

ARE YOU ALREADY A SURNAME EXPERT WITHOUT KNOWING IT?

When it comes to the subject of surnames, we all carry in our heads a very significant amount of raw material ready to be used when the occasion arises. Let me encourage you to lay this book aside long enough to carry out your own mental trawl of the surnames you are familiar with – those of your friends, your relations, workmates and neighbours. Does each person bear a common or a rare surname? Can you guess what all the names might mean, or attempt to establish where they might have originated?

My own view is that if you have even a nodding acquaintance with British surnames, acquired through meeting people, reading, travelling and generally keeping your eyes and ears open, you'll already be more of a surname expert than you might think.

Let's try a short test at the outset. I'm an avid collector of old books which include lists of names, biographies and photographic portraits or sketches of individuals. Some of the most fascinating publications which fall into this category are histories of various non-conformist chapels up and down the country. Using some of these as a basis, let me offer you one or two short lists of names to ponder. The challenge is very simple: can you determine from the group of surnames given in each case where the chapel might be based? A county or region – or even a country within the United Kingdom outside England itself – would constitute a sufficient answer here. I'll begin with the lists, then provide answers at the end.

THE QUIZ

- **Surname List One:**

These men were all ministers at a Baptist Chapel during the 19th and 20th centuries:

> John **Jenkins**; John **Evans**; Rhys **Jones**; Daniel **Davies**; Robert **Williams**; David **Rees**; Thomas **Morgan**; Richard **Lloyd**; Bertie Hubert **Lewis**.

- **Surname List Two:**

The following children were baptised at a Free Church during the second decade of the 19th century:

> Alexander **Grieve**; Margaret **Muir**; Thomas **Fotheringam**; David **Sinclair**; George **Leslie**; Andrew **Davidson**; James **Fraser**; James **Wilson**; James **Thomson**; Isabel **Wallace**.

- **Surname List Three:**

These individuals are 19th-century members of a Methodist church:

> James **Barbet**; Jean **Noel**; H.R.**Angel**; James **Cochrane**; Jean **Le Page**; Jean **Valpy**; Daniel **Knight**; Jean **Ozanne**; William **Clark**; Joseph **Collenette**; Adolphus **Le Cheminant**; Denis **De La Rue**; T.C. **De Putron**; J.D.**Robilliard**.

- **Surname List Four:**

Here are some late 19th- and early 20th-century leaders, trustees and Sunday School teachers in a nonconformist chapel:

> Annie **Sugden**; Florence **Garthwaite**; William **Kershaw**; Edgar **Frankland**; Alfred **Holdsworth**; Sarah Hannah **Murgatroyd**; Herbert **Ridehough**; Edward **Rawnsley**; Joseph **Dewhirst**; Daniel **Holroyd**; Lily **Hardaker**; Annie **Barraclough**; Isaac **Haigh**; Annie **Capstick**; Martha **Pickles**; Asa **Ackroyd**; Eliza **Stockdale**; Skirrow **Beanland**; Fred **Shackleton**; Arthur **Crabtree** – and (no first names provided): Mrs **Sutcliffe**; A.C.**Longbottom**.

Lancastrians and others. These worthy-looking gentlemen were all officials of the Preston (Lancashire) Savings Bank at various times. The surnames *Pilkington* and *Isherwood* are both derived from Lancashire place-names, and *Bibby* [from *Isabel*] is also mainly met with in the county. Robert Benson had been born in Ulverston, and his surname (meaning 'son of *Ben/Bennet/Benedict*', or from *Benson*, Oxfordshire) can be found over a widespread area, but although *Pedder* [a fast runner] would seem not to have its origins specifically in Lancashire, Edward Pedder's family are known to have been in the Preston area from at least as early as the mid-seventeenth century. [From *Souvenir of the Preston Savings Bank 1816-1907*. 1907].

- **Surname List Five:**

These names are taken from 19th and 20th century memorial tablets in a Unitarian Chapel:

> *Gerald* **Allingham**; Louis **Blumfield**; Alexander **Bruce**; William Benjamin **Carpenter**; Mary **Courtauld**; Alice **Drummond**; Gordon **Hollingsworth**; Laurence **Johnson**; Mabel **Montgomery**; Arthur **Roscoe**; Alfred **Schuster**; Thornton **Williams.**

THE ANSWERS

- **List One:**

(South) Wales. From: J.R. Williams and G. Williams, *History of Caersalem, Dowlais, Welsh Baptist Church*. 1967.

Notice the large number of surnames ending with the letter '*s*', which in many cases is a genitive ending meaning *son of*: **Davies** was originally *son of David* and **Jenkins** was originally *son of Jenkin* (John).

- **List Two:**

Scotland (Orkneys). From: *The Centenary Book of the East United Free Church, Sanday* [Orkneys]. 1913.

Some surnames here, like **Muir** or **Sinclair**, are very distinctively Scottish; **Wilson** is not necessarily Scottish, though surnames ending in *-son* are more commonly found in northern parts of Britain than in the South; the spelling of **Thomson** (without a '*p*') is a strong indication that it is Scottish rather than English. **Fotheringham** is an interesting case. It sounds very English, and for a good reason – namely, that the place which gave rise to the surname, *Fotheringham* near Forfar in Scotland, was named after *Fotheringhay* in the English county of Northamptonshire, at a time in the 12th century when the royal family of Scotland held *Fortheringhay* as part of the Honour of Huntingdon. What makes this Orkney list easier to identify as coming from some part of Scotland, of course, is the Christian names *Alexander*, *Andrew*, *James* and *Isabel*; all are used throughout the English-speaking world, yet taken as a group they give a decidedly Scottish feel to the name list.

- **List Three:**

Channel Islands (Guernsey). From: Harry Shaw, *A short history of the Methodist New Connection in Guernsey*.

The mixture of English and French surnames (and some French Christian names) should be a giveaway here. **Noel** could be either French or English, and **Cochrane** is essentially Scottish, but **Collenette** is indisputably French, as are the names which are preceded by the French definite article *Le* (masculine) or *La* (feminine), with or without the preposition *De*.

On the face of it this list could emanate from any of the Channel Islands, and only a person familiar with the region as a whole could be expected to know that **Ozanne**, for example, is a distinctively Guernsey surname.

• List Four:

Yorkshire (West Riding). From *One hundred years of Primitive Methodism in Great Horton: a brief history.* 1924.

Great Horton is near Bradford in Yorkshire. Many of the surnames featured here are based upon Yorkshire place-names, and some – like **Sugden, Holdsworth, Murgatroyd** and others – have been known in the Bradford area for centuries. **Kershaw** is one of the jokers in the pack; it could emanate from a minor place-name in the parish of Halifax, but is more likely to have its origins in a place called *Kirkshaw*, in the parish of Rochdale, Lancashire. Note how typical many of the Christian names are of their period: *Florence*; *Edgar*; *Alfred*; *Herbert*; *Martha* – and even *Asa*. *Skirrow* would seem to be a one-off coinage, a surname being used here as a first-name.

I would say that you've done quite well here if you were able to determine that the names in this list were *northern* in a general way, with a flavour of John Braine's novel, *Room at the top*, about them. If *northern* is the best guess you could make, then further experience should help you feel more confident about ascribing these kind of names to a more precise locality in due course.

• List Five:

(North) London. From: *Rosslyn Hill Chapel: A short history 1692-1973.* 1974.

This has not been a trick question, but one which might take our thinking a stage further. While many individuals who were members of Welsh, Scottish and Yorkshire chapels over the last hundred years or so are still the proud possessors of surnames which have been known in their localities for generations, here in Hampstead, North London, we have an eclectic mix of names, bearing testimony to the long-established pulling-power of the capital city as a place offering new opportunities to migrants from Britain and abroad.

Some names in this list, such as **Allingham** [from place-names in Kent and Lincolnshire] and **Carpenter** [an occupational name], are probably from the southern half of England, while **Roscoe** is from a place-name in Lancashire, and **Hollingsworth** from Lancashire or Cheshire. **Bruce** and **Drummond** are both Scottish, while **Blumfield** and **Schuster** have a decidedly Germanic ring to them. The original English **Courtaulds** were among the more successful Huguenot refugees who fled from mainland Europe to escape religious persecution, and **Courtaulds** has long been a familiar trading name in England.

PART TWO:
Surname Identification –
A Do-It-Yourself Guide

CHAPTER 7

Surname Surgery 1:
The Surname as a Whole

You'll only really know whether you're making progress as a definer and identifier of surnames once you're on your own, removed from any kind of life-support machine. I've chosen the expression 'surname surgery' here because the process of examining a surname seems to me to be something akin to what a surgeon does during an operation, or what takes place during a post-mortem examination.

What follows, then, is intended as a kind of step-by-step do-it-yourself guide. I'm going to suggest that you look at a surname as a whole and then, if necessary, that you examine its component parts. Finally I'll change metaphor from surgery to nut-cracking and offer a number of case studies which suggest ways of approaching surnames that obstinately refuse to yield up their meaning despite the most intense scrutiny.

INITIAL EXAMINATION

Take your surname and prepare to conduct an examination of it. It might be a useful idea to write down the name in question in bold capital letters on a piece of paper, and work on it like a scientist examining a specimen on the laboratory bench. Try to take a holistic view of the name long before you make a closer examination of its various components – in other words, take a general look before resorting to the microscope. Stand back from the name, take a look at it from a distance and let your imagination wander. Speaking it out loud may help unlock its meaning. We can take an example from outside the world of surnames to prove the point: the meaning of the Old English word *Cwen* might not be immediately obvious in terms of its spelling; speak it aloud, and it should snap into focus as the original form of the modern English word *Queen*. Try to pronounce the name which has baffled you using a range of funny accents, if that is one of your party tricks. Try it out on friends and relations. Is it a long name or a short name? Might it have been lengthened or shortened during its lifetime? Is it a crisp, muscular name or a soggy, flabby one? Prod it, change the letters around, read it forwards and backwards, see if you can make it yield up its meaning.

Does it appear to be an English name or a foreign-language name – or a foreign language name adapted for the English language? Might it come from Scotland, Ireland or Wales? You might not have much trouble in deciding that **MacDonald** is Scottish, that **Murphy** is Irish or that **Jones** is Welsh (usually, but not always...) – but subtleties of spelling might take you a stage further, and it's worth knowing, for example, that **Millar** and **Johnston(e)** are common Scottish spelling variants on the names **Miller** and **Johnson** (though Johnstone can also be derived from a place-name in Annandale, Dumfries).

SURNAMES CLASSIFIED

Few writers on surnames have escaped the temptation to come up with a classification system of one sort or another – if only in an attempt to impose order upon chaos. The exercise is certainly a useful one, and I'll offer a classification scheme of my own, with no claim at originality. To concentrate your deliberations at this stage, consider the broad categories given below. Your mystery name clearly fits in here somewhere – but where?

- Surnames which are *patronymic* (based upon a father's given name) or *metronymic* (based on a mother's given name).

- Surnames which are *occupational* (based on a trade or occupation) or are derived from a person's *official status or office*.

- Surnames derived from *physical appearance or personal characteristics*.

- Surnames based upon *places (1): topographical* (based upon general features of the landscape).

- Surnames based upon *places (2)*: *toponymic* (based upon named locations).
- *Miscellaneous* surnames, with a variety of origins.

It may be that you cannot establish the meaning of a surname yourself, despite determined efforts, or else that even so-called experts in the field claim that no such meaning has been unearthed. For your own purposes, then, you could invent a category entitled something like *Origin unknown, unknowable or uncertain*. Do try not to consign too many mystery names to such a dustbin of despair; it's a last resort, and suggests that you've failed despite bringing your best efforts to bear.

Let's take each surname category in turn.

PATRONYMIC AND METRONYMIC SURNAMES

Patronymic surnames

The father's name unchanged
The practice of sons and daughters adding their father's name to their own is the oldest method used to distinguish individuals one from the other. Eventually many *patronymics*, as they are called, developed into full hereditary surnames.

Sometimes the father's given name is left entirely unmodified once it is used as a surname, so **John** or **Thomas** are both surnames in their own right.

A given name that is used in this way might be one that is immediately obvious to you, or it might seem strange and perplexing – either because it has long-since fallen out of use as a first name, or because it is from a language with which you are unfamiliar.

So, looking at surnames like **Fulcher**, **Fulger** or **Fullager**, you could hardly be expected to know that they have their origin in the long-lost given names *Folker* or *Fulker*, without some help from a friendly scholar or a surname dictionary.

Most English people will have heard of the surname **Kinnock**, otherwise spelt **Kinnoch**, **Kinnach** or **Kynoch**. The problem of identification here is that the personal name which gives rise to the surname, *Coinneach*, is not Old English, nor Old Norse, nor Norman in origin, but is Scots Gaelic. The best-known recent bearer of this name, Neil Kinnock, is the descendant of a Scotsman who emigrated to the Welsh valleys.

Male first-names which were popular in England before the 11th century would seem unusual or even quaint to us today, though some survive in a modified form as modern surnames. The Old English *Cenweard* or *Cyneweard* has given us the surname **Kennard**, while the

Old Norse personal name *Thorkell* has survived in a modified form as the surnames **Thirkettle**, **Tuttle** and a whole host of variants. Following the Norman Conquest, such names were steadily replaced by others which were Germanic in origin but which had been adopted by the French, such as *William*, *Robert* and *Richard*. The fact that this new stock of first names was a limited one (by 1350 one third of all Englishmen were called *John*), despite the availability of pet-forms and diminutives, had two major effects: first, that the need to distinguish one man from another became more acute, since so few first-names were being used – and secondly, that it was these post-Conquest names that formed the basis of most patronymics and surnames which developed in mediaeval times.

The father's name modified
Changing other people's names is always regarded as great sport, perhaps because, in a way, it is an activity which reminds us of our childhood, when all language was new, unfamiliar and exciting. School-children can be highly imaginative and even merciless in this regard, but the habit persists into adulthood. We must all know people who are known by a pet-form of their surnames, used almost as a nick-name. I've worked for a man called Mike **Clegg**, referred to by his friends as *Cleggy*; John **Tams**, well-known in Derbyshire and beyond as a song writer and performer, answers to the name of *Tam*; the footballer Paul **Gascoigne** was always *Gazzer*, and at work my father got off lightly, I guess, by being known as *Titty*.

Above all, however, it is first-names that almost cry out to be modified. When I first opened a current account in the 1960s, a name-plate outside the bank would have announced that the manager was *Mr J.K. Smith*, or some such. Nowadays it's likely to be *Jim Smith*, *Jeff Smith* or even *Joe Smith*. I've watched friends of mine struggle very hard to convince new colleagues and acquaintances that they wish to be called *Steven*, *Peter*, *David* or *Valerie*, since everyone falls into the *Steve*, *Pete*, *Dave* and *Val* mode as a kind of fail-safe – almost as if they, not you, are the owners of your name.

This nickname habit goes back for centuries, to a time long before *Terry*s were *Tel* and *Barry*s were *Baz*, and very often it was the pet-form of a first name that gave rise to a surname which was passed on to later generations. Some pet-forms from earlier centuries are still used extensively: Thomas and Richard can still be Tom and Dick – and each of these can be found as surnames with no further modification. The film producer Samuel Goldwyn, the Mrs Malaprop of the United States of America, is once said to have remarked to one of his friends: *Why do you want to call this new baby 'Fred'? Every Tom, Dick and Harry is called 'Fred'* ...

Other pet-forms which gave rise to surnames are less familiar to us today, as will be obvious if you take a close look at any surname dictionary. Our ancestors were especially fond of using rhyme-names, so that *Dick* (Richard) became *Hick*, and *Rob* (Robert) became *Hob* or *Dob* or *Nob*. Each of these in turn could be used as a surname element, though as first-names, at least, *Dob* and *Hodge* were proverbially, if not actually, used to refer to peasants. In mediaeval times one significant advantage of having a wide range of pet-forms available was that the stock of personal names and of the bynames and surnames which sprung from them was thereby greatly increased. For a comprehensive listing of standard and pet-form first-names, both male and female, you should look at *First name variants* by Alan Bardsley (Federation of Family History Societies, 2nd edition, 1996).

We can follow just one example through. *Tibalt* was formerly a common pet-form of the name *Theobald*, and there are still people today who refer to *Theobald's Row* in London as *Tibalt's Row*. We can make an attempt to list some of the surnames which have developed – cascaded, we might say – from the standard name *Theobald* and from various of its pet-forms:

> *Tibalt; Tibald; Tidbald; Tidball; Tiball; Tudball; Tudbold; Tebbell; Tebble; Tibble; Tippell; Tibbett; Tibbitt; Tebett; Tebbet; Tebbett; Tebut; Tebutt; Tibbott; Tippett; Teboth; Theobold; Debutt; Dyball; Dybald; Diboll; Dybell; Dipple; Dible; Dibble.*

The variations I have given here are restricted to those found in English-speaking countries, and I've excluded pet-forms such as *Tebb* or *Tibb* and surnames with a genitive ending such as *Tibballs* or *Tippetts*. Clearly the permutations here are considerable.

Prefixes and suffixes added to the father's name

Adding a prefix or a suffix to the father's name to create a byname or a surname has long been a popular ploy, and is not confined to the English-speaking world. In Roman times *Petrus Martini* was *Peter, son of Martin*; to the Anglo-Saxons, *Alfred, son of Cidda* would be *Aelfred Cidding*; the Spanish *Juan Rodriguez* was *John, son of Rodrigo*, while the Normans made liberal use of the prefix *Fitz*, from the Latin *filius* (compare modern French, *fils*), meaning *son of*. Contrary to popular belief, *Fitz* does not generally indicate that the bearer was illegitimate – or Irish – though the name **Fitzroy** (from the French, *Fils du Roi*) has certainly been used for children born to the mistresses of kings.

● *Prefixes*

In the British Isles, the use of prefixes attached to a father's first-name is particularly associated with Scotland, Ireland, Wales and the Isle of Man, for which see *Celtic naming practices*, below.

● *Suffixes*

** *Adding '-s' to the father's name*
The suffix 's' is frequently added to the formal or pet-form of a given name to create a surname. This is a practice, originally very much favoured in the English Midlands but found more rarely in the North, which should cause us few problems, since the addition of an apostrophe followed by the letter 's' (except in the case of plural nouns already ending in 's') is a familiar marker for the possessive, the grammatical case known as the genitive. So we have the surnames **Roberts**, **Rogers** and **Richards** [ie, Robert's son, Roger's son, Richard's son], based upon the formal version of each first-name, or **Hobbs**, **Hodges** and **Hicks**, from the nickname forms, *Hob*, *Hodge* and *Hick*. Notice how many Welsh surnames follow this pattern, having developed originally from patronymic bynames of Welsh or English origin. **Thoms**, on the other hand [son of Thomas] is more often found in Scotland or Ireland.

Not all bynames or surnames ending in '-s' had the meaning *son of*; **Roberts** could carry the meaning *son of Robert*, but it could also be used to refer to *Robert's widow* or *Robert's servant*. William **Abbotts**, on the other hand, though he may have worked for an abbot, may simply have been an occupier of land which belonged to a monastery.

The German language adds *-es* to form the genitive, and English being, after all, a Germanic language in its origins, we should expect to find the surname **Hobbes** as a variant on **Hobbs** [son of Robert], or **Hickes** as well as **Hicks** [son of Richard].

** *Adding '-son' to the father's name*
A time-honoured form of patronymic surname in English, dating in the main from the 14th and 15th centuries, is that in which *-son* has been added to a father's given name. We will come across obvious examples like **Richardson** or **Thompson**, and ones that need a bit more thought, like **Tennyson** [son of Dennis]. The given name *Andrew* being popular in Scotland, many **Anderson**s [son of Andrew] come from north of the border, while **Thomson**s (no letter 'p') are more likely to be Scottish than **Thompson**s (with a 'p'), and **Hutchison** [from *Hugh*] is more Scottish than **Hutchinson**.

In England itself surnames ending with *-son* were generally more popular in the English Midlands and the North than in the south, a fact sometimes attributed to the influence of Scandinavian invaders. This is not a hard-and-fast-rule, but might help you narrow down your search for a particular surname origin – so if it's **Robson**s which interest you,

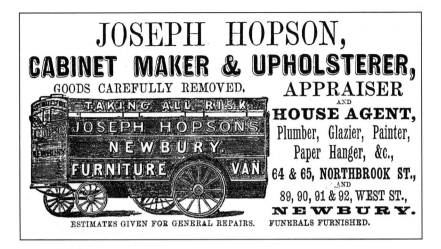

JOSEPH HOPSON,
CABINET MAKER & UPHOLSTERER,
GOODS CAREFULLY REMOVED.   **APPRAISER**
AND
HOUSE AGENT,
Plumber, Glazier, Painter,
Paper Hanger, &c.,
64 & 65, NORTHBROOK ST.,
AND
89, 90, 91 & 92, WEST ST.,
NEWBURY.
ESTIMATES GIVEN FOR GENERAL REPAIRS.   FUNERALS FURNISHED.

Robert's son. The surname *Hopson*, more commonly found as *Hobson*, is derived from the personal name *Robert*. [From Kelly's *Post Office Directory of Bedfordshire, Berkshire, etc.* 1877].

1881 British Census

Dwelling: 34 Bedford Sq
Census Place: Brighton, Sussex, England
Source: FHL Film 1341257   PRO Ref RG11   Piece 1093   Folio 129   Page 48

		Marr	Age	Sex	Birthplace
Jane GIBSON		W	67	F	**Egerton, Kent, England**
	Rel: Head				
	Occ: Lady				
Allice GIBSON		U	36	F	Turncaux Pelham
	Rel: Daur				
	Occ: Lady				
Bernard GIBSON		U	33	M	Turncaux Pelham
	Rel: Son				
	Occ: Timber Merchant				
Bertha GIBSON		U	31	F	Turncaux Pelham
	Rel: Daur				
	Occ: Supposed To Be A Lady				

Supposed to be a lady. There is no mystery about the origin of the surname *Gibson* - it has the meaning 'son of *Gib/Gilbert*' - but what are we to make of the 1881 census enumerator's comment on Bertha Gibson, that she was 'supposed to be a lady'? This entry was spotted by Mrs Chris Sibbald of Cookham Dean, Berkshire, who sent it to Tom Wood of *Family Tree Magazine* for inclusion in his monthly *Miscellany* feature (April 2002). [From the 1881 Census on CD-ROM, a joint venture by the Church of Jesus Christ of Latter-Day Saints and the Federation of Family History Societies. PRO RG11/1093. Reprinted by permission. Public Record Office. © 1998, by Intellectual Reserve, Inc].

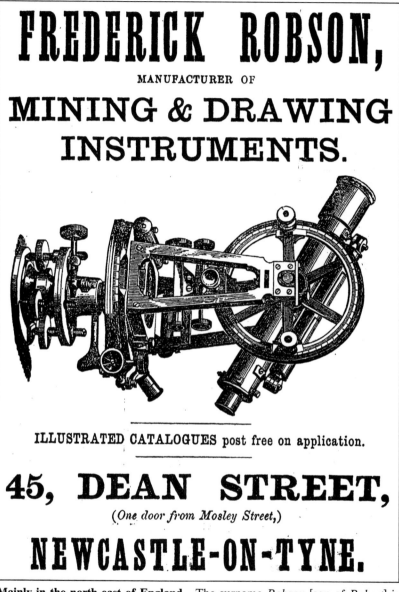
Mainly in the north-east of England... The surname *Robson* [son of *Robert*] is now widespread and not uncommon, but it has always had a particularly strong presence in the north-east of England. [From Kelly's *Post Office Directory of Durham, etc.* 1873].

for example, you'd be more likely to find them in quantity in the north-east of England than anywhere else, and **Hodgkinson**s are more prolific in the Midlands and the North than elsewhere. Surprising as it may seem, then, certain patronymic names can be as localised as some toponymic or occupational surnames are known to be.

In some countries, names ending in *-daughter*, *-dochter* or an equivalent may be found. An example from English records would be the reference to *Cristiana Adamdoughter* in a Poll Tax return for the county of Westmorland in 1379. In essence this is a byname, not a surname; either Cristiana, daughter of Adam, would die as a spinster, in which case her second-name would die with her, or she may get married and take on her husband's last name.

*** Adding diminutives to the father's name*
Another popular method of surname formation was for a diminutive suffix to be added to the pet-form of a personal name:

> *-cock/cox/cott*. **Hitchcock** (from Richard, via *Hitch*); **Willcox** (from William, via *Will*); **Jeffcott** (and other varieties such as **Jephcote**, from Jeffrey).

> *-et(t)(e)/ot(t)(e)*. **Bartlett** (from Bartholomew, via *Bart*); **Willetts** (from William, via *Will*); **Philpott** (from Philip, via *Phil*).

> *-ie/y*. **Davie/Davy** (from David); **Ritchie** (from Richard).

> *-in/ings/ins*. **Tomlin** (from Thomas, via *Tom*); **Jennin(g)s** (from John); **Willin(g)s** (from William, via *Will*).

> *-ken/kin*. **Dicken** (from Richard, via *Dick*); **Jenkin** (from John); **Hodgkin** (from Roger, via *Hodge* – with **Hotchkiss** as another alternative). Similarly, **Wilkin**, **Tomkin**, **Perkin** (from Peter), etc. A genitive '*s*' may also be added, giving us **Jenkins**, **Hodgkins**, etc.

> *-mot(t)/ment/mett*. **Willmot(t)/Will(i)ment/Willmett** (from William, via *Will*).

> *-mough/maugh/muff/mouth/more*. **Watmough** (or **Whatmough**, **W(h)atmaugh**, **W(h)atmuff**, **Wha(r)tmouth** and **W(h)atmore**) means *Walter's relation/brother-in-law*. A similar suffix is used in the name **Hitchmough** (from Richard, via *Hitch*).

Do bear in mind that many surnames found on the mainland of Europe will also be based upon these or similar diminutive forms of first-names.

A very large number of surnames have been created, then, from formal or informal versions of first-names, with suffixes added for good measure. The permutations can sometimes seem almost endless. Here are just some of the better-known variants on the first-names of William and Richard:

> **WILLIAM:** Williams, Williamson, Wilson, Wilcox, Wilcoxson, Wilkins, Wilkinson.

> **RICHARD:** Dick, Dickens, Dickenson, Dickson, Digance, Diggins, Digginson, Diggons, Dixon, Hickin, Hickman, Hickock, Hickox, Hicks, Hickson, Higgins, Higginson, Higgs, Higman, Hiscock, Hitch, Hitchcock, Hitchison, Hitchmough, Hix, Reckett, Ricard, Rich, Richards, Riche, Richer, Richett, Richey, Richie, Richman, Rick, Rickard, Rickeard, Rickett, Ricketts, Rickman, Ricks, Rickson, Ritchard, Ritchie, Rix.

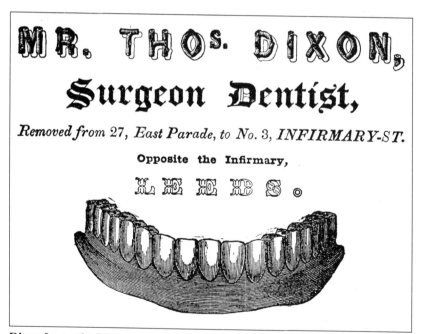

Dixon for teeth. *Dixon* is of one of several surnames derived from the personal name *Richard*. [From White's *Directory of Leeds and the clothing districts of Yorkshire* 1853].

Metronymic surnames

Never discount the possibility that a surname might have been based upon a female name – that of a mother, rather than that of a father.

The female first-name *Annis*, a variation on *Agnes*, has given us surnames such as **Anness**, **Annas**, **Annott** and **Annison**; *Catlin*, a form of *Catherine*, has given **Cattlin**, **Catling**, **Catt**, **Cat(t)on**, **Cattell** and others; **Marger(r)ison**, **Margi(t)son** and **Marget(t)s** are derived from the female name *Margery*, **Ibbetson** can mean *son of Isabel(le)* (via the form *Ibb*), and the once-popular mediaeval female name *Sibley*, from the Latin *Sibilla*, has spawned surnames like **Sibley** itself, and also **Sibbles** and **Sibson**. Despite first appearances, **Billson** means *son of Mabel or Annabel*, and in case we're still wondering about that, it's worth knowing that the male name *William* was not customarily shortened to *Bill* during mediaeval times.

One way of keeping yourself entertained on a long car journey might be to think of all the given names that have both male and female versions: Andrew/Andrea; Henry/Henrietta; Nicholas/Nichola – not forgetting, of course, Nigella Lawson, daughter of the former Chancellor of the Exchequer, Nigel Lawson, who is fast becoming as famous as a television personality as her father was as a politician. So it is that we cannot always be sure whether a particular surname has developed from a male or a female first name. Surnames like **Hibbs**, **Ibbs** and **Ibbetson** could have been used originally for the children of a man called *Hibbert* or of a woman called *Ibb* – a pet form of *Isabel(le)*, which itself was originally a variant of *Elizabeth*. Similarly, **Nelson** can have a male or female origin, meaning *son of Neil/Neal* or *son of Nell (Eleanor)*.

ISAAC PIMBLOTT,
WEAVER BOILER WORKS,
LEFTWICH, NORTHWICH, CHESHIRE

Metronymic and uncommon. *Pimblott* is a diminutive form of a mediaeval female given name, *Pimm*. [From Kelly's *Post Office Directory of Cheshire* 1878].

Surnames derived from trades and occupations or from a person's official status or office

Trades and occupations

Occupational surnames can have a fascinating resonance even at the present day, but to get a glimpse of the genre at its most rich and varied, it's worth taking a brief look at a set of records dating from an earlier period in history than most of us would normally contemplate visiting in our research projects. I'm speaking here about the returns of English Poll Tax payers of the late 14th century. In case you don't think you would feel comfortable with anything quite so arcane, let me set your heart at rest by saying that surviving Poll Tax records for England and Wales from the years 1377, 1379 and 1381 are now being made available in print. The first two such volumes, edited by Carolyn Fenwick (1998, 2001) have already been published, and are easy to access; a planned final volume, to include a name index, is due to appear in the near future.

Glance through the pages of these printed volumes, and you'll find yourself transported into a mediaeval world of weird and wonderful surnames. Some will remain a mystery, but if you examine others closely and try to speak them aloud, they should eventually snap into focus. This is the challenge – and great fun it can be. You might have no difficulty with Johannes **Oylmaker** or Johannes **Wyerdrawer**, both living in Warwickshire, or with Robertus **Pyebaker** or Margeria **Gurdeler** of Southwark in Surrey, and a little thought should make it clear that Galfridus **Fischberar** or his ancestors probably transported fish, or that Nicholaus **Cordwaner**'s name refers to a shoemaker (*cordwainer*). As you grow more confident, you should then feel that you can tackle the surnames of characters like Stephanus **Fleschewer** of Longnor in Shropshire - *flesh-hewer* being a term once used for a slaughterman.

There does seem to be a great preponderance of occupational surnames in use at this period, especially in heavily-populated areas like Southwark. Why should this be so? Perhaps we should answer such a question by asking another one which stems from it. Just how many of these 'surnames' are not really hereditary names at all, but simply 'bynames', second names used by a person during his or her lifetime, which may then die with the bearer? This goes to the heart of the matter. Every 'second name' in these printed Poll Tax books – and there are thousands upon thousands of them – would have its own story to tell. It could be an inherited surname which goes back one or several generations – possibly to a male-line ancestor who was alive in the thirteenth century or even before; it could be a byname which applied only during one person's lifetime – or it could be a byname which would then become hereditary, in that Johannes **Wyerdrawer**, so-called because he drew wire for a living, would pass his second name on to his sons and daughters, and it would then be used by all later generations of **Wyerdrawer**s in the male line as a hereditary surname.

Definitive answers to these questions will have to await a good deal of further scholarly study; relevant records for this period are sparse enough, and a detailed examination of names used in particular towns or villages might offer the best hope of success. We can make at least one generalised observation at the outset, however, which is that there appears to have been some variation across the country at this period in the way in which surnames or bynames were used or written down, and in the balance between surnames of occupational and other origins.

Southwark, located within the county of Surrey but effectively a detached part of London on the south bank of the Thames, would have been bustling with people carrying out a wide variety of trades – a fact which is reflected in the impressive range of occupational names in use there in 1381. Yet the badly torn and faded Poll Tax returns for Westmorland for 1379 tell a very different story. Here there are certainly some second names based on an occupation or location, but in general surnames were clearly at a very much earlier stage of development in this remote northern rural county than they were in London and elsewhere.

Many entries for Westmorland give no second name at all, and relationships between individuals may be expressed purely in terms of the Christian names of each:

> *Willelmo filio Johannis*; *Johanna filia Willelmi*
> [William son of John; Joan daughter of William]

Servants are rarely given second names:

> *Thomas servient Willelmi Smyth.*
> *Mariota ancilla Johannis del Bakhous*
> [Thomas, servant of William Smith; Mariot, servant of John of the Bakehouse. In due course **Backhouse** would eventually become a well-known hereditary surname in Westmorland and elsewhere.]

It is not only in Westmorland that servants are semi-anonymous in this way. Norfolk examples in 1379 include *Stephanus Theparsoneservaunt* and *Robertus Theparsonesman*; at first glance these long descriptive names may look like surnames, but are almost certainly nothing of the kind.

Alternatively, what may appear to be a surname at first glance turns out to be nothing more than a daughter's first name linked to her father's first name:

Cristiana Adamdoughter
[Cristiana, daughter of Adam]

A variation on this theme is represented by:

Johanna Shephirddoghter; Margareta Skynnerdoghter
[Joan, shepherd's daughter; Margaret, skinner's daughter]

It would seem highly unlikely here that we are looking at the daughter of a man called Mr Shepherd and the daughter of a man called Mr Skinner – rather, the fathers of these two women would probably have been the local shepherd and the local skinner – men whose first names are not stated, who probably bore no surname, and may not even have made use of a byname as such.

We move a step closer to inherited surnames in the example which follows, but not all the way. In a fully operative hereditary system, John and Margaret, the son and daughter of Robert Wilson, would be known as *John Wilson* and *Margaret Wilson*, but in Brough with Stainmore, Westmorland, in 1379 we read of:

Roberto Wilson; Johanne filio Roberti Wilson; Margareta filia Roberti Wilson
[Robert Wilson; John, son of Robert Wilson; Margaret, daughter of Robert Wilson]

John and Margaret are the children of Robert Wilson – though with no indication that they had acquired *Wilson* as a hereditary name. In any case, although Robert Wilson himself could be using an inherited surname, he might simply have been known by a patronymic second-name that identified him as the son of a man called William.

The Poll Tax returns for Westmorland, then, would seem to indicate – pending further detailed study – that inherited surnames may have been used only sporadically in that county in the closing decades of the 14th century. Elsewhere in the country there are occasions when we can be rather more confident that hereditary naming patterns were already established, thanks to the fact that some returns helpfully indicate a person's trade next to his name.

We can now take a closer look at an English town: I've chosen Boston in Lincolnshire at random. In 1381, during the reign of Richard II, Boston was a thriving port with an extensive rural hinterland, enjoying great commercial success and with a sizeable population. Nearly all of the men and women who were listed as being liable for Poll Tax in that year are given both first names and second names, of which a significant number were occupational in origin. Broadly-based studies of the subject have indicated that in late mediaeval times fewer than 20% of bynames or surnames used by taxpayers in rural areas were occupational, but that the proportion was significantly higher in towns.

This is no more than a single snapshot, then, of one English town at one point in history. I've extracted most of the second-names which are clearly occupational, but will only mention each such name once. As might be expected, when the same second-name is borne by several individuals, the spelling may well vary, and on occasions there will be two entries for what is apparently the same person, giving two different spellings, almost as if one is an alias or a second attempt at the spelling: so we have double entries for: *Agn.* **Bruster** and *Agn.* **Breuster**, *Agn.* **Tappster** and *Agn.* **Tappstere**, *Robertus* **Ledbeter** and *Robertus* **Ledebeter** and many others. Note that first names may be abbreviated, and that they are rendered in Latin.

Occupational second names featured here are derived from a variety of trades, most of them manual – from individuals who worked with or who sold wool, metal, leather, wood, clothing or food and drink, together with others involved in the construction or furnishing of dwellings and other buildings, and in transportation or other services. Where these second-names are fully hereditary – and, as we have seen, we cannot always be sure that this is the case – they would, of course, reflect the occupation carried out by the original person who first bore the name, who would have been a male ancestor of the man (or unmarried woman) carrying the name in 1381.

Here, first, is a short list featuring bynames or surnames from the Boston Poll Tax returns which have a meaning and origin which should be obvious to us today:

> Rogerus **Barbour**; Constantine **Bedmaker**; Johannes **Bladsmyth**; Adam **Boucher**; Johannes **Capmaker**; Ricardus **Carter**; Johannes **Clerk**; Reginaldus **Coke**; Alanus **Cornseller**; Willelmus **Draper**; Johannes **Fetchewatter**; Johannes **Gardiner**; Robertus **Glasier**; Ricardus **Glover**; Otte **Goldsmyth**; Johannes **Hosyer**; Alicia **Loksmyth**; Willelmus **Mason**; Reginaldus **Mercer**; Willelmus **Musterder**; Willelmus **Nedeller**; Henricus **Paynter**; Alanus **Porter**; Quenilda **Potter**; Henricus **Pouchemaker**; Margareta **Roper**; Willelmus **Sadeler**; Willelmus **Schephird**; Willelmus **Skynner**; Thomas **Smyth**; Margr' **Spicer**; Thomas **Tailour**; Willelmus **Taverner**; Thomas **Turner**; Edus **Tyler**; Johannes **Wolman**; Johannes **Wryght**.

Note that the first-names in this list have generally been given in Latin, whereas the last-names are rendered neither in Latin, nor in French, but in English. Some, of course, are compound names: **Capmaker, Cornseller, Loksmyth**.

Other such bynames or surnames might cause us rather more of a problem, either because the occupation concerned no longer exists, or because the term used to describe it has been changed or re-spelt. I hope that the brief definition I have given after each of the following names might prove useful:

> Johannes **Candeler** [a chandler – originally a maker of candles]; Willelmus **Chaloner** [a maker or seller of blankets]; Juliana **Curriour** [a currier, working as a leather dresser]; Ricardus **Dudder** [a cloth worker]; Willelmus **Ewer** [a carrier of water]; Johannes **Furbour** [a furber – a polisher of metal, especially armour; the surname **Frobisher** has the same origin]; Willelmus **Kalynder** [a calendar, cloth finisher]; Henricus **Latoner** [a person working with *latten*, a yellow metal like brass]; Robertus **Ledbeter** [a lead-beater – worker in lead]; Thomas **Lytster** [a lister, a name for a dyer]; Radulphus **Packer** [a wool packer]; Willelmus **Parker** [a gamekeeper employed in a park]; Walterus **Pesecod** [probably meaning *a seller of peas*]; Johannes **Scherman** [a shearman, who cut the nap off cloth]; Johannes **Souter** [a shoemaker]; Robertus **Spenser** [a servant in a pantry]; Agn' **Tappster** [a maker of tapestries or carpets – or a wine merchant or tavern-keeper]; Thomas **Tawyer** [a dresser of white leather]; Alanus **Theker** [a thatcher]; Ricardus **Walker** [a fuller of cloth]; Robertus **Warner** [the keeper of a game warren – though the name has other possible origins].

For future reference it might be worth pointing out that of the sixty or so occupational surnames I have listed here, only a dozen do *not* end with the letters *-er*, *-or* or *-our*. That is in the nature of occupational names, and may be a useful clue to help you narrow down your search for origins and meanings in difficult cases.

Surname scholars generally agree that in some parts of England

A sea-dog with ancestors who polished armour. Martin *Frobisher* [a polisher of metal or of armour], who was born in Doncaster but died in Plymouth, played a major rôle in the defeat the Spanish Armada in 1588.

occupational surnames which end in the letters -*ster* or -*xter* were based upon terms originally used to describe a female practitioner of a certain limited number of trades. This was not necessarily the case in eastern counties, however, and -*ster* and -*xter* suffixes in Lincolnshire would probably have had as much to do with regional dialect usage as with gender. From the 1381 list for Boston we have Johannes **Baxster** [a baker]; Agn' **Bruster** [a brewer] and Thomas **Webster** [a weaver]. Similar names from elsewhere in the Poll Tax listings include: Mariona **Kempster** [a woolcomber] from Coventry (1379); Rogerus **Blekster** [*Blaxter*, a bleacher] from Edgefield, Norfolk (1379) and Johannes **Songster** [a singer, more commonly found with the spelling **Sangster**; **Sanger** is a further alternative] from Walton, Warwickshire (1379).

If we are trying to make sense of the names borne by the men mentioned above – John **Baxster**, Thomas **Webster,** Roger **Blekster** and Johannes **Songster** – then three possibilities present themselves. If *baxster, webster, blekster* and *songster* were female-specific occupational terms, then they could have been passed on as surnames to John, Thomas, Roger and Johannes/John by a female ancestor; if they were simply local dialectal terms used for bakers, weavers, bleachers and singers of either sex, then they could either have been passed on by a male ancestor, or were simply being used as bynames for each individual. Theorising, of course, is all very well here, but we should not expect total consistency or predictability in the records in question. More often than not we have to be content with intelligent guesswork based upon whatever evidence is available.

One of the commonest -*ster* words in current English usage is *spinster*; originally a female term for a spinner of wool, by late mediaeval times it was beginning to be used to refer to a woman who stayed at home spinning while her contemporaries upped and got married. Strange to relate, **Spinster** is known to have been used as a surname, though in fairly rare cases. Early examples include Amos **Spinster**, son of Amos **Spinster**, baptised at Chilham in Kent in 1595, and John **Spenster** who married Margaret Barnes at Cotgrave in Nottinghamshire in 1587. Unless there was illegitimacy at work here, or *spinster* was used as some kind of a nickname or was applied to males and females alike, it would seem likely that this surname would have come from a female ancestor who was known to have spent her time spinning, not one who was an unmarried woman. This means that when we find *Margareta Spynnester* and *Thomazyne Spynnester* as Poll Tax payers in Southwark in 1381, or *Editha Spinestere* in Somerset in 1379, it is just possible that their second-names are surnames – but more likely, it must be said, that they were so-called because they were spinners of wool, or unmarried women, or both.

What are we to make of Johannes **Fynster** in the 1381 list? Does his second-name belong to the **Baxter/Bruster/Webster** class, with the meaning of 'a (re)finer of metal'? And while we're about it, what about the meaning of the second-names of Johannes **Outener**, said to be working as a *webster*? Or Johannes **Pokbynder/Pok(e)bynder**? Was the name applied to a book-binder, or maybe to a person who bound up small bags called *pokes* (those bags in which you are said to buy a pig, if you're not careful...)? Answers on a postcard, please...

Before we leave Boston in Lincolnshire, it might be of interest to consider what occupational surnames were in evidence there at a point almost mid-way between 1381 and the present day, an easy enough task thanks to the survival of the so-called Protestation Returns for the town. In 1641/2 a nationwide listing was made of all males of the age of eighteen years or over who were prepared to sign an oath *to live and die for the true Protestant religion...* – and also, in theory, of those who would not commit themselves to such an oath for any reason. The extant lists for Lincolnshire were published in 1984 by W.F. **Webster** [a female weaver, remember...?], and so we have a helpful listing of males in the town in the mid 17th century.

What has changed? Well, to begin with, there appears to be a much wider range of surnames, drawn from a variety of sources, and of the sixty-odd occupational names we featured from the 1381 Poll Tax, only twelve can still be found in 1641/2, several of them spelt rather differently. In particular, some of the more unusual and intriguing names have gone: no more **Bedmaker**s, **Capmaker**s, **Cornseller**s, **Fetchewatter**s [notice the clue here to the traditional pronunciation of the word *water*], **Pouchemaker**s or **Latoner**s – neither in Boston itself, nor elsewhere within Lincolnshire, judging by the index to the printed returns.

Yet by 1641/2 it was a matter of out with the old, in with the new, as fresh occupational surnames had made their appearance in the town. There are only a few with obvious meanings this time, like **Baker**, **Brewer**, **Cartewright** and **Ostler**. The rest could benefit from at least a brief word of explanation: **Collier** [as likely to be a charcoal burner as a coal-getter or a coal-dealer]; **Corker** [a maker or seller of a red or purple dye known as *cork*]; **Kitchingman** [someone who worked in a kitchen, or a cook]; **Paternoster** [a maker of rosaries, each of which contains large beads known as *Pater nosters*, Latin for *Our Father*]; **Pedder** [a pedlar]; **Pulter** [poulterer, dealer in poultry; note that the name of the London Livery Company known as the *Poulters* clings more closely to the original spelling]; **Wadsman** [someone who gathered or sold the blue dye, woad].

The fact that so many of the occupational second-names used in Boston in the 14th century seem to have vanished by 1641/2 means that it is possible that some of the 'surnames' from 1381 were really only 'bynames' after all, used by a person during his lifetime and then dying with him. Either that, or some hereditary occupational surnames could have died out for lack of male heirs in certain families, a phenomenon which had certainly been the case earlier in the 14th century, thanks to the devastation caused by the arrival of the Black Death in England in 1348 and subsequent visitations in the 1350s and the 1370s.

It is also possible that some families in Boston and elsewhere might have chosen new surnames to replace their original occupational ones, finding these to be absurdly arcane, especially since it might have been some time since anyone in the family had followed the trade in question. Not everyone, after all, would have been happy to go through life bearing a second-name inherited from Henricus **Stokkefischmonger** of Southwark (1381). Too much of a mouthful for everyday use? In other cases the surname might have been modified, shortened, or re-spelt: so maybe the 14th-century **Capmaker**s of Boston were hiding behind surnames such as **Capp**, **Cappe**, **Cappes**, **Cappett**, **Capps** or **Caps** by 1641/2?

Only a more detailed study than this one could find answers to such questions. It is certainly the case, however, that surnames based upon a place or upon some personal characteristic tended to become stabilised and to move away from being mere bynames at an earlier date than those with an occupational or personal-name origin. Many of the occupational surnames which have survived into the 21st century are those relating to basic and widespread trades; we can find plenty of **Baker**s and **Mason**s around, long after **Stockfishmonger**s have been consigned to the footnotes of history.

Familiar occupational terms

It's now time to leave Boston and to take a more general look at occupational surnames. Of all those in this category which still make perfect sense to us today, few are more familiar than **Smith** or **Wright**.

Smith (that is, a person who would *smite* or strike with a hammer) is not only the commonest surname in England, it is also the commonest in Scotland and in the United States (where, admittedly, a high proportion of **Smith** families had originally borne a different surname, even if it was one like **Schmidt** or **Smed**). This is not a new phenomenon, and in 1853, for example, the six commonest surnames, including **Smith**, accounted for nearly one-sixth of the entire population of England and Wales.

Variants such as **Smythe** are, of course, simply alternative (and sometimes deliberately *olde worlde*) spellings for **Smith**, and there would seem to be no good reason to accord them the luxury of a different pronunciation.

The Latin for a smith is *faber*, which gives rise to the German surname **Faber**, and the very common French surname **Lefevre** or **Lefebvre**;

The commonest of all surnames. Smiths would make and fashion a wide variety of useful objects, and many would make use of a hammer, an anvil and a forge, as the smith in this illustration is doing. [From *The book of English trades*, 1823].

related English names include **Fearon** and **Farrer**. Celtic words for a smith give us **Govan**, **Gowan**, **Cowan** and **Gow**; the Manx equivalent is **Gawne** and the Welsh surname **Gough/Goff** can either refer to a smith or to a red-haired person. The Cornish word for a smith is *gove*, and the related surname **Angove** literally means *The Smith*. The Polish word for a smith gives us **Kovacs** – and so on...

Colin Rogers, in his book *The surname detective* (1995), has an astute observation to give concerning the name **Wright**. He makes a convincing case that the reason why the surname **Carpenter** is not more commonly found outside the southern counties of England is that elsewhere in the country a man carrying out such a trade was known as a *wright* (a word of English origin), not as a *carpenter* (French in origin).

Examples of *smith* and *wright* being used as elements in longer surnames are featured later in this book.

Unfamiliar occupational terms

It's easy enough to make sense of a modern surname like **Baker** or **Butcher**, but all too often an occupation itself, or a term which was commonly used to describe it at the time when surnames were first being adopted, may long since have passed into history. Intuition might tell us that the name **Lockyer** has its origins in a man who was a locksmith, or that a **Needler** made needles (which were usually made of bone in

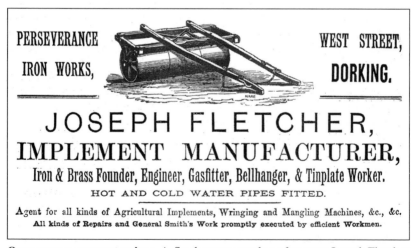

Once arrows, now waterpipes. A *fletcher* was a maker of arrows; Joseph Fletcher of Dorking's skills are different - he makes a range of implements, hangs bells, is a gas fitter and installs water pipes. [From Kelly's *Post Office Directory of Kent, Surrey and Sussex* 1878].

mediaeval times), but we no longer live in a world where a **Bowyer** makes or sells bows, or where an **Arrowsmith** or a **Fletcher** (from the French word for an arrow, *flèche*), makes arrows for an **Archer** to shoot.

Here are some examples of occupational terms which are with us no longer, either because the trade itself has now vanished, or because the term formerly used is no longer familiar to present-day speakers of English:

- *Byron.* A cowman, though it can also be used for a person living near cattle sheds. The poet **Byron**'s ancestor John Byron (?1600-1652) was the first to be elevated to the peerage as Baron Byron.

- *Chapman.* A merchant or trader, especially one travelling from place to place selling small wares. The element *chap* (or *cheap* or *chip*) can often be found in place-names. English surname variants include **Chipman** or **Chapper**, while a German equivalent is **Kauf(f)man(n)**.

- *Chaucer.* A maker of shoes (compare the French *chaussures*) or leggings. Related surnames include **Chauser** and **Causer**.

- *Cordwainer.* A shoemaker, originally working with leather from *Cordoba* in Spain. Related surnames include **Cordner**, **Cordiner** and **Codner**.

- *Crerar.* My father had a life-long friend called Louis **Crerar**, who emigrated to Toronto in Canada as a young man to earn his living as a professional pianist. I'd always thought that his surname might be a shortened form of an Irish name – something like **McCrerar** – but in fact it comes from a Scots Gaelic term for a sievewright. The Crerars were originally a small sept [clan] settled in the Strathspey and Lochtayside areas, and the surname is well-known to bibliophiles thanks to the fact that John Crerar (1827-1889), a Scotsman by birth, endowed a public library which bears his name in Chicago, USA. Related surnames include **Crearer** and **Crarer**.

- *Culpeper.* A spicer or herbalist – someone who originally *culled pepper*. Early spellings include **Col(e)peper**, and the number of '*l*'s and '*p*'s in the name can vary.

- *Earwaker.* A watcher over the wild boars. A surname which will be familiar to anyone who has had occasion to refer to a scholarly work on local history known as *Earwaker's East Cheshire*, written by John Parsons **Earwaker** and first published in 1877. The alternative spelling *Erriker* simply reflects the usual pronunciation of the surname.

- *Falder.* A shepherd, or one who attended cattle. The surname **Falder**

From Scotland to Chicago. The surname *Crerar* comes from a Scots Gaelic term for a sievewright. John Crerar, a Scotsman by birth, endowed a public library which bears his name in Chicago, USA.

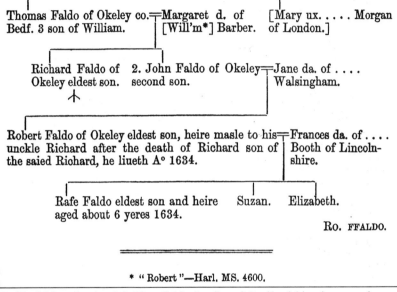

𝔉𝔞𝔩𝔡𝔬

[of 𝔒𝔞𝔨𝔩𝔢𝔶].

ARMS.—*Same as Faldo of Goldington, a mullet for difference.*

William Faldo of Malden╤Margaret d. of .... Pichard
and of Faldo A° 6 E. 6. | of Okeley.

Thomas Faldo of Okeley co.╤Margaret d. of   [Mary ux. .... Morgan
Bedf. 3 son of William. | [Will'm*] Barber.   of London.]

Richard Faldo of   2. John Faldo of Okeley╤Jane da. of ....
Okeley eldest son.   second son. | Walsingham.

Robert Faldo of Okeley eldest son, heire masle to his╤Frances da. of ....
unckle Richard after the death of Richard son of | Booth of Lincoln-
the saied Richard, he liueth A° 1634. | shire.

Rafe Faldo eldest son and heire   Suzan.   Elizabeth.
aged about 6 yeres 1634.

RO. FFALDO.

* " Robert "—Harl. MS. 4600.

Bedfordshire shepherds? The *Faldo* family of Bedfordshire is one of some antiquity. The meaning of the surname has never been satisfactorily explained, though the term *falder* was once used for a shepherd or for a man who looked after cattle. [From *The Visitations of Bedfordshire 1566, 1582 and 1634*, edited by F.A.Blaydes for the Harleian Society, 1884].

is not uncommon in the north of England, but I am still working on the possibility that this occupational term might also be the origin of the surname of Nick **Faldo**, the golfer. The Faldo family has been well-established in Bedfordshire from at least as early as the 13th century, and alternative spellings for the name include **Fal(l)doe**, **Fal(l)dow**, **Fauldo(e)**, **Fawldow**, **Faldew**, **Foldo(e)**, **Fo(u)ltow**, **Foldow**, **Folldo** and **Foltow**. There are also a few scattered examples of Bedfordshire **Falder**s, such as that of Ann **Falder** who married John **Wheeler** in Lidlington in 1689.

- *Hansard*. A maker of cutlasses or daggers. Luke **Hansard** (1752-1828) was the first person to publish the series of official accounts of proceedings in Parliament which still bear his name.

- *Hollister*. A female brothel-keeper, from Old French *holier*, a lecher, with a feminine-*ster* ending. Related surnames include **Hollister** and **Ollister**.

- *Jagger*. A north country term for a chapman, or for a man in charge of packhorses. As a surname it is mostly found in Yorkshire, though Sir Mick **Jagger** of *Rolling Stones* fame was born at Dartford in Kent.

- *Keeble*. A maker or seller of cudgels – or possibly someone built like a cudgel or who behaved aggressively. Related surnames include **Keble** and **Kibble**.

- *Lorimer*. A harness maker, or a maker and seller of metal attachments for horses. Related surnames include **Lorrimer** and **Larimer**, though in London the Worshipful Company of *Loriners* uses an alternative earlier spelling.

- *Parmenter*. Made lace and trimmings. Related surnames include **Parmi(n)ter**, **Parmeter** and **Pammenter**.

- *Phemister*. A fee master, foreman of a herd or flock of animals. Related surnames include **Femister** and **Whimster**.

- *Rackstraw*. A scavenger, someone who *raked straw*. Known varieties include **Raickstraw**.

Workers in metal. William Spurrier's surname indicates that his ancestors made spurs. In 1854, though he is based in Birmingham, he is advertising his skills as a metal-plate worker in Kelly's *Post Office Directory of London*.

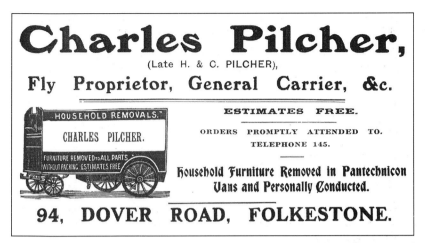

No connection with pilchards. The occupational surname *Pilcher* [a maker of leather garments called *pilches*] is strongly associated with the county of Kent, but although Charles Pilcher of Folkestone had been born in that county and was in business there, his father Henry Pilcher came from Cromer in Norfolk. [From Kelly's *Post Office Directory of Kent*, 1911].

- *Roadknight*. A mounted messenger. Known varieties include **Rodknight**.

- *Runciman*. A man in charge of the *rouncies* (work-horses). Known varieties include **Runchman**.

- *Threadgold*. Someone who practised embroidery using gold thread. Related surnames include **Threadgill** and **Threadgall**.

One American client of mine was descended from a certain Joseph **Billiter**, who arrived in Maryland or Virginia in about the year 1671. Now Billiter is an unusual surname; it means *bell-founder* and appears in mediaeval times in East Anglia and elsewhere – so in Leicestershire in 1327, for example, *Stephen Belyetere* was carrying just such a surname or a byname. There is also a Billiter Street in London, which perpetuates the occupational term if not the surname. In early modern times, however, Billiter simply disappears almost entirely as a surname, reappearing sparsely a number of years later.

The IGI yokes the names **Billiter** and **Belitha** together, and I was increasingly convinced that they really were variants of the same name. Not only that, but the index to wills proved in the Prerogative Court of Canterbury, 1750-1800, includes entries for John Belitha alias **Belitho**, Samuel Belitha alias **Bolitha** and James **Belither** alias **Bolithar**. The

Surname drift. Could *Billiter*, *Belitha*, *Belitho* and *Bolitho* be variations on the same surname? The *Bolitho* family is well-known in Devon and Cornwall, and Richard Foster Bolitho's bookplate features the name of his Cornish country seat, *Ponsandane* (Ponsondine). [From *One hundred book plates engraved on wood by Thomas Moring*, 1900].

surname was dipping, weaving and metamorphosing before my very eyes.

How far do you let what we might call *surname-drift* take you? If you can move from **Billiter** to **Belitha**, from **Belitha** to **Belitho**, before you know where you are you could end up with the surname of **Bolitho**, borne by a distinguished and well-recorded family in Devon and Cornwall. It is possible to change a surname one or more letters at a time, and to end up with a name which is utterly different from the one you started with – rather as you would do in a favourite party game. And, as they say, if a man has an axe and replaces its shaft and then replaces its head, is it still the same axe? For all that, if the alternative is to find no references to a surname whatsoever at a given period in history, extreme measures are often called for.

A listing of obsolete trade terms and their related surnames such as the ones I have just offered could be almost endless. If you are interested in a particular surname and think it might refer to a vanished or very obscure occupation, do consider consulting the full version of the Oxford English Dictionary, published as a multi-volume set of books and also on CD-ROM, which is usually available in good public libraries, or look at a dictionary of occupations such as Colin Waters' *A dictionary of old trades, titles and occupations* (1999).

Sometimes, just to confuse matters further, the same word could once have been used for more than one occupation. So **Brasher** can be derived from a Norman word for a brewer, but can also mean a worker in brass, and a man who acquired the surname **Barker** could have been a tanner, using tree-*bark* in the process, but might well have been a shepherd.

One final complication can arise when a surname seems to be based on a familiar occupational term, but where the term itself has changed its meaning or acquired new ones over the years. This should help to explain why the surname **Farmer** is not as common as you might expect it to be, considering how many English people over the centuries have farmed for a living. In fact written records in times past commonly refer to those who farmed land as *yeomen* or *husbandmen*, leaving the word *farmer* to be used for a person who collected (*farmed*) taxes and revenues, and paid a fee for the privilege.

Regional variations
Different regional terms can be used to describe some of even the most basic trades or occupations throughout the British Isles, and each may have given rise to a related surname.

Several names bear witness to the vital importance of the wool trade in earlier centuries: a person whose job it was to full cloth would be known as a *fuller* in the eastern counties of England, as a *walker* in the

North and as a *tucker* in southern and western areas. All three terms have coined surnames which survive to the present day.

Regional variations of the surname **Thatcher** include **Theaker** (Yorkshire), **Thacker** (West Midlands) and **Thaxter** (a feminine or dialectal form, found mainly in Norfolk). Millers were also essential to the economy, but in this case slight variations on the same word have produced a set of related surnames: there is **Miller** itself, but also **Millward** (more commonly found in the south and west of England and the Midlands), **Milner** (mostly found in the north and east of England and in the Scottish Lowlands) and **Millar** (a Scottish spelling of the word *miller*). The spelling **Meller** may also be found, though the similar-looking surname **Mellor** comes from one of a number of place-names in the North of England and the Midlands.

Official status or office

A number of surnames reflect some civic, legal, administrative or manorial office held by the original bearer on a permanent or temporary basis, rather than any specific trade which he practised as such. This class includes **Chancellor**, **Steward**, **Reeve**, **Sheriff**, **S(e)argent**, **Constable**, **Judge**, **Justice**, **Marshall**, **Butler**, **Purchase**, **Wardroper** and **Chamberlain(e)** (hence **Chambers** and **Chalmers**).

The surname **Knight** could have been applied to a servant or messenger rather than to a dashing horseman of high status, and other surnames which sound very fine, such as **King**, **Duke**, **Lord** or **Squire**, probably reflect the fact that a man of this name played such a role in a pageant. There were plenty of parts to be played, too, in mediaeval miracle, mystery or passion plays. So – need it be said – your ancestor with the surname King would not have been monarch of the realm, but something of an amateur actor.

By contrast, a specific rank in society gave rise to surnames such as **Franklin**, **Freeman**, **Gentleman** and **Vavasour**.

As ever, we should never underestimate the power of metaphor and irony in the process of surname creation. Men called **Chamberlain(e)** or **Judge** or **Gentleman** might simply have behaved like chamberlains, judges or gentlemen – adopted airs and graces, if you like – or have been servants to those of a greater social status than themselves. In the same way, ecclesiastical surnames like **Abbott**, **Archdeacon**, **Bishop**, **Can(n)on**, **Chapl(a)in**, **Deacon/Deakin**, **Dean**, **Friar/Fryer/Freer**, **Monk**, **Parsons**, **Prior** and **Vicar/Vickers**, might have been given to those who acted in a sanctimonious way, or who were employed by such members of the church. Basil Cottle, in *The Penguin dictionary of surnames* (1967) shares with us the alarming fact that George Abbott (died 1633) was the only Archbishop of Canterbury ever to have shot a gamekeeper...

Summoned to appear... The surname *Sumner* owes its origin to an official known as a *summoner*, whose job it was to summon individuals to appear before an ecclesiastical court. George Sumner of Wem in Shropshire, wine and spirit merchant, had a rather more palatable way of earning a living. [From Kelly's *Post Office Directory of Shropshire, Herefordshire, Gloucestershire and Bristol* 1879].

name, the letter '*n*' having removed itself from the indefinite article and become attached to the word which follows) in the heading to this section, but thought better of it. If a nickname is an extra name applied to someone because of something distinctive which marks him out from the crowd, then in a way all bynames are nicknames: Richard with red hair, Richard the courteous man, Richard whose father was called John, Richard who lived near the hill, Richard who came from London, and so on.

In a narrower sense, and moving closer to everyday parlance, we can say that nicknames focus upon a man's physical appearance or aspects of his character, and that is the kind of nickname we will be considering here.

Nicknames have been a fact of life for hundreds of years; they can be used as a sign of affection, to cut a pompous person down to size, or to give a separate identity to each of a number of individuals who bear the same name or names. Even entire family branches have been known to have their own generic nickname. There are still places where such distinctions need to be made even today. In a Scottish village full of *James MacKay*s, or in a Welsh settlement bristling with *Hugh Evans*es, nicknames will be employed in the interests of precision – hence *Evans the coal*, *Evans the bread* – or, apocryphally, *Good Evans* the local minister...

The English of all social classes can play this game along with the rest; here is an example from the Wigan/Warrington area of Lancashire:

*Some little difficulty was occasionally experienced, owing to
the number of scholars with the same surname. At one period,
there were no less than fifteen boys who rejoiced in the name
of 'John Lowe'. To avoid the confusion of identity incidental
to such a similarity of appellation, the boys were characterised
in the register as 'John Lowe John's John', 'John Lowe
Henry's John', 'John Lowe red nob', 'John Lowe white nob',
'John Lowe black nob', and so forth, until, by appropriate
sobriquets, they could all be distinguished from each other.
[The history of Park Lane Chapel by George Fox (1897),
p.83]*

Even more imaginative were the good folk of Gate Pike, near Bolton:

*Amongst the people at Gate Pike there was a strong
propensity to use nicknames. Nearly everyone answered to a
name other than their own. William Fletcher at the coal yard
had a son whom everybody called 'Jimmy Chant'. In one of
the cottages near, lived Jane Markland, who was known as
'Jane Puddin'. The Rothwells were always designated
'Rosins'; Haslams were 'Fowts', because Thomas Haslam
originally came from Tonge Fold (Tum Fowt). Then the
Heaton family were familiarly called 'Yettons', William
Heaton occupying the proud position of reader to the
village, his successor being Joe Smith, otherwise 'Scowie',
the knocker-up.*

*'Saut Bob', whose name was Woods, was the rag and bone
merchant; 'Owd Hardneck' an old army pensioner; and
William Miller was 'Owd Meighl'. And so on, through Fine
John, Bill Blue, Owd Physick, Galloper, Tommy Stump, and
many more such luminaries. [Gate Fell: the story of 80 years'
Methodism, 1843-1923 by Hannah Cottrell (1924), pp. 17-18]*

Nicknames belong principally to the world of oral tradition, of course,
and can often give a fascinating insight into the vernacular speech-
patterns of bygone days, but even in fairly recent times they can be
found in official documents. As late as the 19th century, some
nicknames are known to have been used as if they were hereditary
'surnames' – a theme which I refer to briefly in my book, *Succeeding in
family history* (2001), pages 29-30.

When surnames were first being adopted in mediaeval times, a
number of nicknames which previously would have been used merely as
bynames for particular individuals were elevated in status to become
fully-fledged hereditary surnames, and as such they can be particularly
fascinating in that they often reveal some very personal and intimate

details about the original bearer. Don't despair if you come across a surname like **Silly**, which sounds most unfortunate to modern ears, but which comes from the Middle English *seely*, meaning *happy*. Language moves on, and a good-quality dictionary can be particularly helpful in defining the meaning and the history of words used to describe physical or personal characteristics.

Just as a good many occupational surnames have vanished over the years, so those based upon appearance or character have dwindled in number as certain families, not wishing to be reminded of the more unfortunate physical defects or the moral shortcomings of their ancestors, have abandoned or sanitized their names accordingly.

Physical appearance

Even in our politically correct times, people are still cruel enough to use nicknames like *Fatso* or *Pongo* for their overweight or smelly acquaintances. The parents of a friend of mine once decided that it would be diplomatic to have a quiet word with both her and her elder brother to break the news that little brother Stuart was going to have to wear spectacles. *We don't want you to be cruel enough to call him **Specky four eyes** or anything like that*, said the parents, with great concern. Now this was a sobriquet that the two children had never heard before, but they were grateful to their parents for having suggested it to them, and thereafter they began to apply it to little Stuart with gusto.

Surnames derived from physical appearance are legion, not all of them so very kind. Complexion, hair colour, general build, physical deformities – all were grist to the surname-creators' mill, though it should be stressed that many such names could also have alternative origins. The meaning of **Redhead** or **Bigg** is obvious enough, while slightly more obscure examples include **Foljambe** [afflicted with a crippled leg], **Bunyan** [suffering from a bunion or similar bodily lump, though it can also refer to a baker of fruit tarts], **Camoys** [snub-nosed], **Crowfoot** [deformed feet], **Hamill** [a scarred or maimed person – though in Scotland and Northern Ireland it can also be a toponymic surname based upon a French place-name], **Puddephat** [shaped like a barrel], **Pauncefoot** [big-bellied], **Oliphant** [as large and ungainly as an elephant] and **Ballard** [a bald man]. I don't know that the Scots are particularly heartless in their use of nicknames/surnames, but the country does seem to have its fair share of people called **Campbell** [crooked mouth], **Cameron** [crooked nose] and **Cruikshanks** [crooked legs]. My own **Cruikshanks** ancestors from Aberdeenshire, let it be said, seem to have been upright enough citizens in every way.

The late George Pelling used to deliver a most entertaining talk on surnames. He took great delight in pointing out that although the

His gould complexion... Rev Sabine Baring-Gould (1834-1924) achieved fame as a writer and folklorist, and is perhaps best remembered as the author of the hymn, *Onward Christian soldiers*. The *Gould* element in his double-barrelled surname represents an earlier pronunciation of the world 'gold' - hence the motto on his bookplate: 'Gould bydeth ever bright'. [From *One hundred book plates engraved on wood by Thomas Moring*, 1900].

surname **Blake** can mean *black* (from Old English *blaec* or *blac*) and was thus used for a swarthy person, it can also be a nickname derived from an Old English word *blac*, meaning wan, pale, or white – referring to a fair person. In other words, it's possible to prove that black is white...

One of the various possible origins of the name **Gould** is that it was a nickname for a person with very fair or gold-coloured hair, the *gould* spelling simply reflecting an earlier standard pronunciation of the word *gold*. Consider a line from one of the more famous of Shakespeare's sonnets, *Shall I compare thee to a summer's day..*:

> *And often is his gold complexion dimmed*

At the time when this line was penned, it would have been pronounced by speakers in most parts of the country in the following fashion:

> *And often is his **gould complex-i-on** dimmed.*

Is it any wonder, then, that some surnames seem unfamiliar to us today, despite the fact that their meaning would have been perfectly obvious at the time when they were first used?

Many of our ancestors had animal or bird bynames imposed upon them – either because of their physical appearance, or, perhaps more likely, because they behaved in a way that certain animals are said to behave. When I first arrived at secondary school, the word soon got around that a certain teacher (who has long since departed this life, and I won't mention his real name) was referred to as *Mouse*. We all wondered why this might have been the case – until the school gathered together for the first morning assembly of the new academic year, and the teachers took their place on the platform, flanking the headmaster. There amongst them was a man of advanced years who bore a quite uncanny resemblance to a mouse – lacking only a set of protuberant whiskers. Ever since then I have always been quite prepared to believe anyone who tells me that he or she knows a human being who could be mistaken for some animal or other.

A person from the south of England might be called **Fox**, while the northern equivalent would be **Tod(d)** (**Todhunter**s being those who chased foxes). **Fuchs** is a German *Fox* surname, and a sixteenth-century German botanist of this name gave his name to the flower known as the *fuchsia*. Sometimes an 'animal' surname does not yield up its meaning at first glance. **Vidler** refers unequivocally to a person's appearance, with the meaning of *wolf face*, being derived from Anglo-Norman French, *vis de leu*. A person who hunted wolves might be known as **Pritlove** or **Pretlove** (literally, *prick wolf*). The Scottish name **Veitch** refers to a cow – a fact which becomes more obvious if we compare it with the French word *vache* or the Italian *vacca*. **Doggett** sounds like a tame enough name, but would once have been fairly abusive, a nickname for someone who looked or behaved like a little dog, or was some kind of a *dog head*. **Flea** (also spelt **Fley**, **Flay(e)** and so on) was applied to someone who had a flea-like appearance or character. The mind boggles.

Birds have provided us with surnames like **Duck**, **Woodcock**, **Wren** and **Crow(e)**; where the crow being referred to was a small one, the French-sounding alternative **Corbet** (*Corbeau*) was sometimes preferred. The wild goose, known for being shy and cautious, has given us a charming surname like **Graygoose**, and also **Wildgoose** itself, while East Anglia, for example, though it has comparatively few place-name surnames, seems to be positively brimming with those of the feathered variety, such as **Partridge**, **Pheasant** and **Coe** [from a nickname for a *jackdaw*].

There are very few names with genuinely fishy origins, **Pike**, **Tench** and **Bucktrout** (male trout) being among the possible exceptions. **Salmon** is usually a contracted form of the given name *Salomon/ Solomon*, and Bardsley maintains that '**Salman**, **Chubb**, **Spratt**, **Gudgeon**, etc have no connection with the fishy tribe.'

A rose by any other name would smell as sweet... unless your surname is **Rose**, in which case you may well feel attached to the name, which was probably given to a distant ancestor who was as sweet as a rose, was fond of roses, cultivated roses, looked like a rose, even? There's no evidence of anyone being surnamed **Cauliflower** because of a cauliflower ear, however...

Other plant or flower names include **Flower(s)** and **Lilly** [having very fair hair or skin]. Someone called **Briar(s)/Brier(s)/Brear** may have been

J. J. PARTRIDGE,

IMPORTER OF TEAS,

Family Grocer and Provision Factor, &c.,

93, HIGH STREET,

WESTON-SUPER-MARE.

Birds of a feather. Many if not most bird-names have given rise to surnames. James J.Partridge, tea dealer of Weston-super-Mare in Somerset in 1875, had been born in Witheridge, Devon. [From Kelly's *Post Office Directory of Somersetshire* 1875].

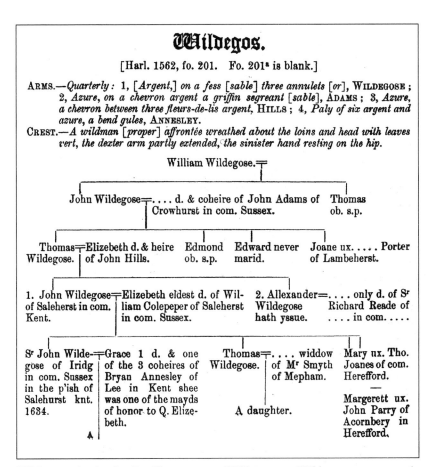

𝕎𝕚𝕝𝕕𝕖𝕘𝕠𝕤.

[Harl. 1562, fo. 201. Fo. 201ᵃ is blank.]

ARMS.—*Quarterly:* 1, [*Argent,*] *on a fess* [*sable*] *three annulets* [*or*], WILDEGOSE ; 2, *Azure, on a chevron argent a griffin segreant* [*sable*], ADAMS ; 3, *Azure, a chevron between three fleurs-de-lis argent,* HILLS ; 4, *Paly of six argent and azure, a bend gules,* ANNESLEY.

CREST.—*A wildman* [*proper*] *affrontée wreathed about the loins and head with leaves vert, the dexter arm partly extended, the sinister hand resting on the hip.*

William Wildegose.⊤

John Wildegose⊤.... d. & coheire of John Adams of Crowhurst in com. Sussex.   Thomas ob. s.p.

Thomas⊤Elizebeth d. & heire   Edmond   Edward never   Joane ux..... Porter
Wildegose. | of John Hills.   ob. s.p.   marid.   of Lambeherst.

1. John Wildegose⊤Elizebeth eldest d. of Wil-   2. Alexander=.... only d. of Sʳ
of Saleherst in com. | liam Colepeper of Saleherst   Wildegose   Richard Reade of
Kent. | in com. Sussex.   hath yssue.   .... in com.....

Sʳ John Wilde-⊤Grace 1 d. & one   Thomas⊤.... widdow   Mary ux. Tho.
gose of Iridg | of the 3 coheires of   Wildegose. | of Mʳ Smyth   Joanes of com.
in com. Sussex | Bryan Annesley of | of Mepham.   Herefford.
in the p'ish of | Lee in Kent shee   —
Salehurst knt. | was one of the mayds   Margerett ux.
1634. | of honor to Q. Elize-   A daughter.   John Parry of
               | beth.   Acornbery in
             ⚓ | Herefford.

Wild geese in the family. The surname *Wildgoose* or *Wildegos* means exactly what it says, the original Mr.Wildgoose having presumably resembled a wild goose in some way or another. Here is the pedigree of a Sussex family of *Wildegose*s as recorded in 1633. [From *The Visitations of the County of Sussex, 1530 and 1633-4*, edited by W.Bruce Bannerman for the Harleian Society, 1905].

as prickly as briar, or have lived near a briar patch, though **Broom** and **Fe(a)rn** almost certainly refer to a place of habitation rather than to an aspect of character or personality.

A person may have been characterised not so much by his appearance, as by his physical prowess. **Armstrong** is a surname closely associated with the borderland between England and Scotland, as is **Turnbull**; the man from whom this name was derived may have been strong enough to turn a strong bull around – or he might have *turned* English bulls into his own Scottish fields, a common enough practice at one time.

Personal characteristics

You might have a surname which gives an indication as to the character or personality of your male-line ancestor. Was he sagacious, faithful and frugal, or was he foolish, feckless and a spendthrift?

The following names are good news in this regard, though people being what they are, any of them could have been used with heavy irony: **Amis** [friend, *ami*; a particularly fine friend would be **Bellamy** (*bel ami*)]; **Bligh** [cheerful]; **Car(e)less** [ebullient, without a care in the world]; **Curtis** [courteous, refined]; **Douce/Douche/Duce/Dowsett** [sweet, pleasant]; **Figgis** [trustworthy]; **Fairbairn** [literally a lovely child, but possibly a variant on **Freeborn**]; **Fairchild**; **Godsal(l)/ Goodsell** [a *good soul* – but easily confused with **Godsell/Godsil**, derived from place names in Hampshire, the Isle of Wight, Kent or Wiltshire]; **Goodlad** [a trusted servant]; **Goodson** [a dutiful son]; **Goodswen** [a *good swain*, or trusted servant]; **Goodwill** [friendly]; **Hendy** [pleasant and affable]; **Jolly/Jolliffe(e)** [jolly, cheerful]; **Lawty/ L(e)uty** [trustworthy]; **Lovejoy** [simply a lover of joy? Bardsley says: *A pretty sobriquet. Just the surname to be handed down. No fear of any*

Scattering good or goods around. A man originally named *Scattergood* would have been generous, if not over-generous, with his wealth, scattering it around to all and sundry. [From Kelly's *Post Office Directory of Derbyshire* 1876].

Sheer Bliss. The name *Bliss* would have been used for a happy or cheerful person, though it can also be a Welsh patronymic surname meaning 'son of Ellis' (*ab Ellis*). This bookplate was used by Philip Bliss of the Bodleian Library at Oxford.

A marvel to behold. The surname of Andrew *Marvell* (1621-1678), M.P. for Hull and a poet, is known to have been used literally or ironically for a wondrous person, but can also be derived from a French place-name, *Merville*. [From *Yorkshire Notes and Queries*, Volume Two, edited by J.Horsfall Turner, 1890].

male member of the family trying to get rid of it. To a generation of television viewers, the name Lovejoy will be forever associated with a likeable but roguish antiques dealer played by Ian MacShane]; **Makepeace** [a wise conciliator]; **Merryweather** [of a sunny disposition; the surnames **Fairweather** and **Foulweather** may also be found]; **Mildmay** [gentle, innocuous]; **Noble**; **Prowse** [brave, valiant]; **Pridham/ Prudhomme** [a prude or sensible person]; **Stallard** [resolute]; **Sweetapple** [apparently a nickname for someone as pleasant as a sweet apple]; **Toogood** [very good – or, ironically, too good by half]; **Standfast** [reliable]; **Va(i)sey** [cheerful].

But here comes the bad news: surnames which imply an insult. As many derogatory names as complimentary ones seem to have survived to the present day, and the fact that more of these have not been abandoned in favour of euphemistic alternatives can be accounted for in part by the change in the meaning of certain words over the years. If you bear one of these surnames yourself, you'll know how unfair each can now seem to be, and how different you may be from the person whose human frailties gave rise to it in the first place.

- *Arrogant.* **Boggis** [boastful, haughty]; **Proud(e)/Prout** [haughty or vain; **Proud** is mainly found in Northumberland, while Prout is Cornish]; **Proudfoot** [strutting around in a haughty manner].

- *Boorish.* **Thewless** [ill-mannered; chiefly a Yorkshire surname].

- *Cheating.* **Fetters** [imposter, cheat]; **Treacher/Tricker/Trickett** [devious, unreliable]; **Wrench** [wily, tricky].

- *Childish.* **Suckling** [childish in behaviour or appearance, like a suckling infant]; **Maliphant** [*mal enfant*, naughty child].

Suckling twice over. The armorial bearings featured on the bookplate of Florence Horatio Suckling reinforce the fact that *Suckling* [a nickname for a childish person] was both her married name *and* her maiden name.

- *Clueless.* **Coote** [stupid, but can also be used for a bald person, the bird of this name being both apparently-bald and proverbially stupid]; **Dwelly** [always making mistakes]; **Geach/Geake/Jeeks/Jecks/Jex** [stupid; Geach is found principally in Devon and Cornwall] or **Samways** [from Old English elements meaning *half wise*].

- *Dandy/Effeminate.* **Blanchflower** [*white flower*, probably used for a man who looked effeminate]; **Damsell** [an effeminate man, like a damsel]; **Lovelock** [from the name for a well-placed lock of hair of the kind favoured by a dandy]; **Peabody** [a flashy dresser: *peacock body*]; **Quantrill** [a dandy].

- *Drunkard.* **Chopin** [English and French surname for a heavy drinker; appropriately enough, the famous composer Frédéric Chopin came from a family of French vineyard owners].

- *Flirtatious.* The name **Lovelace** would appear to have nothing to do with lace, but was used for a philanderer who was *love-less*, entering into relationships with women with no real sense of commitment.

- *Gloomy:* **Droop** [dejected, sad]; **Friday** [as solemn as a Friday fast-day]; **Sadd** [serious, solemn].

- *Greedy.* **Gulliver/Gulliford** [greedy]; **Puttock** and **Gleed** [greedy, from two different Middle English words for a kite, a proverbially ravenous bird].

- *Incompetent.* **Mauleverer** [an inept hunter of hares, from the Old French *mal levrier*. Isn't it difficult to imagine a world long gone by, in which lack of skill in this activity was the most distinctive feature of a man's life and character? A more precise explanation for the origin of the name is offered alongside a **Mauliverer** pedigree in *Ducatus Leodiensis* by Ralph Thoresby (revised by T.D. Whitaker, second edition, 1816, page 191): *This name in ancient Writings is called **Malus Leporarius Mal-levorer**, or the **Bad Hare-hunter;** and Tradition saith, that a Gentleman of this Country being to let slip a Brace of Greyhounds, to run for a great Wager, so held them in the **Swinge**, that they were more likely to strangle themselves than kill the Hare, whereupon this Sir-Name was fixed on his Family.*]

- *Lazy.* **Doolittle** [a man who didn't get around to doing very much of anything]. The **Co(c)kayne** family was hardly noted for its lazy ways, and produced a 17th century Lord Mayor of London and a highly-acclaimed herald at the College of Arms, George Edward Cokayne (1825-1911); too bad, then, that the surname is derived from a nickname for a person whose feet were never firmly on the ground, but who preferred to inhabit a dreamy kind of cloud-cuckoo land.

Not a good hare-hunter. Legend has it that there was once a gentleman who intended to hunt hares with greyhounds for a bet, but who was so totally incompetent at what he was doing that he was named *Mauleverer* [an inept hunter of hares] and thereafter bore three running greyhounds on his coat-of-arms. [From *Yorkshire County Magazine*, Volume One, edited by J.Horsfall Turner, 1891].

- *Lecherous*. Readers of Shakespeare will know that a *plackett* was part of a woman's clothing, but could also refer, by association, to the female sex organs. The colloquial use of the word probably pre-dates Shakespeare's time, and the surname **Plackett**, found today in Derbyshire and elsewhere, is perhaps derived from a nickname for a sexually active person.

- *Miserly*. **Drinkwater** [a miser or pauper who drank water because it was cheap; also possibly used ironically of an innkeeper or heavy drinker of alcohol]; **Pennyfather/Pennyfeather** [a miser]; **Money-penny** [a miser or rich man – someone who had *many pennies*]; **Wimpenny** [a miser or gambler; principally a Yorkshire surname].

- *Obstinate*. **Crust** [hard as a crust].

- *Pusillanimous*. **Doubtfire** [*fear fire* – someone afraid of fire. Admirers of Robin Williams's bravura performance as the eponymous Mrs Doubtfire in the film of that name will be glad to hear that at least the surname itself is not a fictional one but has a long history: so, for example, Johannes **Doutfir** appears in the Poll Tax returns for Whaplode in Lincolnshire in 1381].

- *Reckless*. **Bulleid** [*bull head*, impetuous]; **Hassard** [a risk-runner, prepared to take a chance – especially in gambling games]; **Ventris** [daring, or too daring].

- *Unfortunate*. **Mallory** [from Old French *malheure*, meaning unlucky or unhappy].

There are many other surnames in the same vein: **Atter** means venomous, **Grill(s)** means fierce or cruel, **Haggard** means wild – and so on...

The Oxford English Dictionary, which can be a great help in identifying old or arcane occupational terms, also includes a large number of obsolete words which were once used to describe physical or personal characteristics, and may well help you unlock the meaning of an unusual surname. Do pay particular attention, though, to the date which usually accompanies a word to indicate when it is first known to have been used in written documentation.

Surnames based upon places: topographical

Surnames based upon places form the largest category of all, and here we can usefully separate those which are *topographical* in origin (based upon a general feature of the landscape, be it natural or man-made) from those which are *toponymic* (derived from a place or natural feature which is already defined by a specific name of its own).

Topographical surnames such as **Wood, Hill, Shaw, Heath, Moor(e)** or **Rivers** are not usually difficult to spot, though there are some regional differences: the name **Coomb(e)(s)** [*a valley*] is most commonly met with in the West Country, but the further north you travel into England or Scotland, the more likely you are to come across surnames like **Thwaite** [*a meadow, clearing*], **Clough** [*a slope or ravine*] or **Burn(s)** [*a stream*]. Now here we may encounter difficulties straightaway: does a particular family bearing a surname like Coomb, Thwaite, Clough and Burn have its origin in a man who lived near such a topographical feature, or in one who came from a settlement which carried the place-name *Coomb*, *Thwaite*, *Clough* or *Burn*? Only careful research in written records may yield the answer here, even if one can be found at all. The problem is exemplified by a surname like **Sykes**, which has been the subject of DNA analysis by Professor Brian Sykes of Oxford University. We can say that Sykes is a name principally found in the West Riding of Yorkshire, and that the word *syke*, meaning a stream or ditch (often one serving as a boundary), is very much a north-of-England topographical term. Some families called Sykes, then, may have had an ancestor who lived near a *syke* – but he might also have come from one of a number of small settlements in Yorkshire bearing the place-name *Syke(s)*. The surname specialist George Redmonds has found references to the Sykes surname in Flockton, near Huddersfield, as early as the 1280s, but a Sykes pedigree featured in *Ducatus*

Where else but the West Riding of Yorkshire? Two distinctively Yorkshire surnames yoked together. *Gaukroger* is from a Sowerby place-name, while *Sykes* can have its origins in a feature of the landscape or in one of a number of place-names. [From Street's *Indian and Colonial Mercantile Directory*, 1888].

Leodiensis by Ralph Thoresby (revised by T.D. Whitaker, second edition, 1816) indicates (accurately or not, as the case may be) that a family of this name which eventually became well-established in the West Riding could be traced back to a Richard Sykes of *Sykes-Dyke* near Carlisle. Just when we thought we might have the Sykes family bottled up nicely, this suggestion of a Cumbrian place-name origin comes along to confuse matters. Investigations like this, it would seem, are *never over until the fat lady sings…*

Do look out, by the way, for rather less obvious examples in the topographical category such as **Lyle/L'isle** [*the island*] or the Scottish surname **Innes** [from the Gaelic *Inis*], which also means *an island*.

Many topographical surnames are not at all scarce, and it should be clear that not all **Wood**s, **Hill**s and **Rivers** are necessarily related. It is even said that on one occasion in the 18th century when Kent played Surrey at cricket, every member of the Surrey team had the surname Wood.

Individuals who lived to the north, south, east or west of a given settlement or had arrived from those directions, could acquire surnames accordingly. **Norris** [north] and **Southern/Sotheran** [south] fall into this category.

Once again it can be a fascinating exercise to take a close look at the printed Poll Tax returns for the late 14th century – a time when surnames were first becoming generally established in many parts of the country. Here you will unearth a number of topographical bynames or surnames preceded by a preposition: so in the Wapentake of Kesteven in Lincolnshire we'll find Willelmus **atte Water** and Willelmus **atte the Lane**, while in Norfolk we have Johannes **in the Medewe** and Johannes **atte Grene**.

Some surnames have retained such a preposition, or the rudiments of one, as their first syllable: men who lived at or near a ridge, a wood or a tree could acquire the second-names **Attridge**, **Attwood/Underwood** and **Attree**, and someone dwelling beside a river, stream, lake or pond could be known as **Bywater**. Someone who dwelt near a spring or a well could be known as **At(t)well**, and this in turn could be shortened to **Twells**. It was once a common practice to change the preposition *at* to *atten* when the following word began with a vowel. William who lived near an ash tree would be known as *William atten ash*, and his friend Thomas, who preferred to set up home near an oak tree, would be *Thomas atten oak*. Over time, William's byname or surname would eventually be shortened to **Nash**, and Thomas's to **Noake(s)**. This process is not confined to personal or family names, of course: the amphibious creature which we currently refer to as *a newt* began life as *an ewt*. The Poll Tax returns provide examples of this process in mid-stream, as it were: in Tangmere, Sussex, the name of Johanne **atte**

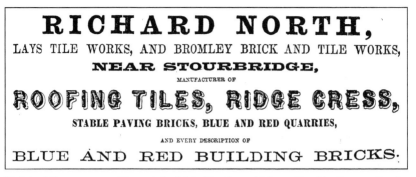

RICHARD NORTH,
LAYS TILE WORKS, AND BROMLEY BRICK AND TILE WORKS,
NEAR STOURBRIDGE,
MANUFACTURER OF
ROOFING TILES, RIDGE CRESS,
STABLE PAVING BRICKS, BLUE AND RED QUARRIES,
AND EVERY DESCRIPTION OF
BLUE AND RED BUILDING BRICKS.

Point of the compass. The original Mr North could have lived to the north of a given settlement, or may have come from that direction in the first instance. [From Kelly's *Post Office Directory of Shropshire, Herefordshire, Gloucestershire and Bristol* 1879].

Nasshe has already had the letter '*n*' removed from the end of the prefix *atten* and attached to the beginning of the word *asshe*; in the fullness of time such a process would yield up the byname or surname we know today as **Nash**.

Since man has left his mark on the countryside over many hundreds of years, it is hardly surprising to find a large group of surnames based upon man-made features. Monosyllabic examples here would include **Hall** or **Church**, while **Town(s)end**, **Mil(l)house** and the rest are rather more sophisticated. Spellings might have changed over time or according to locality, so the surnames **Bridge(s)** and **Brigg(s)** and **Gate(s)**and **Yate(s)** are essentially the same, and a person who lived on a broad street would become **Bradstreet**. I live in a part of England where once-familiar outhouses which used to characterise the urban scene were referred to as the *coal'us* (coal house) and the *wesh'us* (wash house) – not to mention the ubiquitous *shit'us* – and where a village with the official name of *Horsley Woodhouse* is universally referred to as *Ossly Woodus*, so it's no surprise to me to find that people who lived in or near a woodhouse, a bakehouse, a lofthouse or a bullhouse acquired surnames like **Woodus**, **Backus**, **Loftus** and **Bullas**.

Again, we can find several 14th-century Poll Tax payers whose topographical names are based upon man-made features preceded by a preposition, such as Matilda **atte Hall**, Johannes **at the Brygg** and Cristiana **atte the Tounshende**. The name of Isabella **de Hall** of Aunsby in Lincolnshire (1381) is rather more untypical, since the preposition *de* is more usually attached to a toponymic name (as with *Philippus de London*, assessed for tax in Denver, Norfolk, in 1381) rather than a topographical one such as *hall*. In the later Middle Ages, the prepositions *de* and *atte* could be replaced by '*a*'. The Poll Tax returns for Leicestershire in 1381 include John **A Leke** in West Langton, and over time a byname or surname such as **A Gate** would become simply **Agate**.

In theory almost anyone could have lived near a hill, a gate or a millhouse and been named accordingly, so we must not expect that individuals bearing surnames based upon common rural or urban features or buildings will necessarily be related. Nevertheless, some topographical surnames are scarcer than we might think, and can represent a single-family origin in certain cases.

Surnames based upon places: toponymic

If a surname which interests you is *toponymic* in origin – that is, it is clearly based upon a named location rather than a general topographical feature – then you may feel that you have some cause for rejoicing. To learn from a surname that the first person who bore it lived near an unidentified hill or wood is one thing, but to be able to say that such a person came from, or once lived in, a named place is rather more satisfying. Do be cautious: a man with a toponymic byname or surname like **Ashton** may have lived or owned land in a village of that name, but he may only have acquired Ashton as a second-name when he moved somewhere else, his place of origin at that stage being a useful way of identifying him. We could say in general terms that the higher up the social scale a person was, the more likely it will be that he had acquired his toponymic surname because he was a significant landowner at the place in question. George Redmonds makes the telling point, however, that this was not always the case in the uplands, where tenants such as the **Akroyds** of Akroyd, the **Lightowlers** of Lightollers, the **Butterworths** of Butterworth and others took their name from their farm or from a piece of arable ground which they tended.

I should say at the outset that while the great majority of toponymic surnames are easy enough to pin down, several traps do lie in store for the unwary, and you'll find that I'll be entering caveats thick and fast.

Just to prove the point, let me begin with a word of caution. We know that some place-names have given rise to surnames, but it's worth remembering that a number of surnames have themselves been used as the names of places, and that it is sometimes difficult to know which came first. Faced with the problem of identifying a place-name which might have given rise to my own **Titford** surname, and keen to grasp at almost any straw, I initially paid some attention to a tiny settlement which is still named *Titford* on detailed modern maps, and which lies in an area of western Wiltshire which was home to the Titford family from the mid 16th century onwards. I was eventually able to convince myself that I had my chickens and eggs reversed. A yeoman called Richard Titford had farmed the spot called *Titford* in the early 17th century, and it looks all-but-certain that he gave his surname to the place, not the other way around. This was a disappointment, certainly, but also a good object lesson to have learned. If we were to focus upon *Upton Scudamore*, the Wiltshire parish in which *Titford* lies, however, we'd have little difficulty in separating chickens from eggs. Here is one of many examples of a place being given a double name: *Upton* is clearly a place-name pure and simple [*higher farm*], to which has been added the surname of the **Scudamore** family, former property owners in the area. Peter **de Skydemore** is known to have held the manor of Upton in 1216, followed by Geoffrey **de Escudamor** in 1242 and Peter **Scuydemor** in 1275.

Countries within the British Isles

Some surnames seem to indicate very clearly that the original bearer came from one of the countries that make up the British Isles.

The surprising thing about the surnames **English/Inglis/England** is just how often they are found within England itself, but surely the person who was first given the byname or surname of **Scotland** or **Scott** was a native of Scotland who then went to live somewhere else? Well, yes and no. This is true in many cases, but **Scotland** could also be an English version of a scarce Norman given name, *Escotland*, or a Scottish name for a person from a place named *Scotland(well)* in Kinross. **Scott** could refer to a person from Scotland, but is more commonly used within Scotland itself for a speaker of Gaelic, and such people originally came from Ireland...

Surnames of the **Walsh(e)/Welsh/Walch/Welch** class would seem to indicate a Welshman, and they often have been used in such a way, but strictly speaking such names are used for Celtic people in general, being derived from an English word meaning *foreigner*. The original English, who had arrived as invaders from the east as early as the 4th century, had the barefaced cheek to refer to the indigenous population of the British islands as *foreigners*. Of course, to travel abroad and yet still to think of the national population of other countries as *foreigners* is something of a pastime for the English even today. I suppose we might say that Johanna **Walsshewoman**, who appears in the Poll Tax returns of 1379 for Stamford in Lincolnshire, is only one letter of the alphabet away from being a washerwoman (*wasshewoman*), but her name as it stands suggests that she was of Celtic origin. The surname **Wallace** has a similar meaning to those of the Walsh group, and was originally used in different parts of Britain to describe Welshmen, Scotsmen and Bretons. So a Scotsman could be a Welshman... Complex, isn't it?

Gaelic speakers. Sir Walter Scott (1771-1832). The name *Scott* was frequently used for a speaker of Gaelic.

Ireland and **Irish**, by contrast, are simple enough, referring to a person who came from Ireland. Another name sometimes applied to an Irishman in general – though originally used for a bard or poet in particular – is **Tighe**, with variations such as **Teague** and **Teek**.

Surnames which suggest an origin outside the British Isles – like

French – are often easy enough to identify, though **Pettingill** (a man from Portugal) or **Dench** (a man from Denmark) are, perhaps less obvious.

Counties

Although **Kent**, a short and punchy word, sits happily as a surname, many full-bloodied county names like *Herefordshire* or *Kirkcudbrightshire* would sound cumbersome in the extreme if they were to be used in this way. **Westmor(e)land**, **Cumberland** and **Cornwall/Cornwallis**, however, operate successfully as surnames, and so do **Derbyshire** and **Hampshire**. But here come the caveats...

Darbyshire/Darbishire/Derbyshire could refer to a man from the midland county of that name, but it can also be derived from the area of West Derby near Liverpool, which was known in mediaeval times as *Derbyshire*. H.B. Guppy, in *The homes of family names in Great Britain*, published in 1890, reported that **Derbyshires/Darbyshires** were more plentiful in Cheshire than they were in the county of Derbyshire itself, and Kelvin E. Warth found a significant number of Lancashire-based **Derbyshires** listed in telephone directories for the 1980s (Lasker, G.W. and Mascie-Taylor, C.G.N. *Atlas of British surnames* [1990]).

Hampshire as a surname first began to perplex me when I found out that the English county of that name was known as the county of *Southampton* at the time of surname formation, and for many centuries afterwards. How could such a surname emanate from a county which did not then exist? There would seem to be two answers to this non-

Not all Darbishires have their origins in the county of Derbyshire. Charles Henry Darbishire, in business as a quarryman in Wales, had been born in Manchester. The area around West Derby in Lancashire was once known as *Derbyshire*, and is one well-attested source of the surname. [From Kelly's *Post Office Directory of Kent, Surrey and Sussex* 1878].

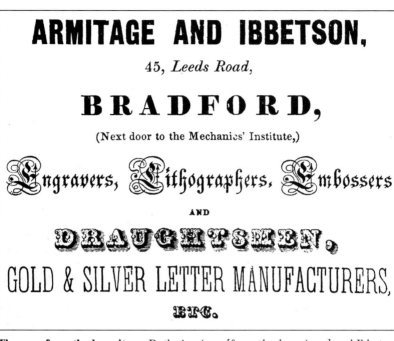

The man from the hermitage. Both *Armitage* [from the *hermitage*] and Ibbetson [son of *Isabel*] are distinctively West Riding surnames. [From White's *Directory of Leeds and the clothing districts of Yorkshire* 1853].

rhetorical question. Firstly, the word *Hampshire* was probably alive and well for many centuries in everyday speech and writing, even if the official county name was *Southampton* – and *New Hampshire*, on the eastern seaboard of North America, was first named and settled as an independent colony in the year 1623. Secondly, an area around Sheffield in South Yorkshire which has long been known as *Hallamshire* was modified to produce the **Hampshire** surname, which is still most frequently found in Yorkshire.

Towns and villages

By far the largest number of toponymic surnames with origins within the British Isles are based not upon a country or a county, but upon a town, a village, a hamlet – or even an isolated farmstead. A fairly straightforward example here would be that of **Priestley**, with its origins in one of a number of minor place-names, of which the best-known is in West Yorkshire. Joseph Priestley (1733-1804) achieved

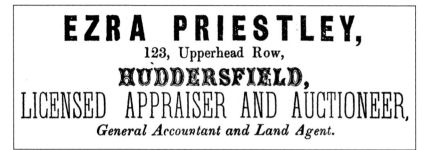

EZRA PRIESTLEY,
123, Upperhead Row,
HUDDERSFIELD,
LICENSED APPRAISER AND AUCTIONEER,
General Accountant and Land Agent.

Priestley, alias Presley. *Priestley* comes from a minor place-name in Yorkshire. Variations on the name include *Presley*. [From White's *Directory of Leeds and the clothing districts of Yorkshire* 1853].

lasting fame as a scientist and writer, but to a generation of people brought up after the Second World War, the surname **Presley**, a variant of Priestley, will probably have an even greater resonance. Elvis Presley (1935-1977) had several interesting ancestors, including a number of Scots-Irish and a Cherokee Indian called *Morning White Dove* (1800-1835), but at present his paternal line, featuring one illegitimate birth in 1896, can be traced back no further than David **Pressley**, a Anglo-Irishman who settled at New Bern, North Carolina, in 1740.

It is a feature of toponymic surnames that a significant number of them seem to emanate from small settlements rather than from large towns. In the 1970s one of my tutors on a Post-Graduate Certificate in Education course at the University of Newcastle-u*pon-Tyne was called David* **Rostron**; it struck me even then that I was as likely to come across his surname (a variant on **Rawsthorne/ Rawstorn(e)/ Rawstron/ Rostern(e)/ Rosthorne**), which comes from the village of *Rostherne* in Cheshire, as I was to meet someone named after the county town of *Chester*.

Even a village like Rostherne, however, is populous indeed compared to the single dwelling-house situated near a *hermitage* which is said to be the origin of the Yorkshire surname **Armitage**. Here we have an interesting example of one of the ways in which pronunciation patterns in England have changed over the years. John Walker uses the introduction to his famous *Pronouncing dictionary*, compiled in the closing years of the 18th century, to protest (on behalf, as he says, of himself and of Richard Brinsley Sheridan, the famous dramatist) that the older pronunciation in a word like *service* was fast disappearing. Originally such a word was spoken as if it was spelt *sarvice*, but by John Walker's time fashions were changing. These days British speakers generally use an *er* pronunciation in words like *service* (formerly pronounced *sarvice*) and in names like *Gertrude* (formerly pronounced *Gartrude*), though they have retained the *ar* sound in words like *clerk* and in place-names like *Derby, Berkshire* and *Hertfordshire*. Imagine how confusing it must be at the present time to live in *Berkhamsted* (*er* pronunciation) in the county of *Hertfordshire* (*ar* pronunciation)! Now our American cousins have handled matters rather differently. They have 'modernised' the word *clerk* to give it an *er* pronunciation, but have generally retained the original *ar* sound in words where the English have abandoned it, such as *wrestle* and *vermin*, which many Americans pronounce as *wrastle* and *varmint*.

We can draw an important general conclusion here regarding the pronunciation of surnames and first-names. You must expect that in times past your distant ancestor *Gertrude Herbert from Jersey* would have described herself as *Gartrude Harbert from Jarsey*. I use this concocted example quite deliberately since, as it happens, I have seen historical examples of all three names spelt *Gartrude, Harbert* and *Jarsey*. In other words, on some occasions the spelling was changed to reflect what was then the usual pronunciation.

An English surname like **Marchant** has a slightly different story to tell; in this case it is derived from Old French via the Middle English word *march(e)ant*, which itself had an *ar* spelling as well as an *ar* pronunciation. As time went by, the Marchant surname remained true to its roots, retaining the *ar* spelling and pronunciation, while in everyday use the word *march(e)ant* became *merchant*, with an *er* spelling and an *er* pronunciation. Modern French, of course, still makes use of the form *marchand*.

If you can find a copy of the fourth edition of Eilert Ekwall's *The concise Oxford dictionary of place-names*, published in 1959, you'll see that the dust-jacket carries a rather splendid colour facsimile of Saxton's map of Oxfordshire, Buckinghamshire and Berkshire, dated 1574, which includes an outline of what is described as being 'Part of *Hartfordshire*' – a spelling which reflects what was then the usual pronunciation of the county name, and has remained so to this day. We may say that in situations like this, something had to give: either the spelling of certain words would have to be changed to *ar* to reflect the usual pronunciation – which is what Saxton was doing in 1574 – or a new *er* pronunciation would have to be adopted to reflect the existing *er* spelling. Matters were coming to a head by the late 18th century; much to John Walker's obvious disgust, the *er* spelling was remaining unchanged, but an *er* pronunciation, which seemed to reflect that spelling so neatly, was starting to win the day. This process of change left a number of place-names (such as *Hertfordshire*) and words such as *clerk* untouched, however – a typical British compromise, we might say.

If your surname is **Garnsey** or **Garnesy**, by the way, you'll already know that this reflects an earlier pronunciation of *Guernsey* in the Channel Islands, quite consistent with the principles I've just outlined. A pullover made of Jersey wool is, of course, a *jersey*, but in parts of the Midlands (and elsewhere?) a similar garment from Guernsey is known as a *ganzie*.

It's all very well for me to expound at length on this subject, but I was recently caught napping myself when it comes to *ar*s and *er*s. I was tracing the ancestry of a Norfolk family called **Bircham**, and had come to terms with the fact that it was sometimes spelt **Burcham** – which represents the same pronunciation as Bircham, after all. What I didn't notice from the outset as I searched through various indexes, but should have done much sooner (a real slapped wrist job, this), was that the family also appeared as **Barcham**. Of course they did, since this almost certainly reflects the way in which they originally pronounced their name!

Now – at last – we can relate this whole process to the **Armitage** surname. George Redmonds in *Yorkshire surnames series, Part Two: Huddersfield and District* (1992) says that the family name seems to have a single source in Yorkshire. A dwelling house near a hermitage in South Crosland, itself also known as the *Hermytage* (1382) was the home of the Armitage family for several hundred years. Early bearers of the name were known as **de Hermitagio**, **Hermitage**, **Hermitege** or **Hermetege**, but by the year 1545 there is evidence in the Subsidy Rolls of a man called William **Armitege**. Here is a case, it would seem, of the surname spelling finally deciding to imitate the usual everyday *-ar* pronunciation, as was the case, we may remember, with our friend *Gartrude* **Harbert**. Henceforward a *hermitage* (still pronounced *harmitage* or *armitage* until the late 18th century) was a building, but a person whose ancestors had lived in or near a hermitage were the Armitages. As if to prove that matters are never quite so simple in surname studies, it's worth mentioning that George Redmonds has found references as late as the 1720s to the surname still being spelt Hermitage by some family branches with Yorkshire connections.

I suppose the defining moment for me when considering the **Armitage** surname came a few years ago when I was driving through Nashville, Tennessee, on my way west towards Memphis. I couldn't avoid the temptation to make a stopover in order to visit The Hermitage, the country retreat of my favourite American President, Andrew *Old Hickory* Jackson. I was checking out next morning at a Holiday Inn close to Hickory Boulevard, when a couple of visitors arrived and asked the lady behind the desk where they could find Andrew Jackson's former home. 'Oh, you mean *th'Armitage*' was her reply. When I enquired politely whether everyone in Nashville used a similar pronunciation, she replied that she didn't know, since she was an

DWERRIHOUSE   AND COMP^Y.,

Watch and Clock Makers,

Formerly of Berkeley Square (and Davies Street), but now of

131, MOUNT STREET.

In consequence of frequent mistakes arising, BELL and SON feel called upon to state that they are the *only Survivors* of the late Firm of DWERRIHOUSE, CARTER, OGSTON AND BELL, and continue to carry on the business as usual, at

131, MOUNT STREET, BERKELEY SQUARE, W.

Established 1760.

Lancashire clockmakers in London. *Dwerrihouse*, a scarce surname, is derived from a place-name near Chorley in Lancashire. Thomas Dwerrihouse was making clocks in Garston as early as the 1770s, and in 1781 John Dwerrihouse was made an honorary freeman of the Clockmakers' Company of London. [From Kelly's *Post Office London and Suburban Guide* 1861].

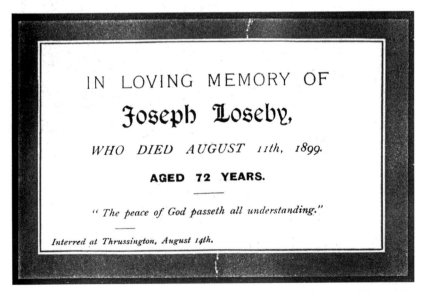

IN LOVING MEMORY OF

Joseph Loseby,

WHO DIED AUGUST 11th, 1899.

AGED 72 YEARS.

" The peace of God passeth all understanding."

Interred at Thrussington, August 14th.

Typical toponymic. The surname *Loseby* is not featured in any of the major surname dictionaries, but a gazetteer shows that *Loseby* (or *Lowesby*) is the name of a village in Leicestershire. Joseph Loseby's family appears not to have moved far from its point of origin: Thrussington, where he was buried in 1899, lies only a few miles north-east of Lowesby.

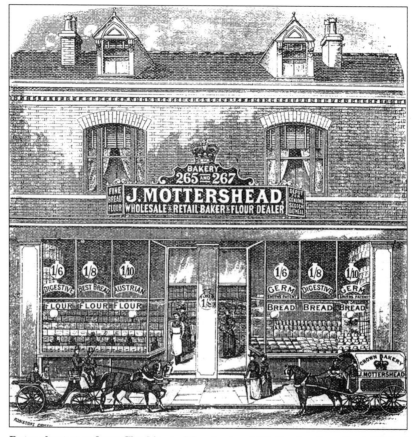

But a short step from Cheshire to Manchester. J.Mottershead, well-established at Hyde Road, Manchester, in the 1890s, would have been happy to sell you all the bread and flour your heart could desire. His surname comes from a now-lost place in the parish of Mottram, Cheshire. [From *The century's progress: Lancashire (Progress and Commerce)* 1892].

outsider herself, having been born and raised in *Jarsey* (New Jersey). I found it very gratifying to discover that an older English pronunciation of this sort is still alive and well in present-day America.

So much, then, for small settlements and even named houses which have given rise to surnames. What of large towns and cities? There is at least one known example of the town of *Ipswich* in Suffolk having spawned a surname in the late mediaeval period. The will of Nicholas **Yepisswich** of Burgate was proved in the Archdeaconry Court of

No connection with kettles. The surname *Kettlewell* is derived from a Yorkshire place-name. The *Kettle* element means 'a deep valley'. [From White's *Directory of Leeds and the clothing districts of Yorkshire* 1853].

Sudbury on 20 October 1445, but only if we were to know that the town itself was originally called *Gipeswic* could we begin to make sense of the fact that he was also referred to as Nicholas **Gypewic**. Relations mentioned in his will carried a variety of last-names: his father was Thomas de **Gippewic**, he had sons William de **Gippewic** and John **Yebyswych**, and two of John's sons were William **Gippewic** and

A Yorkshire surname in London. The Yorkshire surname *Robertshaw* has its origin in a place of this name near Heptonstall. [From Kelly's *Post Office London and Suburban Court Guide* 1861].

Sweet name. The surname of E.H.Bickersteth, one-time Bishop of Exeter, comes from a place-name in Lancashire with the meaning 'beekeeper's landing place'. [From *The Church Missionary Gleaner*, volume fifteen (1888)].

Nicholas **Gipp**. We might say that only a good deal of local knowledge or a flash of almost divine inspiration could have alerted us to the fact that a second-name like **Gipp** could be derived from the place-name *Ipswich*.

Worcestershire and London. Sir Nicholas Throckmorton (or Throgmorton), a courtier and diplomat who died in 1571, might have given his name to Throgmorton Street in the City of London. The Throckmortons have long been a well-known Catholic family, with a surname which comes from a place-name in Worcestershire. Sir Robert Throckmorton of Coughton in Warwickshire was made a Baronet in 1642, and his arms feature the Red Hand of Ulster accordingly. [From *Bookplates* by Edward Almack, 1904].

Certainly the surname **Gipp** or **Gipps** can still be found at the present day, though it is usually taken to be a pet-form of the personal name *Gilbert*. Yet despite the fact that Ipswich was a major town, we could look in vain for any significant number of people who have carried anything approaching **Ipswich** or even **Gippewic** as a hereditary surname during the post-mediaeval period. By contrast, there is no problem finding people with a surname like **Palgrave**, which comes from a more modest settlement altogether. Or rather, to be honest, it can come from one of two settlements with similar names, one in Suffolk and the other in Norfolk – so the chances of a person being called Palgrave after a place-name are theoretically doubled. Francis Turner Palgrave (1824-1897) has been well-known to generations of schoolchildren and poetry-lovers as the compiler of *The Golden Treasury*, first published in 1864, while his father Sir Francis Palgrave (1788-1861), a highly-regarded historian and mediaevalist, was Deputy Keeper of the Public Records. Here comes the caveat: there would be little point in trying to trace the Palgrave ancestry of Sir Francis, because, quite simply, he doesn't have any. Born in London in 1788, he was the son of a Jewish stockbroker called Meyer **Cohen**, but changed his name – and his religion – in 1823, when he married Elizabeth **Turner** of Great Yarmouth, whose mother's maiden name was Palgrave.

Surnames like **Manchester**, **Colchester**, **Exeter** and **Norwich** can be found, but are not common, and although the name **Canterbury** does exist, you will hardly stumble across it very often in a typical lifetime. So why might it be that the names of large cities or towns seem, in general, not to have been favoured more when it came to surname formation, even taking account of the fact that many of today's substantial towns began life as altogether more modest settlements? It could be, of course, that a good number of individuals were in fact named after larger towns, but that a disproportionate number of them died out, and their names with them, at times of pestilence such as the Black Death of the 14th century. We could consider other possible reasons, too. One of the functions of a surname or a byname is to differentiate one individual from another; and to name a man after a small village would identify him quite precisely, whereas there would have been less point in using the name of a large and populous town for this purpose. Demographic patterns must also have played a part here. The general trend has long been for people to migrate from villages to towns, rather than *vice-versa*; a man from Palgrave in Suffolk, arriving in the county town of Ipswich to seek a better life, could well have acquired the byname or surname of Palgrave in the process – but there would have been much less human traffic in the opposite direction.

On occasions, however, we may be staring at a surname which has a large-town origin after all, without realising it. It may not be too difficult

Cohen, alias Palgrave. Robert Harry Inglis Palgrave (1827-1919), an economist and Fellow of the Royal Society who was knighted in 1909, was the brother of Francis Turner Palgrave (1824-1897), compiler of *The Golden Treasury*. Their father, Sir Francis Palgrave (1788-1861), son of a Jewish stockbroker called Meyer *Cohen*, had changed his surname to *Palgrave* in 1823. [From *Anglo-Jewish notabilities: their arms and testamentary dispositions*, published by the Jewish Historical Society of England in 1949].

to surmise that Willelmus **Burmicham**, featured in the 1377 Poll Tax returns for Staffordshire, was named after the town of *Birmingham*, but would the surnames **Glasscowe** and **Edenbrow** be so easy to figure out? The first of these, which looks at first sight as if it might be describing some tasteless ornament or other you would find on a mantlepiece, is in fact derived from *Glasgow*, while **Edenbrow** and its many variants – you guessed already – was used for someone who came from *Edinburgh*. Rev David Jackson and his wife Anthea (née Edenbrow) very kindly sent me copies of a number of entries from Lincolnshire parish registers for Edenbrow and its variants. **Edinburgh** is featured, alongside **Edenbrow** itself, as are the following: **Eddingborrow**; **Eden Borrough**; **Edenbarugh**; **Edenborough**; **Edenborow**; **Edenborrough**; **Edenborrow**; **Edenburgh**; **Edinbergh**; **Edinborough**; **Edinbourrugh**; **Edinbrough**; **Edinbrow**; **Edingborough**; **Ednbrough**; **Edynburg**. The connection between Edenbrow and Edinburgh is clear, then, but in New Sleaford there are 18th-century references to the spellings **Attenborrow** and **Attenbrugh**, and although a marriage entry of 29 November 1791 relating to William **Allett** and Mary **Attenborough** of Leasingham spells her name in this way, the relevant banns register refers to her as **Edenborough**. Now *Attenborough* is the name of a place near Nottingham, and one of two conclusions can be drawn here: either the clerks who registered events relating to the Edenbrow family in Lincolnshire knew, or could somehow intuit the fact, that the surname came originally from *Edinburgh* in Scotland or from *Attenborough* in Nottinghamshire, and spelt it accordingly, or – perhaps much more likely – they used *Edinburgh* or *Attenborough*, place-names with which they were already familiar, when faced with representing the surname being offered to them. This is a classic chicken-and-egg dilemma: was the surname originally derived from *Edinburgh* or *Attenborough*, or was it modified, whatever its true origin, to conform with the spelling of these two known places, centuries after it was first adopted by the family? I can do no more than leave these conflicting possibilities hanging in the air, though I must say that *Edinburgh*-type spellings are very much in the majority in Lincolnshire records, and a Scottish origin for the Edenbrows would seem to be a strong possibility.

Bearing in mind the fact that we now know that there were two places called *Palgrave* in England which could have given rise to a related surname, we should be aware that we may not always have narrowed down the place of origin of a toponymic name as precisely as we might have wished. There are plenty of settlements in Britain bearing names such as *Sutton*, *Langley* and the like. Not only that, but more than one person from any one of these *Sutton*s or *Langley*s could have acquired this place-name as a hereditary surname.

For all that, a number of surnames with toponymic origins are known to have been used by only one single family throughout the centuries. Such is the case with my own toponymic surname of **Titford**. The pedigree of all known Titfords alive today anywhere in the world can be traced back to two men called Richard **Tutford** and Henry **Tutford**, who were living in the village of Bratton in Wiltshire in the late 16th century; they may have been cousins, but they were very probably brothers. This early Tutford spelling should give us food for thought at the outset: vowels in surnames are notoriously unstable, since you do not use your tongue, your lips or your teeth to affect the sound as it comes up from your voice-box. The slightest difference in the shape of the mouth can move you from one vowel to another, so it is hardly surprising to discover that the full gamut of vowel sounds has been used in the Titford name by family members at different times and in different places. We have written examples of them all: **Tatford**, **Tetford**, **Titford**, **Totford** and **Tutford** – a full-house of *a, e, i, o* and *u*, though only the Tatford and Titford varieties are known to have survived to the present day, the former having first been used in Hampshire as comparatively recently as the 18th century. To get the full surname-variety picture, of course, we'd need to throw in the occasional letter '*e*' at the end of the name, or before the letter '*f*', and to substitute a '*y*' for an '*i*' – but that's the kind of thing you'd expect to encounter almost every day when looking at surnames. We even have a Somerset-based family of Titfords who became **Titeford**, then **Titefoot**, and lastly – a final indignity brought about by folk etymology - **Tightfoot**.

When it comes to vowel-sounds in both surnames and place-names, luck may be on our side, since these have often changed over time in predictable, rather than random, ways, and any linguistic historian worthy of the name could happily 'bore for England', as the saying goes, on the subject of *The Great Vowel Shift*, which once affected the language as a whole, and other such arcane matters. Now it's by no means clear which settlement somewhere in England gave rise to the Titford surname: *Tetford* in Lincolnshire is one possibility, as is a very minor place in Hampshire called *Totford*. As to West Country Titfords, we can readily observe a chronological development whereby the surname Totford became Tutford and then Titford. Now this shift in spelling is reflected precisely in the changes known to have affected a number of place-names in Hampshire and Wiltshire, for example. *Totford* in Hampshire eventually became *Tutford*, just as North *Tidworth* in Wiltshire was originally *Todeworth* and then *Tuddewurth*. This is the predictability to which I have referred; there appears to have been a general shift in vowel sounds from '*o*' to '*u*' to '*i*' which affected both place-names and surnames alike.

This *Tuddewurth/Todeworth/Tidworth* example underlines the fact that place-names have changed over the years, just as the toponymic surnames to which they have given rise have also developed and moved on. So we might well find ourselves aiming at two moving targets at once – hence the challenge. Yet surnames have always been under more pressure to change than place-names ever have. The reasons for this are simple enough: each surname belongs to a limited number of individuals only, whereas a place-name enjoys more official status and is 'owned', as it were, by an entire community, which may be resistant to change. Not only that, but surnames have been regularly carried off hither and thither by those who bear them, while place-names – if I may state the obvious here – have always remained rooted to one spot.

At times it seems as if there may be no end to the spelling variations which can be used for even the most straightforward of surnames, a phenomenon which shows no sign of diminishing in an age of mass communication. Correspondence addressed to me in the last few years has spelt my surname in the following ways: **Tidford, Tedford, Tetford, Titferd, Titforth, Titfort, Titfield, Titfeild, Tifford, Tiford, Tittford, Titfordd, Tichford, Titchford, Titfoed, Titfoot, Titlord, Tilford, Telford, Tipford, Tippford, Tiltford, Ttitford, Tictord, Tiffert, Titofrd, Totford, Tidmarsh, Titmarsh, Twyford, Thetford, Litford, Pickford, Pitford, Pitsford, Fitford, Mitford, Citford, Sitford** and **Stitford**. As it happens, some spelling varieties of the name which otherwise would seem to have died out centuries ago have been resurrected here in modern times. It is clear that some of the examples quoted are the result of a typist's finger having hit the wrong key in error, but what can we make of more surreal varieties such as **Thord, Tittoral, Alford** and **Lidgard**? The oddest things can happen: a late lamented cousin of mine, Rear Admiral Donald Titford, was a Fellow of the Royal Aeronautical Society, so an envelope addressed to him in a formal fashion would carry the letters *FRAeS* after his name. It was only a matter of time, then, before he received an item of unsolicited mail from UNICEF bearing the salutation: *Dear Admiral Fraes...*

We must move on. Just as the prepositions *at(ten)*, *under* and *by* frequently precede topographical bynames or surnames in the mediaeval period, so it is not uncommon to find *de* used with toponymic names. This is simply a French word meaning *of*, and its use bears witness to the dominance of Norman French as a literary and administrative language in England during the centuries following the Conquest of 1066. The Spanish, Italian, German and Dutch equivalents, also frequently encountered in surnames the world over, are *de*, *di/da*, *von* and *van*.

Now a man could carry a byname or a surname incorporating the word *de* either because he lived in the place in question, or because he had once lived there but had moved somewhere else. In the late 13th century Philip **de Totford** held two hides of ground in Totford in

Hampshire; we might safely assume that he was called de Totford because he owned land there. Similarly, Willelmus **de Sharnebourne**, the first person named in a Poll Tax return for *Sharneborne* in Norfolk in 1379, would almost certainly have been named after the place where he was living. By contrast, Walterus **de Drayton**, assessed for tax in the same year in Weybourne, on the north Norfolk coast, might have acquired his name while he was still living in *Drayton* near Norwich, but it is equally possible that he began to be known as de Drayton when he first appeared in Weybourne, thus being defined not as *the man who lives in Drayton*, but as *the man who has come from Drayton*.

Over time the *de* preposition was dropped in English surname usage, but where the place-name element itself was French, and if it began with a vowel or a letter 'h' followed by a vowel, then *de* could become attached or 'fused' to it. Thus we have **Daltry [d'Hauterive], Dangerfield [d'Angerville], Danvers [d'Anvers** – ie, the Belgian town of Antwerp], **Darcy [d'Arcy], Darell/Dorrell [d'Airel]** and **Devereux [d'Evreux]. Dando [d'Aunou]**, derived from *Aunou* in Normandy, is a surname now most commonly found in Somerset, and the much-loved British television presenter, Jill **Dando**, was born in Weston-super-Mare in that county. A surname like **Delaney** can exhibit a slight variation on the theme in some cases: here a fusion of the preposition *de* and the abbreviated definite article *l'* may have been added to a place in Normandy of the *Aney* variety, though it should be said that the surname of the Irish Delaneys has a different origin.

Those few names still familiar to us today which contain an abbreviated version of the English preposition *of* – as in John **O'Gaunt** [*of Ghent*] – have little more than curiosity value. John **O'Groats** is well known as the northernmost point on the Scottish mainland; *Groats* may be a corruption of an Old Norse word for a pebble, *grióт*.

One reason why we can usually tell almost at once whether an English surname is toponymic in origin is that we recognise common place-name elements which we have encountered several times before. There are even entire books dedicated to these matters, such as *The chief elements used in English place-names* by Allen Mawer (1924) and *English place-name elements* by A.H. Smith (two volumes, 1956), both published by the English Place-Name Society, which is based at the University of Nottingham. I have included a sample list of common English place-name elements later in this book, which I hope will prove helpful.

We have seen already that certain place-name suffixes like *-thwaite* or *-co(o)mb(e)* can be localised, so you can be fairly certain from this suffix evidence alone that a person called **Haythornthwaite** [from *Hawthornthwaite*, Lancashire] has northern origins, while the Conservative Party politician Ann **Widdicombe** [from *Widdecombe-in-*

the-moor, Devon, from *Widcombe* in Somerset, or from places called *Withycombe* in Devon and Somerset] has her ancestral roots in the West Country. Incidentally, I guess that many of us will recall the song *Widdecombe Fair*, and I was intrigued to read in a book by Jean Harrowven called *The origins of rhymes, songs and sayings* (1977) that the parish registers for Crediton in Devon feature some of the characters whose names are featured in it: there's a Tom **Cobbley** baptised there in the late 17th century, and the same register carries the surnames of some of Tom's mates: **Pearce**, **Stuer**, **Davy** and **Hawke**.

Before we let **Haythornthwaite**s slip away completely, I should say that I was once researching the surname *Eskridge* for an American client; now *Eskridge* is clearly derived from a place-name, and the hard '*k*' sound strongly suggested that I should look in the northern counties of England. **Eskridge**s, it turned out, were well settled in North Lancashire, Westmorland and Cumberland, and one reference I came across in the apprenticeship records of the Brewers' Company in London read as follows: ***Hatharnethawight**, John, son of John, of Caton, Lancashire, yeoman, deceased, apprenticed to Richard **Eskrige**. 27 January 1572/3* [from a transcription by Cliff Webb, in *London Livery Company apprenticeship registers*, vol.36, published by the Society of Genealogists in 2001]. It took me a while to realise that **Hatharnethawight** was an eccentric early version of **Haythornthwaite**, but when it is spelt in this way it is only one letter short of being the longest English surname, an honour accorded to **Featherstonehaugh** (pronounced *Fanshaw*), derived from a place in Northumberland which these days has the good sense to call itself simply *Featherstone*. All this makes the surname of a man I once came across called Shankar **Balasubramanian** seem quite modest in length by comparison. It is worth noticing that the Hatharnethawight spelling has reversed the two letters '*a*' and '*w*', giving us *thawight* rather than *thwaight*. I suppose that this is only to be expected in such a long and cumbersome name, and we find a variety on the theme in the IGI entry for the baptism of Alice, daughter of James **Hathronwhett**, which took place at St Mary, Lancaster, in 1605. Here the '*r*' and the '*o*' have been reversed, leaving us with *thron* rather than *thorn*. These spellings might have occurred by design or by a slip of the pen, but they are evidence of a process known as metathesis, which is worth looking out for in both surnames and place-names alike. You might well know people who inadvertently use metathesis in everyday life, speaking of *aks* not *ask*, *waps* not *wasp* or *bronical* not *bronchial*. We can observe metathesis at work in surnames, too, such as in those derived from the personal name *Absalom*, where an unvoiced '*p*' is substituted for the voiced '*b*', followed by metathesis affecting the '*p*' and the '*s*', giving us **Aspelon**, **Asplen** or **Asplin**. Similarly, the surname **Apps** [from someone who

lived near an aspen tree] can become **Asp** or **Aspey**. Here we're almost
back to our old friends the *wasps* and the *wapses*.

The family of the Earl of Spencer, who live at Althorp in
Northamptonshire, famously use the pronunciation *Althrop*, an
example of metathesis which is nothing more than a reflection of an
earlier spelling of the place-name. Herein lies an important principle at
work in many toponymic surnames – that they may well be based not
upon the present-day form and spelling of a place-name, but upon an
older version which was current when the surname was first developed,
but which may long since have been abandoned completely or only kept
alive by local dialect speakers. Most pupils I once knew at a school in
Jedburgh in Roxburghshire only ever called the place *Jeddart* or *Jethart*,
both of which formerly had been official names for the town before its
incorporation as a borough in mediaeval times. The village of
Perlethorpe in Nottinghamshire is still referred to locally as
Palethorpe, one of its former names. Now it would be tempting to
jump to the conclusion that the present-day surname **Palethorpe** is
derived from an earlier form of the place name, but that would be an
oversimplification. The village appears simply as *Torp* in the Domesday
Survey of the 11th century, then passes through variations on the name
Peverill Thorp before first being known as *Perlethorpe* (its present-day
spelling) in the 14th century. The earliest surviving written record of the
Palethorpe spelling, on the other hand, dates only from the early 17th
century. Now what might appear to have happened is that the
Perlethorpe spelling has settled down to become the present-day
place-name, while the Palethorpe variant has become the modern
surname. For this to have happened, however, the place would have to
have been known as *Palethorpe* at the time of surname-formation,
certainly earlier than the 17th century, or else the Palethorpe surname
could have begun life as **Perlethorpe** and then changed over time.

I would contend that the most likely explanation lies elsewhere. There
is known to have been what we might think of as a mid-way spelling for
the place, *Parle(s)thorpe*, from at least as early as the 14th century, and
parish register entries for Laxton in Nottinghamshire are using this same
spelling (Parlethorpe – and also, with metathesis, **Parlethroppe**) for the
surname in the late 16th century. Thereafter the surname became
Palethorpe and the place-name, after a brief flirtation with the
Palethorpe alternative, decided eventually to stabilise itself as
Perlethorpe. Interestingly enough, several friends of Steve Palethorpe,
musician and railway enthusiast *par excellence*, who now lives at Bargate
in Derbyshire, take great pleasure in applying metathesis to his name
and refer to him affectionately as **Palethropp**.

It never does any harm to consider whatever historical variations on a
place-name you can find. So, armed with the knowledge that the town of

Brighton on the south coast of England was known as *Brighthelmestone* until the late 18th century, you would not be tempted to assume that the surname **Brighton** had its origins there. In fact it comes from a place called *Breighton* in Yorkshire. In not dissimilar vein, it is worth noting that most **Sunderland**s originated at a farm near Halifax, not at the *Sunderland* in County Durham or at other places of the same name – a fact usefully pointed out by David Hey.

The old trick of pronouncing a surname aloud might well lead you to a place-name origin which you had not previously considered. Such an approach could have paid dividends in the case of Palethorpe, had we not found out what we wanted to know by other means, though I was once rather slow to realise that the surname **Ingersoll**, which I was researching for an American client, was based upon the Derbyshire village of *Inkersall*, which lies very close to where I live.

In general terms, do be conscious of the fact that a toponymic surname might reflect an abandoned, alternative or dialectal form of a place-name. Indeed, the place in question might simply have disappeared over the years. There is some debate as to the origin of the name **Skillicorne**; it is said by some to be a Manx name, but is also found in Lancashire, and one possibility is that it might be derived from the name of a small settlement which has simply vanished off the face of the earth. It is not uncommon to find entries such as the following in C.W. Bardsley's *Dictionary of English and Welsh surnames*: **Pavely**.

Ingersolls from Inkersall. Ingersoll watches have been a familiar product for many years. What is less well-known is the origin of the surname: it comes from a village in Derbyshire called *Inkersall*.

Local, 'of Pavely'. I cannot find the place. In this instance there may well
have been a long-lost place in England called *Pavely*, which Bardsley
was therefore unable to find, though in this instance Hanks and Hodges'
dictionary springs to our aid by telling us that *Pav(e)l(e)y* is a variation
of *Pawley*, which itself is a Norman habitation from Pavilly in Seine-
Maritime.

How should you approach the challenge of determining the origin of a
toponymic surname? Do turn to surname dictionaries in the first
instance; they can be most helpful, especially in cases where a place-
name has changed radically or disappeared, though some clearly take
the not unreasonable view that there is little point in informing the
reader that a surname like **Rutherford** probably has its origins in a place
of that name to be found in the Scottish Borders, since a gazetteer of any
reasonable size would provide the same information. The next resource
you should turn to, if necessary, is just such a gazetteer. The index
section of a modern book of road maps might serve your purpose, but
ideally you should try to get access to a substantial Victorian gazetteer
which will give not just names and locations of a wide variety of places,
but also a good deal of historical information as well. In the first instance
I always use *The comprehensive gazetteer of England and Wales* by
J.H.F. Brabner, a six-volume work published in the late nineteenth
century. There are many similar publications; some cover England and
Wales only, others are dedicated exclusively to Scotland or Ireland, and
some feature the whole of the British Isles. The so-called *Topographical
dictionaries* published by Samuel Lewis in the early Victorian period,
now available on CD-ROM, are very strong on historical content, but as
a result they contain fewer place-names as such than many more modest
publications. You can always search the Internet for detailed gazetteers,
but ideally what we really need here is some publication or other which
simply lists a vast number of places, large and small, everything from
major cities to insignificant hamlets. Luckily, help is at hand: substantial
place-name lists of this sort for England and Wales have long been
published alongside various printed reports on decennial censuses. I use
a two-volume work entitled *General Register Office: Census 1951:
England and Wales: Index of place names*, published in 1955, but there
are similar publications for other census years, though not all.
Thousands upon thousands of place-names are provided, arranged
alphabetically and accompanied by information presented in columns,
as follows: Place-name; description (Civil parish, ecclesiastical parish,
'locality', etc.); administrative county in which situated; borough, urban
district or rural district in which situated; number of registration district
in which situated; population in 1951.

Be as flexible as you can about place-name spellings when using
books like this – as flexible as you would be when considering surname

spellings themselves, in fact. Odd things happen. I'm well acquainted with the surnames **Barksby** and **Skelston**, which can be found in the Derbyshire/Nottinghamshire border area. No gazetteer will include either of these as a place-name, and what appears to have happened in both cases is that a letter '*s*' has somehow intruded itself into the surname. I would assume that **Barksby** comes from *Barkby* in Leicestershire, and **Skelston** from a number of places called *Skelton* in Yorkshire or Cumberland.

It isn't always safe simply to take a name and to add a letter to it or subtract one from it at random, alas. I have a friend from the north-east of England called Hilary Good whose maiden name was **Crankshaw**. In the early 20th century Hilary's paternal grandfather left Lancashire to take over Pemberton's paper mill in Gateshead, nestled between the High Level and the Tyne bridges, taking his distinctively Lancastrian surname with him. It is easy enough to determine that the original Crankshaws came from *Cranshaw* in Lancashire, and that its known variants include **Cranshaw**, **Cron(k)shaw** and **Crenshaw**, but we need to be careful not to confuse it with the all-too-similar surname of **Crawshaw** (with variants **Crashaw**, **Crawshay**, **Croshaw** and **Crowsher**), which has its origins in a different Lancashire village by the name of *Crawshaw Booth*.

If you wish to examine earlier or alternative forms of any given place-name in England, then turn to the county volumes steadily being published by the English Place-Name Society (EPNS) – but do be aware that the indexes to these often omit many of the minor place-names and field-names which are featured in the main text. The *Concise Oxford dictionary of English place-names* takes a not-dissimilar approach, in much less detail, but at least it covers a selection of places from the whole of England.

As to ancient and modern dialectal versions of a number of place-names, it's worth taking a look at K. Forster's *A pronouncing dictionary of English place-names including local and archaic variants* (1981) and at *A glossary of dialectal place-nomenclature* by R.C. Hope, which is a modest but very useful publication. A reprint of the second edition of this book was published by Gale Research Company of Detroit in 1968, and is arranged both alphabetically by place-name and also by county. Here you will find – to your amazement, maybe? – that a village in Devon with the official name of *Woolfardisworthy* is known locally as *Oolsery*. Few people, it seems, relish the thought of expending enough breath to pronounce a multi-syllable place-name or surname in full, so *Woolfardisworthy* is shortened in everyday speech to make it more manageable.

Forster's book will tell you (once you've mastered the basics of the International Phonetic Alphabet) that a place-name like *Cromford* in

MR. WM. CRANKSHAW,
First Permanent Secretary.

Crankshaws from Cranshaw. *Cranshaw*s came originally from *Cranshaw* in Lancashire. William Crankshaw, pictured here, was the first Permanent Secretary of the Bolton (Lancs.) Co-operative Society. [From *History of the Great and Little Bolton Co-operative Society, Ltd., 1859-1909*].

Derbyshire was originally pronounced *Crum-ford*, and that the present-day preference for *Cromm-ford* has resulted from people pronouncing the name in accordance with its spelling. There are still people, of course, who prefer to pronounce *Coventry* as *Cuventry*, or surnames like **Compton** or **Cromwell** as *Cumpton* and *Crumwell* (or *Crummell*).

Let me offer a final caveat concerning the use of EPNS volumes. Supposing you are interested in the surname **Readshaw**, for example, which has an unmistakably north-of-England feel to it. Sure enough, the IGI has entries for **Readshaws**, **Reedshaws**, **Redshaws**, **Ridshaws** and **Rudshaws** from several northern counties, including Yorkshire and Durham. In case alternative spellings of the name hadn't occurred to you (surely not, at this late stage?), the IGI has here provided a few – which is just as well, since no major surname dictionary includes an entry for Readshaw. Bardsley is happy enough to mention **Redshaw**: *Local, 'at the red shaw', from residence beside the shaw or wood of a red soil...I cannot find the spot.* Now Bardsley, for all his sterling work, had given up far too easily here, leaving Reaney to make the not-unreasonable supposition that this surname comes from a specific place in the West Riding of Yorkshire called *Redshaw Gill* in Blubberhouses. Sure enough, if we then turn to the EPNS index volume for the West Riding, there is an entry for *Redshaw Gill & Beck (Blubberhouses)*. If you've trained yourself to scan an index more generally whilst looking for a specific entry (and I'd recommend such a practice very highly), an entry lower down the page which says simply *Reedshaw* might jump out at you. Now this could be fun, couldn't it? It would be pronounced in the same way as the surname Readshaw, and maybe it's a possible origin that Reaney hadn't considered? Alas, no. *Reedshaw* appears under the heading of *Cowling*, but whereas the first known reference to *Redshaw Gill* dates from the 13th century, the editor has found no evidence of the *Reedshaw* place-name before the 17th century. Even the first-known written reference to *Reedyshaw*, a lost place in the area of Soyland, only dates from 1485, the year of the Battle of Bosworth.

So please be careful. Do look as closely at the full entry for any place-name which interests you in an EPNS volume as you would at a word featured in a comprehensive dictionary such as the *Oxford English Dictionary*. Both the EPNS and the OED will include a specific year against many of the entries; this represents the date at which the place-name or the word in question has first been located in written records. Now does the date which appears beside a particular place-name post-date the main period of surname formation by years, decades or even centuries? Much work has been done by scholars in this field – but do pay the results of their labours close attention, and try not to come up with toponymic surname howlers that could easily be avoided.

Places outside the British Isles

Many toponymic surnames found within Britain have their origin overseas, which is hardly surprisingly in view of the fact that large numbers of immigrants have arrived in Britain over the years from France, the Low Countries and elsewhere, and that the south and east coasts of England are only a short sea journey away from northern France and from the Netherlands. For some odd reason there are British people who are proud of the fact that they believe (rightly or wrongly) that their French-sounding surname was brought over in 1066 by the opportunistic Normans, led by the man called variously *William, Duke of Normandy* or *William the Bastard.*

Not all those who arrived in Britain from mainland Europe were rapers and pillagers, however; a significant number were seeking refuge from the persecution which beset Protestant dissenters during the 16th and 17th centuries, and in the 18th century there were those who sought to escape the ravages of the French Revolution. All these immigrants brought their European surnames – many of which were toponymic in origin – with them, and either retained them in their existing form or modified them to suit English usage. Many such are easy enough to spot if you give them a moment's thought, and the following three names, offered as a sample, have been around long enough to have become part of the general English surname stock: some **Lyon**s will have come from *Lyons* in France; some (but not all) **Cullen**s will have come from *Cologne (Köln)* in Germany, and even the occupational surnames **Challen** or **Challenor**, originally used for a maker of blankets once known as *chalons* or *shaloons*, has a toponymic origin in the town of *Chalons-sur-Marne* in France, where such blankets were once produced in great profusion.

For an international listing of the names of places and of geographical features you should try to find a copy of *The Times index-gazetteer of the world* (1965). At approximately one thousand pages, with each entry presented in small print, it is a very substantial work indeed.

Surnames of miscellaneous origin

Young and old

The meaning of the surname **Child** is generally clear enough – not that many children would begin a family line whilst still in infancy – though it could also refer to a young man waiting to be elevated to the status of a knight. **Pa(d)get(t)** was a term for a young page or servant. **Gamble**, with its variants **Gambell**, **Gammell**, **Gemmell**, and the rest, comes from a word used for an old man, and **Oldknow** means *old enough (enow)*.

A nephew. The most distinctive feature about a man first given the surname *Neve* might have been that he was the nephew of a famous uncle. [From Kelly's *Post Office Directory of Kent* 1911].

Relationship

Eame was a term used for a maternal uncle, and a man who took care of his nephews and nieces once their parents had died might have acquired this as a surname. Just as our amphibious friend *an ewt* became *a newt* in common speech over time, so *mine eame* [my uncle] could be divided in such a way as to give the surname **Neame**, though this can also be a nickname for a short man. **Neve**, by contrast, means a nephew – perhaps referring to someone who was raised by an uncle, or whose uncle was famous in some way. **Soane** is from Middle English *sone* [son], and was used for someone who shared the same personal name as his father.

In centuries gone by the word *cousin* was a notoriously imprecise term for a relative of almost any degree of closeness, and the surname **Cousin(s)/Cussen/Cozen(s)/Cushing** could have been applied to anyone who was kin to a person of some importance. Similarly, the brother of a person of some social standing could simply – and patronisingly, we may say – have been named **Brother**. **Gossip** is from a word meaning *godfather* or *godmother*. **Od(h)am(s)**, from a word meaning *son-in-law*, could be applied to a man who had acquired a wealthy or influential father-in-law by making an advantageous marriage. **Ayer** or **Eyre** is simply what it sounds like – an heir to a title or fortune – and a man called **Heritage** would have inherited his land from an ancestor rather than having acquired it in any other way. **Bairnsfather/Barnsfather**, a surname chiefly found in northern England and Scotland, was used for the father or alleged father of an illegitimate child.

Times of the year
Christmas: **Midwinter**, **Y(o)ule** [born at *Yuletide*]. **Noel** is the family name of the Earls of Gainsborough, amongst others. Brian **Christmas** of Maidstone in Kent has long been well-known as an indefatigable collector of references to his own and other surnames, and is an active member of the Guild of One-Name Studies (GOONS). The surname is principally encountered in southern England, and is said to have an East Anglian origin.

Easter: **Pask(e)**, **Paish**, **Paskin**, **Patchett**. A servant of someone with such a surname could be known as **Paxman**.

Other seasons and months: **Pentecost**; **Haliday**, **Hallad(e)y**, **Hol(l)iday** and **Holladay** (indicating a connection with an unspecified holiday or *holy day*). The surname **Loveday** comes from a day set aside in mediaeval times for the settling of disputes, while **Hockaday** is based upon an important term-day, the second Tuesday after Easter Sunday, on which rents were due.

As to months of the year, I well remember a firm of estate agents, active in Cambridgeshire in the 1960s, called **January**.

Travellers
Someone who had travelled to the Holy Land or to famous shrines elsewhere might be given the surname **Pilgrim** or **Peregrine**, and such a person who had brought back part of a palm tree to prove that he had travelled to far-away parts of the world could be known as **Palmer**. The surname **Cockell** similarly could be applied to a traveller who had returned from a visit to the tomb of Santiago de Compostela in north-west Spain with a cockle or shell-shaped badge to represent Santiago (St James), whose symbol it was.

Favourite clichés
An intriguing class of surnames consists of those which indicate that a man was particularly fond of using certain clichés, oaths or modes of expression.

A person who used the phrase *good sir* to excess could acquire **Goodsir** as a byname/surname, though this could also be a nickname for a venerable old man. **Debney** is said to be derived from a French phrase meaning *God bless*; **Purd(e)y** is from Old French *pour Dieu* (by God), **Pardoe** is from *par Dieu* and **Purefoy** is from *par foi* (by my faith). **Godbe(a)r/Godbeher** can be *may God be here* (though there are other possible origins, including, prosaically enough, *good beer*); **God(s)help** is from *by the help of God*; **Goodby** is from *God be with you*; **Go(o)dsave** is from *for God's sake*; **Godsname** is from *in God's name* and **Goodspeed** is from *may God speed you*. **Mordew/Mordey** is from the oath *mort dieu* (literally, *death of God*), and in theory **Mothersole/Mothersill** could be a corruption of *on my mother's soul*, though a toponymic origin – from *Moddershall* in Staffordshire – is more likely.

CELTIC NAMING PRACTICES

Several surnames from Celtic areas of Britain – from Scotland, Ireland, Wales, the Isle of Man and Cornwall – are derived from occupations, from places, or from physical or personal characteristics, but many more make use of specific patronymic prefixes, of which *Mac* ('son of') in its various forms is the most common.

SCOTLAND AND IRELAND

Most people living in the British Isles and elsewhere will find little enough difficulty in recognising certain surnames as being typically Scottish or Irish. I use the word *elsewhere* quite deliberately here, since both the Scots and the Irish had a major part to play in the opening up of the former British Empire, having chosen, or been forced, to make their home far from the country of their birth, where they became settlers, soldiers, doctors, nurses, engineers, missionaries or administrators.

The introduction of surnames into Scotland is said to date from the second half of the 11th century, though the fact that many individuals sought to protect themselves by adopting the name of a clan with which they may have had no blood relationship can make life difficult for genealogists and other interested researchers, and until comparatively recent times it was quite common for Highlanders to possess both a clan name and a byname. Many clans were originally territorial, and septs

Simplicity itself. The head of the Chisholm Clan refers to himself quite simply as *The Chisholm*.

(smaller groupings within the clans) would often take new or additional distinguishing names of their own. The head of a clan, meanwhile, will usually prefer to be known by the simplest of names – **The Chisholm**, for example, or **MacLeod of MacLeod** ('**MacLeod of that ilk**').

Some clan names are derived from places in Scotland (**Chisholm,**

Murray) or in France (**Fraser, Sinclair**); others are from the Gaelic language (**Galbraith**), from French (**Fletcher**), English (**Armstrong**) or Scandinavian (**Lamont**). The adoption of clan names has meant that in some parts of Scotland, as in Wales, there have been very few surnames to go around, and nicknames or bynames have become a necessity as a result. To makes matters even more complicated, certain Scottish surnames have been changed, anglicised, abandoned – or even proscribed, as in the famous case of the **McGregor**s in 1603. There has also been a recent trend for those bearing Scottish or Irish surnames to revert to earlier spellings: some Scottish **MacAllister**s have thus become **McCollister**s, and some Irish **Lysat**s have become **McLysaght**s.

Lowland Scots names like **Gladstone** [from lands in Teviotdale called *Gledstanes*] and **Maxwell** [from possessions of that name on the Tweed] are English rather than Gaelic in origin, and several families which are thought of today as being quintessentially Scottish have their origin in an Englishman who moved north many centuries ago. The Scottish **Barclay**s are said to have come originally from *Berkeley* in Gloucestershire; the earliest of the **Lindsay**s, Sir Walter de **Lindissi**, came to Scotland from *Lindsey* in Lincolnshire, while the first **Graham**, a Norman baron called William de **Graham**, was from *Grantham* in the same English county, and the first known Scottish bearer of the surname **Ramsey** came from the place of that name in Huntingdonshire.

In the Highlands matters were different, and it is here that we'll find a preponderance of surnames beginning with *Mac*. Such names were unstable for many years, and even as late as the 19th century a number of Highland families were using patronymic *Mac* names rather than hereditary surnames. *Mac* is the usual spelling of the Gaelic word for *son*. There used to be a charming fiction that *Mac* was used in Scotland, while *Mc* was Irish. This is not the case. *Mc* is simply an abbreviated form of *Mac*, while the letter '*M*' followed by an apostrophe is a further contraction – one that initially bewildered me at school when I tried to make sense of a character given the fictional name of *Mr M'Choakumchild* by Charles Dickens in his novel, *Hard Times*.

In some cases experience will tell us whether a *Mac* or *Mc* surname is Scottish or Irish – so we are normally safe in ascribing **MacDonald** [son of Donald] to Scotland, but would know almost instinctively that **MacCarthy** [son of Carthaigh] was Irish – the most numerous *Mac* name in Ireland, as it happens. Matters are not always so simple, however. The Scots were Irish originally, in any case, and two-way human traffic over the centuries – particularly between the Province of Ulster and the West Coast of Scotland – has succeeded in mixing up Irish and Scottish surnames quite effectively. **Kennedy**s [ugly head] were prominent in South Ayrshire in Scotland in mediaeval times, though the name is now thought of as almost exclusively Irish. Some surnames, helpfully enough,

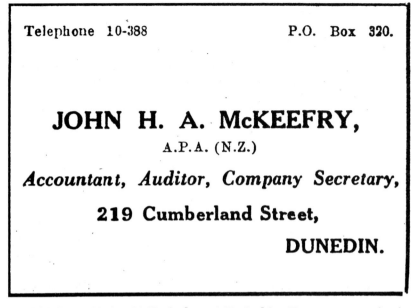

Telephone 10-388   P.O. Box 320.

JOHN H. A. McKEEFRY,

A.P.A. (N.Z.)

Accountant, Auditor, Company Secretary,

219 Cumberland Street,

DUNEDIN.

The Irish Down Under. *McKeefry* [son of *Fiachra*] is a Tyrone surname, but by 1932 John McKeefry had set up business in Dunedin, New Zealand. [From Wise's *New Zealand Post Office Directory*, 1932].

have adopted a different form on either side of the Irish Sea – so **McDiarmid** and **McDermott** are Scottish and Irish variations on the same name, with the meaning *son of Dermid/Diarmada*.

Mac- names have a long history; the Irish were using this prefix for hereditary surnames as early as the 11th century, the same era that brought us those old Scottish favourites, **MacBeth** and **MacDuff**. Sad to relate, MacDuff, Shakespeare's Thane of Fife, was never anything more than a character of fiction, while the surname MacBeth was not originally patronymic, despite appearances. The *Mac* element in MacBeth still means *son of*, but the original bearers of the name were not so-called because they were sons of a man called *Beth*; the meaning is *son of life, a religious person*. In other words, the name is not truly patronymic, and was given to a number of unrelated individuals. Of course that didn't stop MacBeth, like **MacRae** [son of grace, prosperity], being used as a hereditary surname in the course of time. In not dissimilar vein, the Irish **MacDowell** (originally **MacDubhghaill**) means *son of the black stranger*, no specific father's name being mentioned. *Mac* could also be added to an occupational name, giving us the Scottish surnames **McCosh** [son of the footman], **McIntyre** [son of the carpenter/ wright/mason] and **McGowan** or **MacNokard** [son of the smith] and the Irish **MacWard** [originally **Mac an Bhaird**, son of the bard]. We might have imagined that early church dignitaries were celibate; if so we might be somewhat surprised to come across Scottish surnames like **MacNab**, **MacKellar**, **MacBrair**, **MacPherson** and **MacTaggart**, which appear to mean *son of the abbot, son of the prior, son of the friar, son of the parson* and *son of the priest* respectively, but were very probably used originally for individuals who were servants employed by such churchmen.

Not all Scottish patronymic surnames beginning with *Mac* are based upon Gaelic given names. I have a friend called Robb **Watson**, who is the *Sennachie* or family historian and archivist for his Scottish family, known traditionally as the **MacWatties**. Now *Mac* is a Gaelic prefix, but *Wat* or *Wattie* is a pet form of the given name *Walter*, which is of Germanic origin and was introduced into England by the Normans. The oft-repeated story that the MacWatties were named after Walter **Buchanan**, Laird of Leny in the 16th century, would seem to be something of a fiction, since the surname can be found at a much earlier period than this. The full-blooded Gaelic form of the surname is **MacBhaididh**, and **MacQuatty**, **MacQuattie** and even **MacWalter** are alternative modern-day equivalents.

The Danes and Norwegians who settled in Britain in the 9th and 10th centuries brought their own language, now referred to as Old Norse, and also their own personal names. Some, often twisted almost beyond recognition, have become Scottish surnames: the Old Norse *Thorkell*, still recognisable in the English surname **Thurkettle** (most commonly found in East Anglia), has also somehow twisted and changed itself enough to give us the Scottish **McCorquodale** and **McCorkindale**.

The prefix *O'*, which has traditionally been more common in Ireland than *Mac* and which pre-dates it, has the meaning *grandson of* or, more broadly, *descendant of*. Just to confuse matters, you will find various Irish surnames which sometimes include an *O'* or a *Mac* prefix, and sometimes omit it. The common Irish surnames **Murphy** and **Doyle** are rarely found with a prefix, whereas **Gallagher** and **O'Gallagher** [descendant of *Gallchobhar*] are both viable alternatives of the same name, as are **Nally** and **MacNally** [**Mac an Fhailghigh** – son of the poor man]. There is a little ditty which (translated) runs:

> *By Mac and O*
> *You'll always know*
> *True Irishmen, they say;*
> *But if they lack*
> *Both O and Mac*
> *No Irishmen are they.*

This is a catchy but inaccurate little rhyme. Many Irish surnames do indeed begin with *Mac* or *O'*, but by no means all. It is fortunate for those genealogists and historians interested in such things that many surnames which have their origins in the Irish language are still localised to those regions of the country in which they first arose. Not all surnames found in Ireland have a Gaelic origin, however. We have the Normans to thank for such unmistakably 'Irish' names as **Burke** (with its various spellings), **Dillon** and **Cusack**, together with several names beginning with *Fitz* (son of), such as **FitzGerald** and **FitzGibbon**.

There are also a good number of Scottish surnames in Ireland, as we know, and English settlers brought their own names with them when they came as conquerors or settlers. Some English surnames have been in Ireland since mediaeval times, but many came with the so-called *plantations* in Ulster in the early 17th century or with the *Cromwellian Settlement* of the 1650s, which was more widespread throughout the country. In more recent times – and especially in the wake of the potato famine of the 1840s – there has been a good deal of emigration from Ireland, with the result that Irish surnames have become familiar in many British towns and cities, as well as in the United States of America, Australia, New Zealand and elsewhere.

The Roman Catholic people of Ireland, under pressure to abandon, to anglicise or otherwise to change their Irish surnames from the 17th century onwards, frequently dropped the *O'* or *Mac* prefix. In other cases a radical change was made, or a 'translation' attempted, yielding up grotesque forms like **Mucklebreed**, a mere caricature of the Irish name **Mac Giolla Bhrighde** – which in itself must have given a linguistic headache to many an English bureaucrat posted to Ireland. For further details of such changes, see the introduction to *The surnames of Ireland* by Edward MacLysaght (sixth edition, 1985).

From the 19th century onwards, many Irish families chose to re-adopt their original surnames, and a rich – not to say confusing – mixture of names was the result. In 1901, almost in despair, we may guess, Robert E. Matheson, the Registrar-General for Ireland, published a small book entitled *Varieties and synonymes of surnames and Christian names in Ireland: for the guidance of registration officers and the public in searching the indexes of births, deaths and marriages*. This is a useful book for students of Irish genealogy, giving, as it does, extensive listings such as this one for the surname **Bermingham**:

Birmingham; Birminghan; Bremigam; Brimage; Brimagum; Brimmagem; Brimmajen; Brimmigan; Brumagem; Brumigem; Brumiger; Brummagem; Brummagen; Caorish; Corish; Korish; MacFeerish; Magorisk; McGorish; McGorisk.

No.	Surnames, with Varieties and Synonymes.	No.	Surnames, with Varieties and Synonymes.
2045	WHARTON. Faughton. 303(b). Warton. Werton. Wherton.	2054	WHITTAKER. Whitaker. 333. Whiteacre. Whiteaker. Whitegar. Whittacre. Whittegar.
2046	WHEATLY. Whately. Wheately. Whitly. Whittley.	2055	WHOLY. Holey.
		2056	WHORISKEY. Horisky.
2047	WHELAN. [Hyland]. 40. Peelan. Pelan. 306. [Phelan]. 40, 101, 117, &c. [Philbin]. 252. Whalan. Whalen. Whealan. Whealon. Wheelahan. Wheelan. Whelahan. 172, 249, 291. Wheleghan. 312. Whelehan. 136. Whelen. Whelon.	2057	WHYTE. See [White].
		2058	WIDDICOMB. Widdecombe. Withecomb.
		2059	WIGHTMAN. Whiteman.
		2060	WILDE. Wild. Wildes. Wyld. Wylde.
		2061	WILKINSON. M'Quilkan. 43. M'Quilkin. 44. Wilkie. 55. Wilkison. Wilkisson.
2048	WHIGHAM. Whigam. Wiggam.	2062	WILLIAMS. [Williamson].
2049	WHITE. Banane. 501. Baun. 488. Bawn. 76, 136, 210. [Galligan]. 153. Whight. [Whyte]. 393.	2063	WILLIAMSON. [Williams].
		2064	WILLOUGHBY. Wilby. 102.
		2065	WILMOT. Willmott. Wilmitt. Wilmont. 177.
2050	WHITEHEAD. [Canavan].	2066	WILSON. Willison. Willson.
2051	WHITELY. Whitla. 112. Whitley. 346.		
2052	WHITESIDE. Whitsitt. 429.	2067	WINGFIELD. Winfield. Winnfield. Wynfield. Wynnfield.
2053	WHITFIELD. Whiffle. 249.		

The Irish Registrar-General tries to bring order out of chaos. In 1901 Robert E. Matheson published a small book entitled *Varieties and synonymes of surnames and Christian names in Ireland: for the guidance of registration officers and the public in searching the indexes of births, deaths and marriages*, in which he made a bold attempt to group surname variants together.

Surname stability is perhaps less commonly found in Ireland, then, than it is in England. Leonard R.N. Ashley quotes what he says is a well-known example of an Irish tombstone on which a father and mother and their four children are listed as **McEneaney**, **McAneany**, **McAneny**, **McEnaney**, **McEneany** and **Bird** – the last being based on the mistaken notion that the surname has something to do with the Gaelic *éan*, meaning *bird*.

Before we leave Irish surnames, one further point with a more general relevance may be made. It's always worth remembering that surnames were spoken aloud long before most of them were written down. Spelling, then, is playing catch-up, and alternative written forms such as **Callahan**, **Calligan** and **Callaghan** could constitute different attempts at representing one single spoken pronunciation of this Irish surname. If this is the case, note that it would seem to make no appreciable difference whether the letter '*a*' or the letter '*i*' is used to indicate the short vowel which makes up the second syllable in the name, and also that the guttural consonant sound which is most fully represented by the letters *gh* may appear as simply '*g*' or '*h*' in some cases. Misunderstandings can result. From 1976 to 1979 Jim Callaghan served as the British Prime Minister. Few, if any, English speakers pronounced the *gh* in his name with its full guttural value, but would opt for an '*h*' sound or a hard '*g*' according to whim, as if his surname were either *Callahan* or *Callagan*.

Once a name is written down, of course, it is very tempting to pronounce it in the way that the spelling seems to indicate. Some Americans are notorious for their uncompromising approach to foreign language words and phrases, offering a rendition of the French *Notre Dame* that rhymes with *Voter Game* – but the British are sometimes little better, pronouncing the name of the Caribbean island of *Antigua* to rhyme with *how big you are* (instead of *Anteega*), and intruding a full hard '*g*' into a word like *Nicaragua*, to the amusement if not the bemusement of Spanish speakers.

WALES

Most Welsh surnames are patronymic in origin, but not all. Yellow hair (Welsh *melyn/felyn*) could give rise to the surname **Melling** or **Mellens**; a man whose hair or clothing was grey might be called **Lloyd**, and a Welsh nickname for a red-head was *coch*, giving us the surname **Gough**. The surnames **Saer**, **Sare** or **Sears** can be derived from the Welsh word for a carpenter (*saer*), and **Wace** is based upon *Gwas*, a servant. Welsh surnames with place-name origins are few and far between, though you may come across examples such as **Mostyn**, **Conway** or **Kyffin**.

The majority of Welsh surnames, however, are taken from a personal name, with minor adjustments or additions made as necessary – so the surnames **Richard**, **Richards** or **Pritchard** are all derived from the one personal name *Richard*. **Tudor** is a Welsh form of *Theodore*, but personal-names-turned-surnames such as *Hugh(es)* and *Lewis* were English or French equivalents of the Welsh names *Howell* and *Llewelyn*. Sometimes distinctive pet-forms of personal names, such as *Bedo* (from *Maredudd*) or *Mady* (from *Madog*) might find their way into the stock of surnames as **Beddoes** and **Maddy**.

Patronymic surnames are found in Wales in great abundance; in centuries past many were not hereditary surnames at all, but were bynames inherited from the bearer's father, which died with the individual concerned and were not passed on to the next generation. So Hugh, son of William, might be called *Hugh Williams*; his son David would be called *David Hughes*, while David's son Evan would be called *Evan Davies* – and so on. Each father's personal name, in other words, was hereditary, but was passed down to the next generation only, no further.

When what may appear to be a surname is nothing of the kind, but only an individual byname, it can prove difficult, if not impossible, to trace a large number of Welsh pedigrees, though the Welsh have long been famous, in common with members of other strongly oral cultures, for being able to recite many generations of their own male-line ancestry by heart – always a useful trick to have up your sleeve in case

Good Evans. The surname **Heaven** isn't as heavenly as it sounds, but is a variant on the Welsh personal name, *Evan*. [From Kelly's *Post Office Directory of Somersetshire*, 1875].

there is any dispute over the inheritance of property or land. Indeed, it would appear that it was sometimes made perfectly clear to members of families who lived in Wales but who had an English-style surname that it was about time they adopted the 'proper' patronymic way of doing things.

There is nothing particularly Welsh about the patronymic byname practice I have outlined, of course, but the Welsh continued to use it for a much longer period of time than did the English, and many did not adopt hereditary surnames until the mid 17th century at the earliest – or considerably later in areas distant from English influence. The English themselves, meanwhile, had used bynames at an earlier period in their own history – had *been there, done that*, as we might say. So in 1252, at a time when hereditary surnames were not fully in operation in England, King Henry III granted a weekly market and an annual fair to be held in the town of Ilkeston, Derbyshire, to *Hugh, the son of Ralph* – otherwise known as *Hugh Fitz Ralph*. The good news is that this weekly Thursday market is still regularly held, as is the fair, the date of which is computed each year by the time-honoured formula: *The first Thursday after the first Sunday after the eleventh of October.*

In parts of Scandinavia the use of patronymic bynames was only abandoned as late as the 19th century, and it is still favoured in Iceland – though it may not have escaped the notice of ardent television viewers that the Icelandic-born *Magnus* **Magnusson** has used the Magnusson element of his name as a hereditary surname, passing it on to his daughter *Sally* **Magnusson**, a television presenter in her own right. It can sometimes come as a shock to anyone brought up on English forenames and surnames to come across a double use of the same name in the *Magnus* **Magnusson** or *Kris(toffer)* **Kristofferson** mould, but the Italians, for example, are fond of such duplicate naming, and I myself have a Scottish cousin called *Archibald* **Archibald** and a much more distant forebear called *George* **George**.

Here we need to return to our old friend, the *Mac* prefix, meaning *son of*. The original Welsh language version of this was *mag*, changed eventually to *map* (later shortened to *ap*) before an 'h' or r/rh, or to *mab* (later shortened to *ab*), which was often, but not exclusively, used before a vowel. A slow but steady development took place over time: *Hugh the son of Richard*, originally represented as *Hugh mag Richard*, would move through *Hugh map Richard* to *Hugh ap Richard*, finally settling down as *Hugh Pritchard*. The *Pritchard* form could then become an inherited surname rather than a patronymic byname. Surnames with a similar origin include **Parry** (ap Harry), **Powell** (ap Howell), **Pryce** (ap Rhys), **Protheroe** (ap Rhydderch), **Prosser** (ap Rhosier/Roger), **Probert**, **Pumphrey** and **Pugh**, together with **Benyon/Beynon** (ab Einion), **Bedmond**, **Bellis**, **Bevan**, **Bowen** and **Broderick**. A variation on the

DAVID RHYS PHILLIPS

Mrs. BETTY POLLITT

EDWIN PRICE

The Hon. DAVID RHYS

THOMAS MORGAN RICHARDS

Rev. E. G. ROBERTS, M.A.

Full house. A typical page from *Who's who in Wales* (1937) features five men with characteristically Welsh patronymic surnames, while the maiden name of Betty Pollitt, a married lady, was *Davies*.

Welsh in all but name. The much-loved singer and comedian Harry Secombe was something of a professional Welshman, though his surname (derived from a place-name in Devon) was totally English. [Photograph by John Titford].

theme is evidenced by the surname **Upjohn**, where the vowel sound in *up* (ie, *ap*) has been retained.

For an excellent introduction to the study of Welsh surnames, complete with a glossary, you should refer to *The surnames of Wales* by John and Sheila Rowlands (1996).

ISLE OF MAN

It was some years ago that I bought a book which carried a rather handsome armorial bookplate relating to a previous owner whose surname was Mylchreest. I had no special interest in surnames at the time, but this did seem to me to be a particularly unusual name. How was it pronounced? What did it mean? Where did it come from?

A bit of delving produced the answer eventually: **Mylchreest** is a Manx name, a variant of the patronymic **MacGilchrist**, meaning *son of Giolla Chriost* (*Christ's servant*). *Giolla* and other name-elements similar to it can be found in several Celtic bynames and surnames, and the word *gillie* is still in Scotland for a servant who attends hunting or fishing expeditions.

I have since sold the book in question (wish I hadn't, really...), but have always treasured the memory of this most striking surname, one that can sit alongside **Quilleash** [**MacCuillais**, little Paul], **Corjeag** [black-eyed], **Joughin** [son of the dean or deacon] and the rest as being unmistakably Manx.

Manx surnames are a fascinating and complex study in their own right, as may be seen from the system used by J.J. Kneen in *The personal names of the Isle of Man* (1937) to classify those in use on the island:

Gaelic patronymics in 'O-'; Gaelic patronymics in 'Mac-'; Exotic patronymics in 'O-' or 'Mac-'; Welsh patronymics in 'Ap-'; Norman patronymics in 'Fitz-'; English patronymics in '-son'; Patronymics usually without prefix or suffix; Gaelic occupative names; English occupative names; Local names (from estates, villages, or towns); Local names from 'spots' or other circumscribed areas.

Other works on the subject include *Manx names* by A.W. Moore (1903) and *Surnames of the Manks: a review* by Leslie Quilliam (1989).

Manx Gaelic, of course, is a fully-fledged Celtic language, and it is clear that the island has a number of surnames which it can count as uniquely its own; others originated there but are also found elsewhere – especially in Ireland, Scotland and the Hebrides – and, as you would expect, some names have been imported by settlers from outside. It is worth noting that surnames are not commonly found in Scotland until the 16th and 17th centuries, whereas they were widely used in the Isle of Man as early as the beginning of the 15th century.

A quick glance at *Manx worthies: or, biographies of notable Manx men and women* by A.W. Moore (1901) would make it clear just how many Manx surnames are based upon first names, and that several begin with a hard '*k*' sound, represented by the letter '*k*' itself, by the letter '*c*', or by '*qu*', giving us **Callister, Clucas, Kewin, Kinnish** and **Quilliam**. **Quiggin** is a surname well-known to those who are addicted to that splendid confection known as *Kendal Mint Cake*, but although the *Quiggins Mint Cake* works can be found at Kendal in Cumbria, the surname itself is Manx – meaning **Mac Uigeann** (son of *Uige*). It is claimed that a confectioner from the Isle of Man, Bill **Quiggen**, was the first person to make lettered rock; he produced a special batch for Prince Albert's visit in 1847 with the text *Welcome, Prince Albert, to Mona* running all the way through each stick.

What can we make of such names? Yet again we need to renew our acquaintance with the Celtic *Mac* prefix, which was in use in the Isle of Man as early as 1098, in which year there is an entry in the *Chronicle of Mann* for a man named *Macmaras*.

Over the years the Manx *Mac* underwent significant changes. Sometimes it was retained, but often it was simply omitted altogether, **MacGibbon** becoming simply **Gibbon** (or, in this case, being anglicised

---

Corrin, William George, born June 14th, 1861. Left Sept. 1877. Son of T. Corrin, The Parade, Castletown, I.O.M. Day boy.
> Died at Sunderland, March 22nd, 1916.

Christian, William Finch, born April 2nd, 1850. Left Oct. 1870. Son of W. Christian. Principal's.
> Praepositor. Cricket XI., Football XV. Christ's Coll., Camb., 1869. Died Jan. 12th, 1871, at Douglas, I.O.M.

Nosworthy, Frederick Ernest, born Nov. 9th, 1853. Left Midsummer, 1870.

Nosworthy, Richard, born Dec. 8th, 1854. Left Midsummer, 1871.

Helsham, Edward, born March 24th, 1852. Left Christmas, 1870.

Quilliam, William Hughes, born March 28th, 1855. Left Midsummer. 1871. Son of S. Quilliam, Elizabeth Street, Liverpool. Scott's.
> In business.

Mylchreest, Thomas, born Sept. 11th, 1858. Left Midsummer, 1873. Son of J. Mylchreest, The Green, Castletown, I.O.M. Day boy.
> In business. M.B.E., 1920. County Councillor for Lancs. Daisy Bank, Old Trafford, Manchester.

Manx born, Manx educated. Part of a list of names of boys who entered King William's College, Isle of Man, in 1869, from a register (1833-1927) published in 1928. *Corrin, Christian, Quilliam* and *Mylchreest* are typical Manx surnames.

to become **Gibbonson**). Frequently, however, the letters '*m*' and '*a*' were no longer pronounced, leaving the hard '*c*' to be attached to the element of the name which followed it, turning **MacAlister** [son of Alister/Alexander] into **Callister**, **MacJohn/MacEoin** [son of John] into **Kewin**, **MacEnys** [son of Anghus] into **Kinnish** and **MacWilliam** [son of William] into **Quilliam**. Further examples, such as **Clucas** [originally **MacLucas,** son of *Lucas*] and **Kneen** [originally **MacNene,** son of *Naoimhin*] prove that this practice was not only adopted when the second element in the surname began with a vowel. The entire process here is similar to that which occurred in Welsh, of course, where *map* was shortened to *ap*, and the '*a*' was then also abandoned, allowing the '*p*' which remained to be joined to the given name which followed, producing surnames like **Pritchard**.

In the Isle of Man this process could also apply when the second element in the surname was not Manx in origin, but Old Norse, as in **Cottier**, which was originally **MacOttar**, from the Old Norse given name *Ottar* – or **Costain**, originally **MacAusteyn**, a devolved form of the Old Norse name *Thorsteinn*.

The Isle of Man is not alone in adding the vestigial '*k*' sound of *Mac* to the element of the name which follows it, and the Irish surname **Keogh** was originally **MacEochaidh**. A variation on the same theme in Ireland can be observed in the name of what was once my father's favourite pipe tobacco, *Mick McQuaid*. The original name was **MacUaid** (son of Walter); in this case the spelling **McQuaid** has retained the *Mac/Mc* element, but as if it weren't enough to have a hard '*k*' at the end of *Mac* already, the same sound has been further reinforced by the addition of the letter '*Q*' – a case of belt and braces, we might say. Meanwhile the Manx, predictably enough, prefer to drop the *Mac* in their own version of *son/kin of Walter* (originally **MacWhaltragh**), using the spelling **Qualtrough**. This *-ough* suffix (*-ach* in Manx), meaning *kin, family* is one we have come across before in the English surname **Whatmough** [Walter's nephew/kin]. In recent times two men have helped to make the surname **Quayle** [originally **MacPhayle**, son of *Paul*] famous throughout the world. The well-loved actor and stage director Sir (John) Anthony **Quayle** (1913–1989) was born in Ainsdale, Lancashire, of a family with Manx roots, and the male-line ancestors of former U. S. Vice-President (1989–1993) James Danforth (*Dan*) **Quayle** also came from the Isle of Man.

Before we leave the Isle of Man and its surnames, we should say a word or two about one of its famous sons, Fletcher **Christian** [**MacKristinn**, son of *Kristinn*, a Christian], who came from a family of significant social status long settled on the island, where they were Deemsters from as early as 1408. Charles Christian, attorney, fifth son of John Christian of Milntown, Isle of Man, married Ann Dixon on 2 May

Still close to home. An entry in a Manx telephone directory for 1936 shows Quiggin & Co., builders' merchants, still doing business in the island whence the surname originated. The meaning is 'son of Uige' (*Mac Uigeann*).

1751. Ann's mother's maiden name was **Fletcher**, and when Ann gave birth to the seventh of her children in her ancestral home of Moorland Close, near Cockermouth in Cumberland, on 25 September 1764, he was taken for baptism the same day to the nearby parish church of Brigham and was named *Fletcher* **Christian**. Any possibility that Fletcher might have followed the family tradition by entering Cambridge University once his earlier education at Cockermouth Free Grammar School and St Bee's School was completed were dashed by a family bankruptcy. Robbed of his security, his education and his inheritance, he decided to join the navy, becoming a pupil and protégé of William Bligh and acquiring significant skills as a navigator. In 1787 Christian was appointed master's mate aboard the discovery ship *Bounty*, Captain Bligh commanding. So the die was cast: Fletcher Christian would achieve notoriety as the leader of the famous mutiny, only to die some years later on Pitcairn Island in the Pacific Ocean – the victim, it would seem, of a murderous attack.

CORNWALL

Even the casual visitor to Cornwall will soon be aware that this is a county – a 'country', almost – with a fascinating cultural heritage all its own, with its remarkable range of saintly place names like St Ives, St Austell, St Germans, St Michaels and the rest, and an intriguing collection of surnames, many of them unique and some of them positively foreign-sounding. The Cornish language, which is Celtic and close to Breton, but which lacks the kind of substantial corpus of literature which would have assured it a place on the world stage, is said to have died out as a spoken language in the 18th century, but in its way is nevertheless still alive and well – and attracting new converts by the day.

Just as patronymic surnames predominate in other Celtic countries within the British Isles, so Cornwall is especially rich when it comes to those derived from place-names. The good news is that, as a result, there are infinitely more Cornish surnames than will be found in Wales, for example. Luckily help is at hand in the shape of a well-known little ditty:

> *By Ros-, Car-, Lan-, Tre-, Pol-, Pen-,*
> Ye may know most Cornish men.

This spot of doggerel is helpful, certainly, though it overstates the case somewhat. For all that, there are a thousand or so surnames which are specifically Cornish, and many do begin with these prefixes. Let's see how they work in practice, with a couple of examples for each:

Ros (heath, promontory): **Roscarrock**; **Roskruge**.
Car (fort, camp): **Carthew**, **Carkeet**.
Lan (enclosure): **Landeryou**, **Lanyon**.
Tre (homestead): **Trelawny**, **Trewolla**.
Pol (pool): **Polglaze**; **Polkinghorne**.
Pen (head or end): **Pendray**, **Pendarves**.

We might usefully add three more such prefixes: *Ker-* (fort, camp, a variant of *Car-*), as in the surname **Kernick**; *Bos-* (dwelling), as in **Bosanko** and several similar names and *Nan-* (valley), as in **Nancarrow**.

You could hardly mistake any of these surnames as being anything other than Cornish. Caution is advisable, however, as so often in such cases. The following surnames, among others, carry the prefixes we have been considering, but are not Cornish after all: **Rossington** [from a place in Yorkshire]; **Carmichael** [from a place in Lanarkshire, Scotland]; **Lansdown** [from a place in Somerset]; **Tremlett** [Norman, from a place-name in Calvados, *Trois minettes*]; **Polly** [Norman, used for a courteous and polite person or, ironically, for someone who lacks such qualities]; **Pennington** [from places in Lancashire, Cumberland and Hampshire]; **Kersey** [from a place in Suffolk]; **Bostock** [from a place in Cheshire] and **Nangle** [an abbreviated form of *atten angle* – a dweller by a corner of land].

Matters are little easier when it comes to an undeniably Celtic surname like **Penrose**. Admittedly there are settlements of this name in ten parishes in Cornwall, but it can also be found as a place-name in Wales and Herefordshire, all of which could, in theory, have given rise to the surname. The surname **Penruddocke**, on the other hand, although it proudly bears its *Pen-* prefix, comes from the Celtic place-name of *Penruddock* – but this is situated in Cumberland, not in Cornwall.

So this is the first caveat to enter when applying the little *Ros- Car- Lan-* ditty – namely, that not all surnames beginning with the prefixes listed are Cornish, or at least not exclusively Cornish, even when the name in question sounds, or is, unimpeachably Celtic.

The second caveat is simple enough: we should be aware that

although many Cornish surnames have a place-name origin, several do not. Some are based on personal characteristics, such as **Tallack** [*big browed*] or **Connock/Cunnack/Cunnick** [from Cornish *connek*, clever]. Others are occupational in origin, like **Angove** [the smith], **Hellier** [a tiler or thatcher] or **Trahair** [a tailor].

There are several surnames which are undeniably Cornish in origin, but which may have also developed quite separately in other parts of Britain and Europe. **Morgan**s, **Trevor**s, **Trahern**s and **Gwynn**s can have their origins in Cornwall or in Wales; **Anderton** is a Cornish name meaning *oak hill*, but the Lancashire **Anderton**s are named after a township in that county; Cornish **Lanyon**s originally came from a place with this name in Gwinear, but *Lannion* in northern France also gave rise to a similar surname.

A number of Cornish men and women over the years have made their regional surnames famous. Amongst the ranks of what we might call 'Professional Cornishmen' can be numbered the writer A.L. **Rowse**,

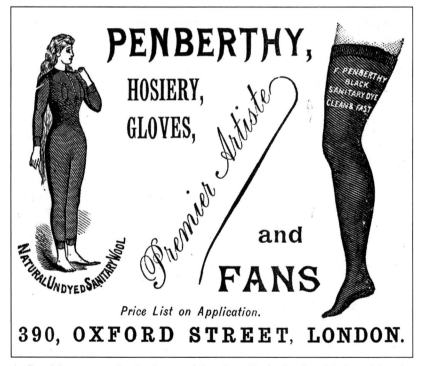

A Cornish surname in the heart of London. Typically Cornish in origin, the toponymic surname *Penberthy* seems very much at home in the heart of London's West End in the 1890s. [From *London of today* by C.E.Pascoe, 1891].

born in St Austell in 1903, whose books include *A Cornish childhood* (1942) and many more in similar vein. The Rowse surname, widely spread throughout Cornwall, comes from *ros*, a heath or promontory, and can also be found with the variant spellings **Rouse** or **Rows**.

Then there is the eminent man of letters Sir Arthur **Quiller-Couch**, born in Bodmin in 1863, who was universally known simply as '*Q*' and whose entry in the *Dictionary of National Biography* begins by describing him simply as a *Cornishman*. Both elements of his double-barrelled surname are Cornish, but if we were expecting any general consensus on their meaning, we'd be sorely disappointed. The few surname dictionaries or similar scholarly works which do choose to list the name Quiller claim variously that it has a French origin and means *a maker of spoons or ladles*, that it comes from a nickname for a fledgling bird, that it refers to a maker of quill pens, or that a person who washed up the *escuelles, porringers and bowls* was surnamed **Squiller** or **Quiller**. The same writer who makes this last claim (the highly-regarded hymn writer and folklorist, Sabine Baring-Gould) then offers another totally different explanation elsewhere in his book, *Family names and their story* (1910):

> *Quiller, also Keeler, the dresser of quilled ruffs and collars, such as were worn in the reign of Elizabeth. Mr Quiller-Couch has in his name references to two trades – the starcher who quilled collars, and the coucher who stuffed beds.*

'Mr Quiller-Couch' would no doubt have been amused if not confused to have read such harmless nonsense. The *quilled ruffs* theory was also espoused at one time by that most charming and erudite of writers, Ernest Weekley (the poor man whose urbane wit seems to have been lost on his wife Frieda, who promptly left him to spend the rest of her life with D.H. Lawrence) in the first edition of *The romance of names* (1914), but by the time he published the second edition of the book which he called simply *Surnames* in 1917, he had seen the error of his ways:

> *The ruff came after the surname period...Hence the explanation I have given of **Quiller** in my* Romance of names *(p.171) is wrong. It is simply the queller, i.e, killer – also **Keller**.*

So now we have a *killer* to add to the list of possibilities. It would seem, without being too unkind, that no one has the foggiest idea what the surname really means. If it's open house for imaginative suggestions, I'll modestly add one of my own: that if the Manx **Quilliam** is a shortened form of **MacWilliam** and the Scots and Irish **Quill** or **Quillan** means **MacCuill** (son of Coll), then it must at least be possible that

Quiller has a Celtic patronymic origin - *Son of William*, perhaps? One essential fact which must be taken into account – and seems not to have been considered by other guessers and theorizers – is that Quiller is almost exclusively a Cornish name. Practically all Quiller entries in the *International Genealogical Index* relate to Cornwall, the earliest being for Jone Quiller, daughter of John Quiller, baptised at Saint Dominick in 1599, and there are Quiller wills proved in the Archidiaconal Court of Cornwall from as early as 1588 (John Quiller of St Dominick). As if to reinforce the point, it is said that both the Quiller and the Couch ancestors of Sir Arthur had been settled in Polperro, Cornwall, for generations.

What of **Couch**, pronounced *Cooch*, a surname which Sir Arthur inherited from his grandfather, the doctor-naturalist Jonathan Couch (1789-1870)? This could be a nickname for a lazy man (the original *couch potato*?) or a bed-stuffer, as Baring-Gould alleges. *Cough* being the Cornish word for *red*, however, we might do well to stick with such an origin for a known Cornish name, and consider the possibility that the original Mr Couch was a red-headed person. The Welsh surname **Gough** can have the same meaning.

Cornwall can offer some glorious surnames for you to get your tongue around – though before you attempt to pronounce some of these, do try to find out from those in the know which syllable should take a stress. Usually the accent is on the second syllable, as in **Rose*warne***, **Chen*o*weth**, though speakers in the rest of England can soon corrupt these into **Rose*warne*** and **Chen*o*weth** – or even to **Chenworth** or **Chinworth**. The first two letters in Chenoweth, in any case, are properly pronounce *Sh*, not *Ch*, as spelt.

Plenty of Cornish surnames can sound unusual or exotic to the uninitiated: **Baragwanath** refers to a baker of fancy bread, **Curnow** is *Kernow*, a Cornishman, and the following are taken from place-names: **Andrewartha**, **Cargeege**, **Carnsew**, **Cawrse**, **Godolphin**, **Nancarrow**, **Vellanoweth**, **Trevorva** – and **Tregloaa**, which even has the rare distinction of being a surname which ends with a double letter '*a*'.

Some Cornish surnames are even more exotic: we could be forgiven for believing that **Bevetto**, **Bolitho**, **Bosanko**, **Carvosso**, **Colenso**, **Lansallos** and **Santo** were Italian in origin, or arrived with survivors of the Spanish Armada in 1588 – though there were no known shipwrecks on the Cornish coast at that time. A reporter for BBC East Midlands television news at the present time is called Rebecca **Spargo**, and I was quite gratified recently to have guessed – correctly, as it happens – that her surname is Cornish, based on a place-name spelt in the same way. More often than not the final letter '*o*' in many of these surnames, which makes them sound foreign to our ears, is nothing more than a Cornish plural or adjectival ending. So **Bennetto**, **Clemo**, **Jago** and **Kitto** are

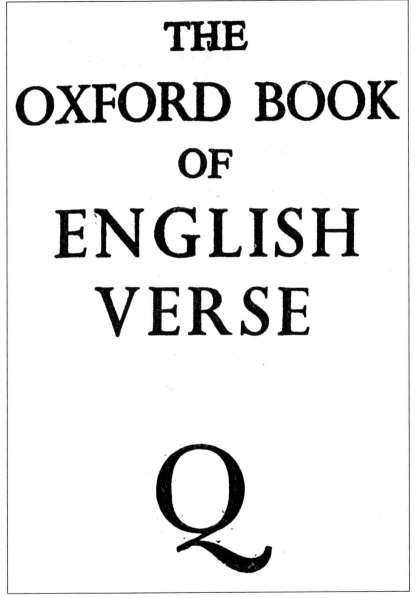

THE

OXFORD BOOK

OF

ENGLISH

VERSE

Q

True fame. Sir Arthur Quiller-Couch, professional Cornishman and editor of the *Oxford Book of English Verse*, was famous enough to be known simply by the initial letter of his surname.

used for the children of Benedict, Clement, James and Christopher respectively, while the well-known Cornish surname **Pasco(e)** means *Easter child*.

In a modest but very useful book, *A handbook of Cornish surnames* (1972, third edition 1999), G. Pawley White laments the fact that many charming surnames are no longer to be found in the county. This is a generally accurate statement, but although there may well be no more **Killigrew**s, **Carminow**s, **Besawsacke**s, **Halvossa**s or **Lancolla**s still living in Cornwall, other names he mentions appear to survive elsewhere in Britain – not to mention other places in the world. There are plenty of **Greep**s still in Devon and **Curnock**s in the Bristol area and elsewhere, and although the few surviving **Trenow**s are in far-away Colchester in Essex, there is no lack of **Trenowick**s in Cornwall itself.

Another helpful dictionary of Cornish surnames, preceded by a thirteen-page preface, is *Patronymica Cornu-Britannica* by R.S. Charnock; originally published in 1870, it was reprinted in 2000 in paperback by Willow Bend Books of Westminster, Maryland, USA.

Cornwall has been affected, of course, by a great deal of emigration and immigration over the centuries, and surnames have come and gone in the process. For all that, the county can take a great deal of

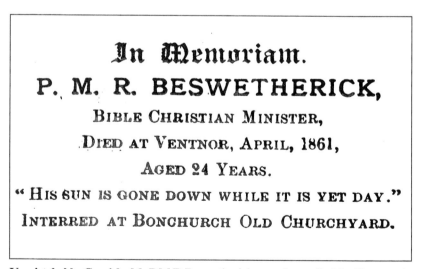

In Memoriam.
P. M. R. BESWETHERICK,
Bible Christian Minister,
Died at Ventnor, April, 1861,
Aged 24 Years.
" His sun is gone down while it is yet day."
Interred at Bonchurch Old Churchyard.

Unmistakably Cornish. Mr.P.M.R.Beswetherick may have died in Ventnor in the Isle of Wight, but his surname, which is derived from a place-name, is unmistakably Cornish. [From *A history of the Bible Christian Churches on the Isle of Wight* by Rev.J.Woolcock, 1897].

satisfaction from the fact that not only has it sent its surnames far and wide throughout the world, but that it has also kept within itself a core of names which are unmistakably its own.

The implications of all this for the surname enthusiast are clear. As a general rule of thumb, if the meaning of a name escapes you, and if it sounds very unusual but could be from the British Isles – then it is quite likely to be Cornish.

CHAPTER 8

Part-Way Quiz

I hope that by the time you reach this stage in the book, you'll feel that you are better equipped to answer some questions in a part-way quiz.

THE QUIZ

This is very simple. All you have to do, on your own or in discussion with family and friends, but *without* consulting books or databases at this stage, is to try to establish the meaning and origin of the following surnames. In each case think about the general groupings of surnames that we've talked about, and try speaking a name aloud if you're still having difficulties with it.

Here are the surnames to be deciphered:

1. **Potticary**
2. **Farmery**
3. **Boleyn**
4. **Foster**
5. **Faulkner**
6. **Jenner**
7. **Brett**
8. **Flinders**
9. **Pickard**

Once you've tried to decipher each name for yourself, then carry on reading the text below for answers and further thoughts.

THE ANSWERS

1. Potticary

What can it mean? Could it be derived from a man or woman with a first name *Potty'* or *'Ary*? Could it have a connection with the river *Cary* in

Somerset, or places called *Cary* Fitzpaine, Lytes *Cary* or Castle *Cary* in the same county? Could it be a nickname for a person who was *potty*, slightly on the crazy side? This might be lively (if far-fetched) brainstorming stuff, but it falls short of the mark. It may be only when we come to the *occupation* category, speaking the name aloud with a bit of a lisp on the *tt* sound, that the penny will finally drop. **Potticary** is a variant on the word *apothecary*, with the letter 'a' missed off the front of it, just as the surname **Prentice** was used for an *apprentice*.

An *apothecary* was originally a shopkeeper who sold a range of medicinal products and spices; the term later became used for a person who manufactured and sold medical drugs.

There's something rather odd about Potticarys: although the surname (or one of its variants) is known to have been used in both Oxfordshire and Yorkshire as early as the 13th century, it eventually settled down to become an almost exclusively Wiltshire surname. Not only that, but it was localised even within Wiltshire itself, the great majority of Potticarys being found in and around the Wylye valley. There must have been plenty of apothecaries around in times past, up and down the country, so why is the Potticary surname so rare and so narrowly localised? The same question might be asked regarding my mother's maiden name of **Buckler**, for example; it's not as rare as Potticary, but all present-day Bucklers would seem to be related to each other, however distantly, with a common line of descent from a single Dorset-based ancestor – who was a buckle maker, presumably. How was it that buckle-makers all over Britain didn't spawn the Buckler surname?

Look for no easy answers here. Clearly the overwhelming majority of apothecaries and buckle-makers acquired surnames which were based upon a father or mother's name, a place of origin or some personal characteristic, rather than upon their occupation. The process whereby each of these categories of surnames was favoured for different individuals in different places and at different times is still something of a delightful mystery to us at the present day. What we can say is that the uneven impact of epidemics such as the 14th-century Black Death upon mortality rates in urban and rural communities might hold some of the answers here, and it is just possible that Potticarys and Bucklers were wiped out in disproportionate numbers when pestilence struck. I'm not totally convinced by such a theory in this case, though it is clearly one that is able to answer some of the questions that surname scholars set themselves.

2. **Farmery**

Anything to do with farmers or farming? No. We need to make a comparison with surnames of both the Potticary and the Armitage type

An apothecary. This common-enough trade has given us an uncommon surname. [From *The book of English trades*, 1823].

Anne Boleyn or Bullen. What can be the origin of her surname?

here: **Farmery**, like Potticary, has lost letters at the beginning (two, in this case), and the *ar* spelling represents an earlier pronunciation of a sound which has become *er* in modern speech. Add two letters at the front, change *ar* to *ir* (pronounced as if it were *er*) and you have *infirmary*. So a man called Farmery worked at a hospital, probably within a monastery. Elementary?

3. Boleyn

Here's a surname which most British readers will recognise as that of
Ann **Boleyn** (daughter of Thomas **Boleyn)**, who married King Henry
VIII in January 1532/3, but was relieved of her head on the scaffold on
19 May 1536.

It may help – or it may hinder us – to know that there are well-
attested variations on this surname: **Bullen; Bulleyn; Bullon; Bullin;
Bullan; Bullant; Bullent; Boullen; Boullin** and **Bollen**.

Did a man with a first name *Bull* have a son and start an ancestral
line? Was a *bullen* a bull-keeper? Was a bull-headed person nicknamed
Bullen? Look again at the variations, of which **Bullant** and **Bullent** are
perhaps the least helpful, with **Boullen** and **Boullin** the most helpful.
Speak them out loud.

We know that England became home to a number of settlers from
France – at the time of the Norman Conquest in 1066, but also later.
Northern French towns lay conveniently close to the coast of England
and none more so than the sea port of *Boulogne*, a favourite destination
for English day trippers to this day. One of Ann Boleyn's ancestors in
the male line, then, would have been an immigrant from Boulogne.

From here on it might get easier, since both **Foster** and **Faulkner** are
occupational surnames, while **Brett**, **Flinders** and **Pickard** have
toponymic origins.

4. Foster

A forester (a man in charge of a forest). Alternatively, the name could
refer to a person who lived near a forest, or who worked in wood, made
scissors, or was a foster parent. A forest worker or dweller could also
acquire a surname such as **Forster**, **Forest** or **For(r)ester**.

5. Faulkner

A falconer (someone who tended falcons). More obscurely, it can also
be derived from a person who operated a gun known as a *falcon*.
Variant spellings include: **Faulkener; Faulknor; Falk(i)ner; Falconar** –
and, simply, **Falconer**.

6. Jenner

Not *sojourner*, nor from the French word **déjeuner**, but an *engineer*
(someone who designed or made machines for use in war or peace), a
surname principally found in the south of England. Variant spellings
include **Ginner**, **Genner** and **Jenoure**. Rather more of a challenge, this
one? As with Potticary, the trick with **Jenner** is to guess that an element
at the front of the word *engineer* has been omitted.

A surname with an obvious meaning once you know? Falkiner Fine Papers of Southampton Row in London is a Mecca for bookbinders and others. [Photograph by John Titford].

7. Brett

A Breton, someone from Brittany. Folklore having determined that Bretons were generally stupid, the name can sometimes be used for a dim-witted person. **Brett** as a surname is most common in East Anglia, where many Bretons made their home after the Conquest. Variants: **Britt**; **Breton**; **Bretton**; **Brittain**.

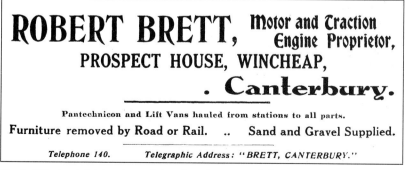

ROBERT BRETT, Motor and Traction Engine Proprietor,
PROSPECT HOUSE, WINCHEAP,
. Canterbury.

Pantechnicon and Lift Vans hauled from stations to all parts.

Furniture removed by Road or Rail. .. **Sand and Gravel Supplied.**

Telephone 140. *Telegraphic Address:* "*BRETT, CANTERBURY.*"

Brett. What might be the origin of such a name? [From Kelly's *Post Office Directory of Kent*, 1911]

8. Flinders
A Fleming, someone from Flanders. Many weavers and others from Flanders settled in England and established families there. Variants include **Flanders**.

9. Pickard
A person from Picardy in Northern France – where, in the words of the song, roses are blooming... Significantly, Picardy is close to Normandy, home of William the Conqueror.

CHAPTER 9

Surname Surgery 2: The Parts of a Surname

Today we have naming of parts ... **(Henry Reed, 1946)**
Today we have parting of names ... **(John Titford, 2002)**

If the holistic approach to the surname which interests you fails to yield results, and you seem to be getting nowhere by looking at the name as a whole, then it might be time to attack it with a scalpel and start carving it up into its component parts. Cut it in half, or into three or more pieces; consider its beginning, its middle and its end as separate elements, and generally set about it mercilessly. It might be messy, but it could end in a successful conclusion.

MAKING THE FIRST CUT

Even the most skilled of surgeons or pathologists may not be quite sure exactly where to make the first cut, and you might find the same problem once you've sharpened up the knife and are ready to do battle with your surname specimen.

It could be that the surname is of two-part compound variety, and that you'll need to break it more or less in half. There is some debate as to whether the names **Shakespeare** and **Wagstaff** could have been bawdy nicknames in origin; was it a spear or a staff – or something more intimate – that the original bearer was shaking and wagging in public? In any event, it is clear that such two-part names consist of a verb followed by a noun, just as **Whitehead** or **Barefoot** can be broken down into an adjective and a noun. Mr **Longstaff**, bearing a surname composed in a similar manner, might have carried a big stick, but could have been particularly well-endowed in the nether regions. **Strongi'th'arm**, a feisty name which even carries within itself its own Midlands/Northern dialectal pronunciation, is more complex: here an adjective (*Strong*), a preposition (*in*), the definite article (*the*) and a noun (*arm*) have been compressed to create a striking surname which has survived to the present day.

Dividing up a surname at the appropriate point may not be so simple. Where would you split the surname **Benskin**? In my youth I was familiar with boards outside pubs and off-licences advertising the products of Benskin's Brewery, and if I'd stopped to think about the meaning of surnames in those days, I probably would have made a division between *Ben* and *skin*. In reality the cut needs to be made at a different place: Benskin is a diminutive of the personal name *Benn/Bennet/Benedict*; we can think of it, if you like, as *Ben's kin* – nothing to do with skin…

Singleterry

Then what about **Singleterry**, a surname which I first encountered in the Cambridgeshire Fens? Most English **Singletary**s [the earliest-known spelling of the name] featured in the *IGI* were living in Lincolnshire, the earliest reference being to the birth of Joan **Singletary** at Surfleet in 1549, and they would appear to be members of one single family group. The English **Singletary**s/**Singleterry**s are vastly outnumbered, however, by their American cousins; the www.placesnamed.com web-site on the internet provides us with the mind-numbing information that **Singleterry** is the 19,970th most popular last name (surname) in the United States, and follows this up with the even more bewildering fact that its frequency is '0.000%'. Riveting stuff. The original *paterfamilias* of the great horde of American **Singleterry**s seems to have been Richard **Singletary**, who is known to have been in Salem, then in Newbury, Massachusetts, from as early as 1637 – a very early transatlantic immigrant indeed, who is said to have been 102 when he died in 1687.

At first sight, there would appear to be two components in the name, *Single* and *Terry*, and we could certainly split the name in this way, just as we could with the byname or surname **Syngalday**, found at Hallaton in Leicestershire in the late 14th century, which appears to be quite simple *Single/day*. When a member of the extended **Singleterry** family in America was granted five hundred acres of land in Berkley County, South Carolina, in 1703, his surname is indeed split into two parts, and he is described as *Richard* **Single Terry**. Even if this were to be what we might call a 'name of two halves', however, the challenge of interpreting each half would still remain. That's a task for another day.

I always like to bear in mind the lessons which can be learned from the stirring story of Crick and Watson and their discovery of the double-helix structure of DNA. It worked to their advantage, I believe, that one was English and the other was American; they were at that cutting edge

Ben Skin or Ben's Kin? The surname *Benskin* has nothing to do with *skin*, but is derived from the personal name *Benn*. (From Kelly's *Post Office Directory of Kent, Surrey and Sussex* 1878].

of science where logical thinking has to give way to a leap of imagination (surname researchers, take note...) and the different life-experiences and cultural norms which each brought to the task in hand must have been invaluable. Not only that, but it is said that in the evenings they took a well-earned rest from their endeavours by frequenting Cambridge city public houses; here they chatted and argued with a range of friends from a variety of academic disciplines, each with a different take on life and work. Several heads being better than two, they finally broke the code and built their model.

In an ideal world, we would seek help from a surname expert, preferably one with an in-depth knowledge of a specific locality which interests us, whenever we are confronted with a thorny problem that cries out for a solution. Failing that luxury, it is still possible for us to exercise our thinking processes by discussing possibilities with friends and relations. We all bring some kind of mental baggage to our studies – or, to change the metaphor, we all think within our own strait-jackets, whereas an outsider who is not so close to a problem might have ideas about a troublesome surname which had never occurred to you.

I tried the name **Singleterry** out on two people whose opinions I valued. The first took the name as a whole, and wondered out loud whether it might have some connection with *swingletree*, a Standard English word for the cross-bar on a plough, with dialectal variants including *single-tree*. In some dialects a *swingletree* was the stock over which flax is beaten, or the movable part of a flail. Was the original Mr. **Singleterry** a ploughman, or a man who worked with flax or wielded a flail?

My second helper instinctively split the name in a place that hadn't occurred to me, coming up with the not-unreasonable suggestion that the first meaningful component might be *Sin*, not *Single*. Could *Sin* be a close approximation to the French word Saint (a saint), which is pronounced *San*, and so might the surname be a corrupt form of a French place-name such as *Saint Gaultier*, pronounced in the original as *San/go/teeay*? Another intriguing line of enquiry ...

Incidentally, since the earliest-known spelling of the surname in England was **Singletary**, and bearing in mind the fact that a word like *clerk* is still pronounced as *clark* even today, we could expect that the *ar* prounciation in the second part of the name was probably the one originally used, whatever the spelling may have been.

You'll see that I have assiduously avoided being bold enough to offer a definitive conclusion as to the origin of the **Singleterry** name, and given the fact that it appears in no surname dictionaries, only a close study of other surnames and place-names in the localities where the first-known members of the family were known to be living might stand a real chance of unlocking its meaning. What I do hope to have done, however, is to suggest that flexible thinking processes can pay dividends: apart from considering the name as an indivisible whole, we can then try splitting it up at more than one point and see what transpires. This is the kind of procedure which just might give you the breakthrough you need when it comes to a surname which seems determind not to yield up its meaning without a fight.

Tolliday

Let's turn our attention briefly to another of the surnames which, like Singleterry, I first encountered when I was a teacher at the former March Grammar School in the Fens of Cambridgeshire. What can we make of a name like **Tolliday**? If we take it as a whole, we might notice that it seems to rhyme nicely with the word *holiday* – which itself was originally a compound of *holy* and *day*, but which was subject to the same kind of shortening of its initial vowel that also affected a word like *bonfire*, which was originally spelt and pronounced *bonefire* – a fire on which you would burn *bones*. A connection with *holiday* might be a charming thought, but is perhaps not so very useful?

Henry Alfred Long, author of *Personal and family names* (1883), whose explanations as to the origins of surnames usually beggar belief, has an imaginative suggestion to make concerning Tolliday:

> **Tolliday**. *Born on St Olave's day, gives* **Tully**, *when English, Tooley Street [London] named from St Olave's church.*

The surname **Tully**, as it happens, is said by Hanks and Hodges to be an anglicised version of the Gaelic names **O'Taithlagh** or **O'Maol Tuile** ('descendant of the devotee of *St Tuile*'), so Tolliday could conceivably have one of two possible saintly origins.

Ernest Weekley makes it clear in his book *Surnames* that he is as perplexed by Tolliday as we might be, though he makes no mention of St Olave:

> *The Lincolnshire name* **Tolliday** *or* **Tollady** *is very puzzling. It may mean 'Tolley the dey' or the 'dey of Tolley'. In Leicestershire Borough Records occurs the name of Richard* **Tollidenoit** *(Anglo-French, 'toille de noit', toil by night). Was the first* **Tolliday** *the opposite of this? Or does the name represent 'toil dey' – compare William* **Delveday** *(City of London Letter Books, 1275), and William* **Plouday** *(Hundred Rolls, 1273).*

I would by no means reject these 'born on St Olave's day' or 'toil by day' explanations out of hand here, but I would like to explore further possibilities, nevertheless. When it comes to wielding the surname-surgeon's knife, Messrs Long and Weekley have both decided to make a cut between *Tolly* and *day*. There is certainly something seductive about such an approach, and we could develop it further by pointing out that **Tolley/Toly** exists as a surname in its own right, based upon the Middle English given name *Toll*, and that it can also be a shortened form of the personal name *Bartholomew*. A language dictionary, meanwhile, isn't much help when it comes to *tolly*, but it does indicate that the word *toller* was a term used to describe a toll-collector or a person who tolled a bell. Surely it would be a bit far-fetched, however, to claim that the surname means something like *The day the rent-man called*?

While I was pondering all this, I came across a reference to a much-admired Pre-Raphaelite tomb in Abney Park Cemetery in North London, erected in memory of Elizabeth **Tollady**, wife of William Tollady of Dalston. This chance encounter with what appeared to be a variant spelling of Tolliday jogged my mind out of its lethargy, and I remembered that Weekley's book had indeed yoked Tolliday and Tollady together. Rev Henry Barber's dictionary of surnames makes a bold attempt to derive Tollady from *Tolladine* in Worcestershire – a stab in the dark which the author has the good grace to enter with a question-mark against it, and which seems to owe more to inspired guesswork than to any attempt to localise the surname or to think of any alternative forms. The discovery of the Tollady spelling was good news for me, however, because I could now try splitting the name at an earlier point, and consider the possibility that *lady*, rather than *day*, might be the final element. It was a case of 'good-bye' to *Tolly/Tolli* followed by *day*, and 'hello' to *Tol* followed by *lady*.

Now all I had to do was to change one letter, and I could turn Tollady into **Toplady**, a well-established name with a known meaning which has earned its place in most surname dictionaries. Of course there are times when simply changing one letter in a name to suit your own convenience is a shameless case of intellectual dishonesty, but in this instance I felt justified in doing so, if only because it is clear that euphemism has been at work overtime on the Toplady surname, which has its origins in a bawdy nickname. Scholars are agreed that the original Mr Toplady or **Tiplady** had achieved fame or notoriety thanks to an ability to *tip* ladies over, or to be found a-*top* them... In other words, the surname is derived from a term used for a libertine, referring especially to someone who succeeded in making love to a woman of higher rank than himself. The surname **Shacklady** may have a similar origin.

Some brave souls, mainly in Yorkshire and County Durham, remained loyal to the uncompromising Tiplady name, while Nottinghamshire is the home of most of the **Topladys/Topladies/ Toplodys**. The more euphemistically-minded **Toplises** are almost all confined to Derbyshire, while **Tolliday** (an alternative spelling of the same name, if my theory about its origins are correct) is more widespread geographically – though strongest in East Anglia in general and Cambridgeshire in particular – and its spelling more varied: **Tolliday, Tolledy, Tol(l)ady, Tolloday, Tol(l)aday, Toleday, Tollardy, Towleday** and **Tilledy**. In 1754 a member of the Cambridgeshire Tollidays, Rebecca by name, married a Thomas **Wilberspin** at Histon, Cambridgeshire. We will have something further to say about the **Wilberspin/Wilderspin** family before our story is at an end.

So my own theory in all of this is clear enough, I hope. While some families were happy enough to stick with Tiplady or Toplady, regardless of the fact that it referred originally to a womanizing bounder (who may, for all we know, have been much admired by some of his contemporaries despite, or even because of, his amorous adventures), others preferred euphemistic alternatives such as Toplis or Tolliday.

It might be the case, as with the surname Singleterry, that all this theorizing about Tolliday may be taking us further from the truth, though I think not; again it is the importance of flexible thinking processes which counts.

The *Countdown Conundrum* syndrome

Learning to think flexibly about surnames is a harder task than it may at first appear, for at least one very good reason. We owe part of our success as human beings to the fact that our brains create and store clusters of information, ready-made packages which save us the trouble of approaching every problem entirely from scratch. If I ask you whether you have ever come across the imaginary surname **Rippleflick** before, it wouldn't take you more than a fraction of a second to say 'No, I have never heard it or read it in my life'. Presumably what your brain has done here, working at frenetic speed, is to compare Rippleflick as a whole, or elements of it, with all the names and name elements it has stored over many years, and has failed to find a perfect match. Of course these trusty brains of ours can become mesmerised by groupings of letters which they think they do recognise, which they find familiar and comforting. They are very eager to divide Singleterry into *Single* and *terry* or Tolliday into *Tolli* and *day*. If we want to think flexibly, we'll have to strip out some of this cerebral wiring, vitally useful as it may be to us in most everyday situations, and start over again with modified wiring or very little wiring at all. Our experience of life will not have prepared us for such an activity, so it comes hard!

Consider the so-called *Conundrum* feature which forms part of the Channel 4 Television programme, *Countdown*. The nine letters of a chosen word have been reassembled, and two contestants vie with each other as to who can unscramble the conundrum and identify the original word in the fastest time – if at all. Now what makes this task so much more difficult than it might otherwise be, is that the cunning compilers, knowing that the human brain loves to settle onto patterns it finds familiar, usually manage to include at least one recognisable word as part of each conundrum. *STOPPEDNO* includes the word *stop*, and *GRIMPAINT* contains not one, but two, known words, *grim* and *paint*. To stand any chance of answering each of these teasers correctly (yes, I'm sure that all readers immediately came up with *POSTPONED* and *IMPARTING* without any difficulty...), you first have to ignore or unscramble the 'words' which are there already – and how the poor brain hurts at having to do that!

The TV contestant who solved the *GRIMPAINT* conundrum in four seconds must have been taking mental gymnastics lessons!

So it is with surname interpretation: very often you'll need to unwire and rewire your brain, and try to eradicate preconceived patterns as far as you can.

Many surnames, we know, have already been altered by folk etymology to fit into a familiar mould, into the kind of 'preconceived patterns' we have been talking about, and this has possibly been the case with Singleterry. We are very keen, as students of the subject, to make some sense of a name, and so were people in earlier generations; but unlike us, they may have had the power to take their own or someone else's surname and to change it to suit their expectations. In this way, as I shall argue later in this book, the name **Pennicott** can become **Petticoat**, and **Habershon** can end up as **Haversham**.

PREFIXES AND SUFFIXES

Rather than dividing a surname neatly in the middle, it may be more useful to pay some attention to its beginning or to its ending – in other words, to consider prefixes and suffixes. This is a topic which has been touched upon already at various stages in this book, but here I'll try to make a consolidated listing of some of the more commonly-encountered prefixes and suffixes. Please note that some letter combinations appear in more than one list, and do be aware that prefixes and suffixes are not set in concrete, but have been subject to minor or major modifications over the years. George Redmonds makes a further vital point here: *An unaccented suffix was particularly susceptible to change, and could be confused with almost any other frequent suffix.* The third appendix to George's book, *Surnames and genealogy*, provides a series of examples of this process at work, one whereby **Snawsdale** can also be **Snawsell**, **Stockdale** can be **Stockton**, and so forth.

Patronymic and metronymic surnames

Prefixes and suffixes can be added to the full version of a male or female personal name, or to one or other of its pet-forms.

Prefixes

Fitz-. Doesn't necessarily indicate illegitimacy.

Mac-, Mc-, M'-. Scots and Irish, *son of*.

O'. Irish. *Grandson* or *descendant* of.

Mag-, Mab-, Map-, Ab-, Ap. Welsh, *son of*. Suffixes like these can be abbreviated and attached to the name which follows: **Probert** has evolved from **ap Robert**.

Qu- (followed by a vowel); *C-* or *K-* (followed by vowel – or by a consonant, as in **Clulcas, Kneen**). Manx, *son of*, an abbreviated form of *Mac/Mc*. Similar features can also be observed in some Scottish and Irish surnames.

Notice also that Welsh and Cornish surnames with an adjectival origin may begin with the letters *Gw-* (**Gwatkin, Gwilli(a)m**)

Suffixes

-s or *-es*. A genitive ending, as in the modern *'s*.

-son, -ason, -eson, -ison, etc. More commonly found in the North of England than in the South.

-daughter, -dochter. Usually found as part of unstable bynames.

-cock, -cot, -cott, -cox; -at, -ate, -att, atte, -et, -ete, -ett, ette, -it, -ite, -itt, itte; -ot, -ote, -ott, -otte; -ut, -ute, -utt, -utte; -ie, -y; -in, -ing, -ings, -ins; -ken, -kin; -lin; -ment. These are diminutives, some of which are capable of being used alongside other suffixes, giving us **Tomkins**, but also **Tomkinson**.

-mough, -maugh, -muff, -mouth, -more. With the meaning of a relation in general, or a brother-in-law in particular.

* Traps for the unwary

Qu-. These initial letters are by no means limited to Celtic patronymics. The surname **Quarles**, for example, while it might look as if it could be a Manx version of **MacCharles** (son of Charles) is of English origin, from a place in Norfolk.

Many English speakers make no attempt to pronounce the 'h' sound in names or words beginning with the letters *wh*, whereas in Scotland a pronunciation such as *hwither* for *whither* is commonplace. Note that in this case the 'h' is pronounced before, not after, the 'w', which is totally in keeping with the Old English original, which was *hwider*. It seems clear that the pronunciation of *wh* has had a more guttural quality to it in certain places at certain times, which would help to explain why *Quarmby* and *Wharmby* are variants of the same surname. The origin here is a place now called *Quarmby* in the West Riding of Yorkshire, which was *Cornebi* in the Domesday Book of 1086, *Querneby* in the 13th century and *Whernby* or *Wharnby* in the 15th century. The present-day spelling is first known to have been used in the early years of the 16th century. The surname *Quarmby*, then, though it begins with the letters *Qu*, is English through and through, with not a hint of the Celtic about it.

-s. This suffix was originally applied to personal and occupational bynames and surnames, but then became more widespread, and may be found, for example, in topographical surnames such as **Briggs** [the bridge], **Yates** [the gate] or **Mills** [the mill].

-son. This suffix was usually attached to a personal name (or to its pet-form), but not always. The son of a wright could be known as **Wrightson**, the son of a smith could become **Smithson**, the son of a shepherd could become **Sheppardson** or **Shepperson**, the son of a clerk could be **Clarkson** and the son of a man who worked at a monastery or was known for being pious might be named **Frearson** [son of the friar].

Several place-names ending in *-ston* were shortened, officially or unofficially, to give *-son. Ilkeston* in Derbyshire, for example, is always referred to colloquially as *Ilson*. Some toponymic surnames also dropped the '*t*' in this way, whether or not the place-name also underwent such a change. So look out for toponymic surnames which look as if they might be patronymic in origin but which are really nothing of the kind, such as **Beeson** (*Beeston*) or **Marson** (*Marston*). The surname **Benson** can be a patronymic name with the meaning *son of Benne/Benedict*, but it can also be derived from a place in Oxfordshire called *Benson*. **Pinson** (with variants such as **Pinsent**) is also not patronymic, but comes from an Old French word for a finch, and could have been used to describe a cheerful person, or one who made or used pincers.

The non-patronymic suffixes -*sall* or -*soll* can sometimes be changed to -*son*, and I have found instances of the surname **Inkersall/Ingersoll** [from *Inkersall* in Derbyshire] being written as **Ingerson**.

-*cock*. Some names ending in -*cock*, such as **Peacock** or **Woodcock**, are derived from the names of birds.

-*cott*. The -*cott* element in a toponymic surname like **Vellacott** [from a place in Devon] is from an Old English word for a *cottage*.

Occupational surnames

Occupational bynames or surnames in mediaeval records will frequently be preceded by the French definite articles *le* or *la*. In principle a gender differentiation is adhered to, *le* being used for males and *la* for females, but in the Warwickshire Hundred Rolls of 1279-1280, for example, while men are listed using the formula *Ricardo* **le Tannur** of Warwick or *Thomas* **le Wodeward** of Brandon, the masculine form *le* is also used for women such as *Margareta* **le Porter** of Kenilworth and *Emma* **le Smokere** of Bishops Itchington.

Suffixes which can also stand as occupational surnames in their own right

● *Smith and Wright*

Smith and **Wright**, as we know, can happily act as stand-alone surnames, but each can also be used as an element in a longer name.

A **Whitesmith** worked in tin, a **Naysmith** made knives or nails, and a **Sixsmith** was possibly a maker of sickles. A **Siev(e)wright** made sieves, an **Arkwright** (a Lancashire surname) made chests, and a **Wainwright** made carts or waggons – think of the well-known painting by John Constable entitled *The hay wain*.

We might tend to assume that wrights and smiths have always

worked in hard materials, but certain surnames indicate that this was not always the case. **Cheesewright** refers to a maker of cheese, and no doubt Johannes **Botersmyth**, who appears in the 1381 Poll Tax returns for Holbeach in Lincolnshire, made butter for a living.

* Traps for the unwary

Woolwright is not an occupational surname, but comes from the Old English personal name **Wulfric**, which has also spawned names like **Wolveridge**, which looks for all the world as if it has toponymic origins.

● *Herd*

Herd/Heard/Hurd as a surname originally referred to a man responsible for tending animals. A few rare surnames have *He(a)rd* as a first component (**He(a)rdman**, **He(a)rder**), but many more carry it as a final element, giving us **Shepherd** or – from the 1381 Poll Tax returns for Spalding in Lincolnshire - *Robertus **Calfhird*** and *Thomas **Oxhird**. Herd* as used at the end of a name, however, has a nasty habit of disguising itself, as it does in the following surnames: **Calvert** (calf herd), **Co(u)lt(h)ard** (colt herd), **Coward** (cow herd), **Geldard** (gelding herd), **Goddard** (goat herd), **Gossard** (goose herd), **Hoggard/Hoggart** (hog herd), **Nothard/Nutter** (a keeper of oxen, from Middle English *nowt*), **Oxnard** (ox herd) and **Stoddard/Stoddart/Stothard** (a *herd* in charge of *stots* – that is, horses or steers). **Stobart**, by contrast, does not belong to this *herd* class of names, but comes from a medieval given name, *Stubart*.

● *Ward*

The surname **Ward** comes from a word used for a watchman, for someone who keeps guard, so a person who watched over a wood was a **Woodward**, and a **Hayward** was responsible for protecting stretches of land or forest. Hayward, of course, can often be pronounced in the same manner as the toponymic surname **Haywood**, and can readily be confused with it. I must confess, in similar vein, that as a young boy I always thought that the surname of Mr **Woodward**, our TV repair man (in the days when televisions needing repairing...), was *Woodwood*. As such it struck me as very odd – why would someone have the name *Wood* repeated in this way? A **Forward**, despite appearances to the contrary, looked after swine (from *for*, an Old English word for a hog or pig).

● *Man*

Man(n) can stand as a surname on its own, but we are as likely to come across it as the final element in a longer name. **She(a)rman** [a sheep-shearer, or someone who cut the excess nap from cloth with shears] and **Chapman** [a dealer in small wares] are straightforward enough occupational surnames, as are **Spel(l)man** [also **Speller**, a teller of tales or weaver of spells], **Twentyman** [someone in command of twenty men], **Bannerman** [a standard-bearer] and **Kidman** [a goatherd or a seller or faggots]. **Kidman** is a well-known name in Australia, and although the film actress Nicole Kidman, formerly the wife of Tom Cruise, was born in Honolulu, Hawaii, in 1967, her family is Australian and she was brought up there from the age of four.

Sometimes, however, the *man* element in a surname means *servant of*. **Hickman** was Richard's man or servant, and **Addyman** worked for a man called Adam, but the name **Fentiman**, intriguingly enough, includes the surname of the master – in this case, Mr **Fenton**. The surnames **Pask(e)**, **Paish**, **Paskin**, **Patchett** are derived from a word used for Easter, and a servant of a family with such a name could be called **Paxman**. Jeremy Paxman is a well-known television presenter, quizmaster of *University Challenge* and famous for his acerbic interviews with the powerful and pompous. The not-dissimilar name **Packman**, though it can refer to a pedlar who carried a pack of goods with him ready to sell, can also denote a man who acted as a servant to someone called *Pack*. **Coleman** could be a charcoal burner, but also a servant of the **Cole** family, and the original **Hayman** could have lived near an enclosure, been a tall man, or worked for a man called **Hay**. The meaning of **Berryman** [servant at the manor house] is rather more general, informing us where it was that a man worked, rather than stating the name of his employer.

* Traps for the unwary

Not all names ending in *man* are occupational. I have Scottish ancestors from Huntly in Aberdeenshire whose surname, **Jessiman**, is said to come from the *Jesmond* area of Newcastle-Upon-Tyne. **Godleman** describes a person from *Godalming* in Surrey, while **Tru(e)man** simply refers to a trustworthy chap, and **Muddeman**, a variant of **Moody**, was used of a courageous or impetuous person.

Other occupational surname suffixes

-*maker*. A byname or surname ending in -*maker* clearly has an occupational origin. The meaning will be clear enough in most cases, but not all. What a person originally named **Slaymaker** made for a living was not *sleighs* to use in the snow (different spelling), but *slays* – that is, implements used in the weaving process. The related surname **Slaywright** is now apparently extinct.

-monger. Although the words *fishmonger, costermonger* (originally a seller of *costard apples*) and *ironmonger* are still in use today, only the last of these is still commonly met with (in a variety of spellings) as a surname.

-ster and *-xter.* These suffixes are strongly indicative of an occupational surname, sometimes being derived from a dialectal usage, but often referring to a female practitioner of the trade in question. So a **Dexter** (or **Dyster**) was a dyer, and a **Simester/Simister** was a tailor or sewer - *sempstress* or *seamstress* being the modern female term.

-er, -or and *-our.* Suffixes like these will sometimes suggest an occupational origin, but not always. The English name **Turner**, for example, may be found as **Turner, Turnor** and **Turnour**, though the element *-our* used in this way, which is far from common, looks very French to us today. Names like **Fielder** or **Bridger**, on the other hand, have a topographical origin.

Surnames derived from physical appearance or personal characteristics

Bynames or surnames which are based upon physical or personal characteristics can also, like occupational surnames, be preceded by the definite articles *le* or *la* (*the*) in mediaeval records, though examples are rather harder to come by. Nigellis **le Sherp** of Chadshunt, Johannes **le Wise** of Burton Dassett and Nigellus **le Broune** of Tysoe appear in the Warwickshire Hundred Rolls of 1279-1280; it would seem likely that they were so-called because they were sharp, wise and of a brown complexion respectively.

It would be misleading to attempt to identify a significant number of common elements used in surnames which originally described some physical or personal characteristic, though *love, fair, good* and *mal* are found fairly frequently, and some names which are adjectival in origin will end with the letter '*y*' or '*ie*'. Surnames of this sort are very varied, and so are the elements of which they are comprised.

Topographical surnames

Topographical bynames or surnames were often preceded by a preposition in mediaeval records – so in the Warwickshire Hundred Rolls of 1279-1280 we read of **Walterus atte Townsende**. Many such names would eventually drop the preposition entirely (giving *Walter Townsend*), but in other cases it would become attached to the last name itself, *Walter **atte Water*** becoming *Walter **Attwater*** and *John **atter Eaves*** [at the edge of a wood] becoming *John **Reeves***. Less commonly, the French definite article *le* can be found with topographical second-names: *Johannes le Halle* is listed as holding one cottage in Moreton in Warwickshire in the Hundred Rolls; but although he was then occupying a cottage, we might presume that either he or one of his male-line ancestors had lived in or near a hall.

Toponymic surnames

Toponymic bynames or surnames featured in mediaeval records will often be prefaced by the preposition *de*. In the Warwickshire Hundred Rolls of 1279-1280 we have Thomas **de Folebrok/Fulbroke** of Warwick, Johannes **de Kyrkeby** of Kenilworth and a host of others. *Galfridus Scot* of Brandon is preposition-less, but it might perhaps not have been appropriate to preface his name with *de* (*of Scotland*), since, if anything, he was something more akin to *Galfridus le Scot* (*the Scotsman*), rather in the style of *Cristiana la Irisshe* (*the Irishwoman*) of Harbury, who is featured in the same lists.

The fact that a surname is derived from a place-name might be immediately obvious to us, or it might not, since these do come in many shapes and sizes. The elements which make up place-names are themselves very large in number; many closely resemble each other yet have different origins, and generally it falls to scholars who specialise in such matters to make sense of what can be a complex subject. Sometimes a recognisable element appears at the beginning of the place-name, and it should soon dawn on us that the *Brad* of *Bradford* or *Bradley*, for example, is simply the Old English word for *broad*. Above all, however, it is suffixes which really give the game away. Many English place-names include commonly-found suffixes taken from Old English (*-ley*, *-ham* and the like) or from Old Norse (*-by*, *-toft* and so on). Immediately, then, we have something of a geographical dimension, since English settlements which eventually came under the control of the Danelaw are quite likely to include an Old Norse suffix; it is immediately evident, for example, just how many towns and villages in Lincolnshire, Leicestershire, Nottinghamshire and Derbyshire end in the Old Norse element *-by*. We'll also find that Scandinavian settlers in England were not happy with the kind of soft consonant sounds which appear in Old English words like *church,* and were happier with *kirk*, giving us a whole host of place-names such as *Kirk Ireton, Kirk Langley* and others. Don't for one minute assume that *kirk* is some kind of Scottish word, for all its popularity north of the border! *Kirkham* in Lancashire, meanwhile, combines the Old Norse *Kirk* with the Old English *ham*. Look out for this hard '*k*' sound in both place-names and surnames for evidence of Scandinavian influence; although there are places called *Shipton* (sheep farm) in several counties of England, only in the area of the old Danelaw – in this case, in North Yorkshire – do we find the Old Norse version of the same place-name, *Skipton*, complete with its hard '*k*' sound.

In presenting the alphabetical list of place-name components which follows (taken largely from *The chief elements used in English place-names* by Allen Mawer [1924]), I'm going to play safe by not referring to them as *elements* as such, which is a word that carries a precise meaning within place-name scholarship. Rather, I'll suggest that you look out for the combinations of letters presented in this list, just in case they might indicate a place-name origin for a surname which you are investigating. Such letter-combinations may be found at the beginning, at the end, or in the middle of a place-name: there are places called **Kirk**ham but also *Fal***kirk**; **Ford***wich* but also *Thet***ford**; *A***bing**don but also *Brading*; **Hamp**stead but also *Sea***ham** and *Seven***hampton**. Very often the first component in a place-name consists of a human rank or occupation (*Bishop, King, Priest*) or some kind of vegetation (*Ash, Birch, Wheat*); animals are sometimes favoured (*Crow, Cow*), as are personal names, giving us, for example, **Grimble***thorpe* in Lincolnshire (the thorp where *Grimkell* lived) or **Grimes***thorpe* in Yorkshire (the thorp where *Grim* lived).

The following list is Anglocentric, I'm afraid: these are combinations of letters found principally in English, rather than Celtic, place-names. Welsh, Scottish, Irish, Manx and Cornish place-names have all been the subject of academic study in their own right, and an impressive body of relevant published material may readily be found. I will make one exception right at the start, however: given the fact that many Cornish surnames have a place-name origin, I'll provide a list of some of the commoner prefixes found in Cornish place-names, which are so numerous because they act as they equivalent of English suffixes:

* Some Cornish place-name prefixes

Bos-, Car-, Ker-, Lan-, Nan-, Pen-, Pol-, Ros-, Tre-.

* Some English place-name components

A surname which includes one or more of the following letter-combinations might have its origins in an English place-name. This is a selective list only; various other permutations of consonants and vowels of this sort may also be found.

> *acre; age; all; apple; aps; ash; asp; ast; ba(t)ch; bag; ban; bank; barrow; beach; beck; beech; ber; berg(h); big; bil; birch; black; boar; boro(ugh); borth; bottom; bourn(e); brad; breck; brick; bridge; brook(e); brock; broad; buck; bud; bul; burgh; burn;*

JAMES BUSBY and CO.
WIRE DRAWERS,
WIRE WORKERS,
AND
TIN PLATE MANUFACTURERS,
NEW-STREET, BIRMINGHAM.

Origin both known and unknown. Scholars generally agree that the surname *Busby* comes either from a place of this name in North Yorkshire, or from a settlement called *Bushby* in the Midlands, but no one seems to know the origin of the term *busby* as used for an item of military headgear. [From Wrightson's *New Triennial Directory of Birmingham* 1818].

bury; bush; by; cal; carl; caster; castle; cester; chad; chal; che(a)p; ches(ter); chev; chil; chip; church; clay; cliff(e); clough; comb(e); con; coney; cook; cop(e); cor; cot(t); cran; cress; croft; crook; cross; dal(e); dam; dean; deep; del; den(e); dern; dike; ditch; don(e); down; dray; dung; durn; dyke; east; edg(e); elm; end; ern(e); est; fair; fal; far; feld; fen; field; fint; firth; fish; fleet; fold; ford; forth; f(o)ul; gar; garth; gate; gill; g(o)at; god; gold; gor(e); gos; gr(e)at; gr(e)ave; green; grove; had; hag; hale; (h)all; (h)am; hanger; har; hard; hat; haven; hay; head; heath; heb; hen; hes; hey; high; hill; hin; hirst; hol(d); holm(e); holy; holt; honey; hope; horn(e); hors(e); hough; house; how; hunt; hurst; hyde; hyth(e); ing; keld; kil(l); king; kirk; knight; knoll; lade; lake; lamb; land; lane; lang; lay; lea; lee; leech; leigh; ley; lick; light; lin; ling; lip; lit; little; lock; loe; long; loft; low; lyn; mal; map; mar; ma(u)l; marsh; me(a)d; mell; mer(e); mes(s); michel; mickle; mid; min; minster; monk; moor; more; mouth; nal(l); nes(s); nether; nettle; new; nor(t)(h); nut; oak(en); op; over; ow; pad; park; pen; peth; pit; plum; pol; pond; pool; port; pres; quar; rain; r(e)ad; ram; ran; rat; raw; red; ret; rid; ridge; ring; road; rock; ro(y)d; rom; rook; ros; row; rush; ry(e); sal; salt; sam; sand; saw; scar; scough; sea; sel; sey; shad; shal; shap; shar; shaw; she(a)d; sheep; shel; shen; sher; shil(l); ship; shir(e); shor(e); shute; sid(e); skip; sla; slade; slap(e); slo; slop(e); smar; smer;

snape; sne(a)d; snod; som; south; spon; spring; stall; stan; stang; staple; star; stathe; ste(a)d; sten; still; stock; stoke; ston(e); stow; strad; str(e)at; stre(e)t; sud; sul; summer; sut; swan; swin(e); tang; thing; thorn(e); thorp(e); thwait(e); throp; tin; toft; ton; tong; tre(e); trow; try; t(e)y; tyne; under; up; vant; ville; wad(e); wal(l); war(e); ward; wardine; wark; wash; wat; water; wath; way; weal; wed; wel(l); wen; west; wet; wheat; whet; whit(e); wich; wick; wid; wil(l); win; winch; with; wood; worth(y); wray; yar.

* Traps for the unwary

We shouldn't expect that all the above letter combinations will have survived in all their pristine glory, either in place-names or in surnames. Look out for *-house* being shortened to *-us, -is,* or *-ers,* for example, or *ham* being abbreviated to *am, um* or *on.*

By no means all surnames which include one of the above components are toponymic in origin. Some are based upon personal names, like **Gutt(e)ridge** (from the Middle English names, *Goderiche* or *Cuterich*), **Wadlow** (a form of **Waddilove**, said to be a corruption of the personal name *Wadelief*), **Rickwood** (from the Norman names *Richold* or *Richward*), **Ottoway** and **Ottewell** (from one of two Norman personal names, *Otoïs* or *Otewi*) and **Caton/Catton** (from the mediaeval female given-name, *Catlin*). **Stallwood/Stal(l)worthy** are variations on **Stallard**, from an Old English word for a valiant person; **Pridham/Prodham/ Prudham/Purdham** come from the French, *prudhomme*, referring to a wise man, and names in the **Gulliford/Galliford/Galliver/Gulliver** group are not derived from a place-name, nor from a trade, but were originally used for a glutton, from Old French *goulafre*.

Some elements found in non-English surnames

Surname elements derived from other European languages are many and varied; a full study of these would be a lifetime's work, but most of us would expect names ending in suffixes like *-sen, -poulos, -ez, -aldi* or *-berti* to have their origins outside the British Isles, and would recognise elements such as *-mann, -t(h)al, -dorf* and *-stein* as being German; *-steen,* on the other hand, has something more of a Dutch flavour to it, and endings such as *-ov, -ow, -vich, -czyk, -wicz, -nko* and *-ski/sky* should alert us to the possibility of an Eastern European origin. The suffix *-ski* can be found attached to place names, given names, nicknames or occupational names, while *-ovski* is normally used with a habitation name. Many Russian surnames taken from given names, nicknames or occupational names will end in *-ov*, *-ev*, or *-in* (for names ending in a vowel), while the Polish equivalents are *-ow*, *-ew*, and *-in*.

Thanks to the impact of the Norman Conquest of 1066 and the influx of various groups of later immigrants like the Huguenots, a number of surnames which are now thought of as being essentially English may contain one or more French elements. Many, but not all, surnames beginning with *De* (*of*) or *Du* (*de* + *le* = *of the*) are French in origin. In France itself, a toponymic surname such as **De Beauvais** would keep the *De* element separate from the place-name, but a shorter place-name such as *Blois* would often have the preposition attached to it, giving us the surname **Deblois**. Similarly, a person living in or near a wood or a valley might be called **Dubois** or **Duval**. Suffixes such as *-ac*, *-ad*, *-ain*, *-ard*, *-art*, *-at*, *-aud*, *-au(l)t*, *-aux*, *-el*, *-en*, *-et*, *-eux*, *-ier(e)*, *-in*, *-oin*, *-on*, *-or*, *-ot*, *-our* and many others may also indicate a name which is French in origin, and several French nouns (especially if they are grammatically female) and proper names end in a double consonant, followed by the letter '*e*', giving us endings like *-lle*, *-mme*, *-nne* *-rre* *-sse* and *-tte*.

The fact that a name includes a French-looking element may mean that it has been imported from France in the distant or more recent past, or, sometimes, that it represents the deliberate Frenchification of an English name in an attempt to give it some kind of kudos. Many surnames which are genuinely French in origin have developed in the opposite direction, of course, and have adapted their form or spelling to the English language in order to become more easily assimilated.

Finally, before we get our lines crossed, what of a Dutch surname like **De Wit**? In this case *De* does not mean *of*, as in French, but has the sense of *the*: **De Wit** is literally *the white* – that is, a man who has a pallid complexion or white hair.

CHAPTER 10

Surname Surgery 3:
Hard Nuts to Crack

Some surnames are hard nuts to crack – and some, alas, seem to be simply uncrackable no matter what you do. You might have relished the challenge of looking closely at a surname and at its component parts at the outset, only turning to a dictionary of surnames for help or confirmation afterwards, or you might have chosen to consult a dictionary right at the start. What if neither approach achieves the desired result?

Let's think first about the reasons why a particular name may not be featured in one of the major surname dictionaries. A number of possible explanations present themselves:

- The name is so rare that it is felt to be hardly worth a mention.

- The dictionary compiler is simply not aware of the existence of the name.

- The compiler is well aware of the name, but can offer no explanation as to its meaning and so doesn't wish to include it.

- The surname was edited out for reasons of space. No dictionary can include every surname that ever existed, and there was simply no space to include the one which is proving elusive.

- The surname does lurk within the dictionary somewhere, but in a different form, or under a different spelling.

If we are to proceed with any degree of optimism, we must hope that the last explanation is the one which applies to the surname we are puzzling over. It's certainly a good idea to give your imagination free rein, to play around with spellings, or to speak a name out loud in a variety of different accents, and see what you come up with. There's no guarantee that this will work in the way that you hoped it would, however. **Brumell** [from a place-name] and **Brunel** [nickname for a person of brown complexion] may look and sound similar enough, though each has an entirely different meaning and origin. **Brumell** and **Bromell**, on the other hand, are known variations on the same name. In this case a change of consonant alters the name completely, while a change of vowel simply moves us into an alternative form of the same name.

You may choose to read through the material which follows as a guide to ways of tackling particularly difficult surnames. Alternatively, you might choose to use it by way of a *Final Quiz*, a test of what you've learned, in which case I should say that the names we'll finish with are difficult to make sense of and that none appears in any of the principal surname dictionaries. I've tried my best to come up with an explanation of a name's meaning which I hope you will find convincing, though some areas of uncertainty still persist. If no definitive final solution is forthcoming in these and similar cases, all is not lost. It's rather like those mathematical exercises we all had to do at school: if you show your workings, you get some marks even if the final answer is wrong, or is not forthcoming at all. We are concerned here, above all, with defining a series of processes rather than arriving at a 'correct' answer each time. A mildly clichéd phrase such as *Process is more essential than product* could perhaps stand as our motto in this instance. In any event, we may never have the satisfaction of knowing whether a suggested solution is correct or not; these can be lonely slopes we are climbing, and there may be no companions to guide, to comfort or to reassure us during the final stages of our journey. Grown-ups, alas, generally cannot expect to have a tick from teacher to reward them for their efforts and to reassure them that they have arrived at the right answer.

A number of worked examples or case studies follow. It has not been my intention to conduct an in-depth genealogical investigation of each surname for its own sake; in the first instance I have used the kind of readily-available books, CD-ROMs or Internet databases which are listed at the beginning of this book, but I've turned to more arcane source material when all else has failed. If you have a particular interest in certain 'difficult' surnames of your own, you'll no doubt wish to pursue each one in greater depth, and I hope that some of the sources and some of the approaches I have adopted here may act as a helpful guide.

A FINAL QUIZ

In case you would like to treat the surnames which follow as a Final Quiz, I will list them here at the beginning; feel free to use any resources at your disposal in order to come up with an explanation of the meaning and possible origin of each:

- **Stonhold** of North London.

- **Goakes** of Cambridgeshire.

- **Wilderspin** of Cambridgeshire.

- **Petticoat** of Maryland, USA.

The first three case studies featured here are based upon surnames I encountered during my formative years in North London and then, later, as a teacher in the Fens of Cambridgeshire, whilst the fourth is taken from research I once conducted for an American client.

Case Study One: STONHOLD of North London

Brian **Stonhold** was a classmate of mine at secondary school, though I haven't seen or heard of him since the 1960s. Everyone, of course, had to fight off the temptation to call him *Stronghold*; his surname is – what shall we say – sort of English but not English all at the same time?

Stonhold can't be found in any surname dictionary, even if we take a flexible approach to its form and spelling, so some kind of genealogical approach is the only one that might reap rewards.

The *National Burial Index* has no relevant entries, while the *1881 Census* on CD-ROM features only four Stonhold families and one 'stray' individual. The oldest Stonhold, listed as **Stonehold**, was Henry, a seventy-four year old newsvendor, born in Colchester, Essex, and living in 1881 at Great Coggeshall, between Colchester and Braintree, with his daughter Rosina as housekeeper. Other Stonholds had left Essex, stating on the census that they had been born there: Ebenezer Stonhold, boot maker, aged 37, born in *Ford Street, Essex* (five and a half miles north west of Colchester) was living with his wife at Henfield in Sussex, and Philip Stonhold, 42, unmarried, a gardener, born in Colchester, was lodging with the Deane family in Wonersh, Surrey.

That leaves only two further Stonhold families, both living in Stanhope Street in the St Pancras area of London. William B. Stonhold, 42, a tailor's assistant, born in St Pancras, was with his wife Jane and six of their children at number 52, and James Thomas Stonhold, described as a *Hall keeper (Office)* aged 48, born in St Pancras, was at number 65 with his wife Mary Ann (from Guernsey), with their two children, a boarder and a lodger.

The scarcity of Stonholds in this nationwide census for the late 19th century is highly significant: we are almost certainly looking at just one extended family, probably with Essex origins in the short to medium term, at least.

The *International Genealogical Index* both confirms and develops the findings from the census. There are only thirty-five entries for Stonhold and its close variants in the British Isles – convincing enough corroboration that we are probably dealing with different generations of one single family, with maybe just the odd stray or two thrown in for good measure. All but nine of the entries are for Colchester, where Stonholds were clearly committed Protestant nonconformists, taking their children for baptism at Lion Walk Independent Meeting House from the 1780s onwards, and moving thereafter to the Helen's Lane Meeting.

The IGI can help us make more sense of some of the Stonholds we found in the 1881 census. As we might have guessed already, it would appear that William B. Stonhold and James Thomas Stonhold of Stanhope Street, St Pancras, were probably brothers; certainly James Thomas was the son of Zechariah Stonhold, who himself had been baptised in Colchester in 1800, had married Ann Bigmore at the church of St Bride, Fleet Street, London, in 1828, and whose other known children included Zechariah Stonhold junior (baptised 1833) and Samuel Bigmore Stonhold (baptised 1836).

Moving back a generation, we note that Zechariah of Colchester and London (baptised 1800) was the son of William and Ann **Stonehold**, and that Henry (baptised 1806), newsvendor of Great Coggeshall in 1881, was Zechariah's brother. The parents, William and Ann, had begun baptising a series of children at Lion Walk (Congregational) Meeting House in 1792, and it would seem on the face of it that James **Stonehole** who married Ann Lawrence at St Mary the Virgin church in Colchester by licence in 1775, and John Stonehold who married Ann Harden at St James's church in the town in 1783, and whose children also feature in the Lion Walk registers from 1785 onwards, could well have been William's brothers.

Because we have been dealing with an unusual surname – not to mention distinctive Old Testament first-names like Zechariah, so much favoured by nonconformists – we can be confident about the general accuracy, for surname research purposes at least, of the family story we have outlined so far, one which has taken us back from 19th century London to the closing decades of the 18th century in Colchester, where male Stonholds were married and having children.

At that point anything like a step-by-step genealogical investigation based upon readily-available sources has to come to a temporary halt, since the family seems to vanish from view for a while. There were twelve parish churches of early foundation in Colchester, and the IGI has not indexed all their registers. In any case, although the Stonholds would need to have been married in an Anglican church following the stipulations laid down by Hardwicke's Marriage of 1753 (unless they had

> 6. Ysbrand, s. van Olivier VAN STEENHOLEN en Catharina. *Get.* Adriaen van Steenholen en Catharina van Steenholen. Geb. 26 Oct. Nov. 3.

Olivier Van Steenholen, alias Oliver Stoneholt. Olivier Van Steenholen and his wife Catharina, who took their son Ysbrand for baptism at the Dutch Church in Colchester in 1717, would be referred to as *Oliver and Catheren Stoneholt* when they baptised their daughter Ariah at St Nicholas's parish church in the same town six years later. [From *Register of baptisms in the Dutch Church at Colchester 1645-1728* by W.J.C.Moens, Huguenot Society of London, 1905].

been Quakers at that time, a fact which is not indicated by any relevant Quaker register entries), they might have been quietly getting on with their nonconformist lives in the local chapel, giving the Colchester parish churches and their registers a wide berth when it came to family baptisms and burials. There are no references to the Stonhold surname, unfortunately, in three short histories of Lion Walk Meeting House, Colchester, written by E.A. Blaxill, copies of which are held by Dr Williams's Library in London.

Here, however, it is the surname in general which interests us, not the detailed genealogy as such, and we can renew our acquaintance with the Stonholds of Colchester in the year 1723, when Oliver **Stoneholt** and his wife Catheren took their daughter Ariah for baptism at St Nicholas's parish church. The only other early references on the IGI which might interest us are baptism entries for two sons of John and Ailse **Stanhold** or **Stanhould** at Donington-in-Holland, Lincolnshire: John was baptised in 1707 and William, eleven years later, in 1718. It is not easy at this stage to fit these Lincolnshire entries into the scheme of things, but the Christian name *Ailse* should give us food for thought, as should both the first-name and the surname of *Ariah* Stoneholt, daughter of Oliver and Catheren of Colchester. If even the modern surname Stonhold might have sounded mildly exotic at the start of our investigations, the family now begins to sound altogether less English the further back in time we go.

Clearly no family can suddenly spring to life from nowhere in the early 18th century, as if by spontaneous combustion. Earlier Stonholds/ Stoneholes/ Stanholds/ Stanhoulds or Stoneholts may have been living in parishes in Lincolnshire, Essex or elsewhere not conveniently covered by the IGI; either that, or the family had changed its surname significantly at some point, or they were immigrants from elsewhere in Britain or abroad – or both. At this stage it would seem sensible to consider the possibility that the Stonholds might have arrived in England from elsewhere in Europe – at the start of the 18th century or earlier. Speculation, without evidence at this stage, could suggest a link with the German surname **Steinholt** or **Steinhol(t)z**; there are also **Steinholt**s in Norway, **Steenholt**s, **Steenholdt**s and **Stenholt**s in Denmark and **Steinholt**s in Sweden.

Having taken my theorising thus far, and having already laid down my pen and my word-processor keyboard, I was suddenly blessed by a visit from my dear old friend, Serendipity. I give the first letter of his (or her) name a capital letter, because Serendipity sometimes acts in a God-like fashion, bringing chance discoveries to brighten up the researcher's life.

I was rummaging around in the book-room at home where I keep items that are being offered for sale, when I stumbled across a cheap reprint copy of W.J.C. Moens's *Register of baptisms in the Dutch Church at Colchester from 1645 to 1728*, which is volume 12 in the main series of publications of the Huguenot Society of London (1905). From the 16th century onwards, Huguenots and other Protestant refugees from the Low Countries, including French-speaking Flemings or Walloons, made a new home in England, safe from the persecution they had suffered in their native lands. Some arrived by a direct route, while others settled first in the Netherlands or elsewhere. Several of them followed weaving and allied trades, and many favoured the east coast of England as a place to live – it was an area that reminded them of home, and was easily accessible by way of its sea ports. Such Protestant immigrants from Europe made a new home in Norwich, Thetford, Halstead, Yarmouth and Colchester itself, while many later settlers favoured Canvey Island, Hatfield Chase and Thorney in Cambridgeshire. Two events on the mainland of Europe prompted the greatest influx of such refugees: first, the massacre of European Protestants which took place on St Bartholomew's Day in 1572, and then, in 1685, the revocation by Louis XIV of France of the Edict of Nantes, which up to then had afforded a degree of protection to the non-Catholic population.

Now usefully enough, the register transcripts in Moens's book, though they are all in Dutch (but not impenetrable, for all that) are indexed by name. Here I found, not Stonholds, but entries for a family known as **Steenhole**, **Steenholen** or **Van Steenholen**. Adria(a)n Steenhole or Steenholen and his wife Catherina were taking their children Adriaan, Catharina, Jacobus and Anna for baptism at the Dutch Church in 1699, 1701, 1703 and 1707, but – more significantly – were acting in 1717 as witnesses at the christening of Ysbrand, son of Olivier Van Steenholen and his wife Catharina. You might describe this, colloquially, as a direct hit. *Olivier **Van Steenholen*** and *Catharina* are surely identical with the *Oliver **Stoneholt*** and his wife *Catheren* who took their daughter Ariah for baptism at St Nicholas's parish church in Colchester in 1723? There's more than an even chance of this being so, wouldn't you say? Olivier could well be the son, or else the brother, of Adrian. Oliver and Catheren's use of the parish church for the baptism of their daughter at this time is perhaps not surprising: by 1723 the Dutch Church had become much less active than it had been, and it finally closed its doors for worship in 1728.

Yet we can soon disabuse ourselves of the thought that this family might have arrived in Colchester direct from the Netherlands in 1699 or thereabouts, by consulting another printed book (this time by design, not by serendipity): *The marriage, baptismal and burial registers, 1561 to 1874, and monumental inscriptions, of the Dutch Reformed Church, Austin Friars, London,* also by W.J.C. Moens (1884). Here we find Adrian and Catherina (later of Colchester) again, this time bearing the surname **Van Steenkolen**, baptising their children Olof, Cornelia and Isbrant in 1695, 1696 and 1698 – neatly leaving the couple free to make a move to the Dutch Church in Colchester, where their son Adriaan was taken for baptism the following year, 1699.

Now that we know that the family were in London as early as 1695, it does look at least possible, if not likely, that they were amongst those Protestant emigrants who left the Netherlands for England once the Edict of Nantes had been revoked in 1685.

Let's remind ourselves again, finally, that this has been a surname study using fairly readily accessible digital and printed source material, not a fully-sourced piece of pedigree work as such. The principles at work here, I hope you'll agree, are sound ones: that using a surname dictionary or playing linguistic guesswork with a name may take you only so far. There may be no substitute, ultimately, for even the most cursory and generalised examination of a family's genealogy, followed – if that is where your interest lies – by a comprehensive genealogical treatment based upon original source material.

The approach I've taken to studying the Stonhold surname has consisted of trying to establish where and when the name is first known to have occurred, and what its form and spelling might have been in centuries gone by. No matter how hard and how long you stare at a surname which puzzles you, you might make no sense of it at all if it has changed and developed over time in ways which are not immediately obvious. This is where a genealogical approach may be essential, allowing you, as it does, to move back in time through the generations and to approach ever closer to the surname in something approaching its original form.

Here, using fairly readily-available sources and at no great expense, we have been able to observe the behaviour and development of the **Stonhold** name – from **Van Steenkolen** to **Van Steenholen** to **Steenholen/Steenhole** to **Stonholt** to **Stonehole** to **Stonehold** to **Stonhold**. The final stage in this search for the origin and meaning of the surname is in many ways the easiest one. There is no need to refer to a surname dictionary in order to make sense of the earliest known manifestation of the name, Van Steenkolen. The *Van* element, though it can be said to be the equivalent of the English word *from*, has no particular significance in such a name, but a Dutch-English dictionary (and such a thing is available, like so much else, on the Internet) will tell us that *steenkolen*, like the German *stein kohle*, simply means *coal* (literally *stone coal*). The Van Steenkolen surname, then, might have been applied to a person who worked with coal, who was a collier or a coal-seller, or to someone who lived in an area renowned for its coal deposits.

So this little story has taken us from a boy in a North London school in the 1950s and 1960s whose name seemed to be something like *Stronghold* back to an everyday Dutch word for *coal*, used as a surname by an immigrant from the Netherlands living in London in the late 17th century. Surname research journeys can sometimes be like that. It is fortunate for us that the Van Steenkolens were happy enough simply to anglicise their name – or to have it anglicised for them – over the years. Many other families, not wishing to be stigmatised by virtue of a foreign-sounding surname, or tired of carefully pronouncing it out loud over and over again, simply abandoned it in favour of an unrelated English alternative. So it is that a surviving list of *strangers and foreigners* living in Walbrook in the City of London in the year 1567 has a section headed *Dutchemen* which includes not only men with distinctively Dutch names such as *Anthouny* **Van Hoven** and *Peter* **Vanenock**, but others who sound English to the core, such as *Martyne* **Stronge** and even *John* **Smythe**. So it was, also, with Italians in this list: we might guess the origins of *Baletesar* **Santes**, but not of *John* **Grey**, *broker*, though both are described as *Italeons*. I'm reminded of an Italian gentleman called Domenico (*Tony*) **Manfredi** [from a personal name] who manufactures very tasty ice-cream in Clay Cross, Derbyshire. He tells me that when he first set up in business some years ago, he decided that his Italian surname might not be ideal for his purposes – though I must say myself that I think it might have had a suitably exotic ring to it. Tony opened a telephone book at random to choose himself a trading name – and so **Smith**'s *Creamland Ices, Clay Cross* was born.

Case Study Two: GOAKES of Cambridgeshire

The surname of my friend Paul **Goakes** has long been familiar to the inhabitants of March in Cambridgeshire because of his family's involvement with the building trade. The **Goakes**es, the **Ogden**s, the **Lord**s, the **Morton**s and the **Grounds** – these and other families are all well-known in the town, some being inter-related. It was an object lesson to me, as a London suburbanite born and bred, newly arrived in a middle-sized town like March, to find that I never knew who might be related to whom by blood or by marriage, so I soon learned to be very circumspect in my conversation with strangers.

The surname of Goakes appears in no surname dictionary, so if we wish to determine its meaning and origin, we shall have to do a bit of historical digging. Let's adopt an uncomplicated research strategy and see what transpires, bearing in mind, at the start, that the IGI does not provide a very healthy coverage for the county of Cambridgeshire.

A nationwide search in the IGI for Goakes, Goake or Goaks produces a fairly short list of names, and the earliest relevant parish register entry for Cambridgeshire dates from as comparatively recently as 1759, in which year Ann, daughter of William **Goaks**, was baptised in the parish of Doddington. March, incidentally, was originally a chapelry within Doddington parish, but was elevated to rectorial status in 1856.

What if we omit the letter '*a*' from the surname, changing the spelling to **Gok(e)(s)**, and search the IGI again? The result: Gok(e)(s) are found in the counties of Buckinghamshire and Kent from the 16th century. No great excitement here, but let's bear these in mind in case nothing better turns up.

Now let's take a leap of faith by switching to **Gook(e)(s)**. This time the IGI can offer us a significant number of entries with these spellings for counties which border on Cambridgeshire, such as Norfolk (1567 onwards) and Lincolnshire (1569 onwards). Further than that, given the fact that we already know that there were Goakses in the parish of Doddington in 1759 if not before, it is highly significant to discover that in the year 1720 Jacob **Gooks** married Ann Hobson in Doddington. It looks as if the surname Gooks might well have been changed to **Goak(e)s** in Doddington sometime between 1720 and 1759. This can now be our working hypothesis, though ideally it would be useful to have some more corroborative evidence. The original Gook(e)s spelling, incidentally, would continue to be used in the area in some instances, so in 1810 we find that William Gookes married Alice Shipley in March itself.

Taking things a step further, we find that the so-called *Boyd's Marriage Index* for Cambridgeshire (available on-line at the www.origins.net web site) features a marriage of 1624 which is not on the IGI – that of Susan Gooks and Brice **Lackson** at Wisbech St Mary, not far north of March and Doddington. This now becomes our earliest-known reference so far to a family called Gooks within Cambridgeshire.

We can now consult the printed probate calendars for the Diocese of Ely, published by the British Record Society (1994-1996) for the full range of Goakes-related surnames. These calendars hardly provide a rich haul of Goakes (or similar) testators living within the Diocese during the years 1449 to 1858, but we do discover that the will of Thomas Goake *of March in the parish of Doddington, husbandman* (named as Goaks in the probate inventory), was proved in 1725. This is good news: now we can narrow down the apparent surname change in Doddington, from Gooks to Goake(s), to the period 1720 (Jacob Gooks marries) to 1725 (Thomas Goake's will is proved).

The only other entries in these probate calendars for Goake(s)-type spellings are those for Thomas and Audrey Goake of Tydd St Giles (1604 and 1605) and for a further Thomas Goake, of the same place (1693). So 1604 now becomes the first-known reference to anyone called Goak(e)(s), and Cambridgeshire is still the county in question. No one called Gook(e)(s) is featured in the probate calendars, though we may notice in passing that a family or families called **Goat(e)(s)**, **Gootes**, **Gotes** or **Gottes** were living in Ely (1541), Littleport (1558 onwards) and Wentworth (1726 onwards).

The printed probate calendars for the Consistory Court of Lincoln (British Record Society, 1902 and 1910), meanwhile, have entries for **Gooke** as early as 1535-7, and include details of a 17th century Horncastle family which was known variously as **Goake**, **Gooke** and **Gouke**. So one way or another, a family or a series of families with the surname Gooke (possible precursors of the Goak(e)(s)) can be said to have had a presence in the eastern counties of England from the 1530s, if not before.

A good line of enquiry now might be to consult the recently-published printed volume of *1664 Hearth Tax Returns for Cambridgeshire* (British Record Society, 2000). The Hearth Tax returns list those who were charged according to how many hearths they had in their house(s); those too poor to pay are also sometimes listed. Here, and it was worth waiting for, is the final corroboration that Goakes and Gookes were indeed variants of the same surname. In 1664 Matthew Goakes was being charged for two hearths in Wisbech, with the additional annotation: *Now Mary Gookes*. The two alternative spellings are yoked together in an unmistakable way. We must not always expect to be so lucky!

As it happens, there is evidence of a *Matthew Goake* (almost certainly the same man as *Matthew Goakes* the Hearth Tax payer) living in Wisbech even earlier than 1664, since he appears in a chancery case at some unspecified date during the period 1642-1660, defending himself against charges brought by the plaintiff, Matthew **Laxon**, in matters concerning the personal estate of Brice Laxon in Wisbech. This seems to have been a family squabble, *Brice Laxon* being presumably the *Brice* **Lackson** who had married Susan Gooks at Wisbech in 1624. Taking the chancery case and the Gooks/Lackson marriage together, we would appear to have further evidence that in Wisbech, at least, Goake and Gooks were variant spellings of the same surname.

The 1664 Hearth Tax return for Wisbech also features our old friends the **Goates**: *Thomas Goates* was charged on four hearths, while *Thomas*

Gootes, *junior* was charged on two. The Goates, like the Goakes, it seems, also had problems with their '*oa*'s and their '*oo*'s.

We might not normally pay more than passing attention to these Goates entries – but if we return to the IGI to try to establish the birth and parentage of Matthew Goakes of Wisbech, Hearth Tax payer in 1664, then the only possible candidate turns out to be a Matthew Goate, son of William Goate, baptised at Upton, Norfolk, on 2 April 1621. Maybe some of the Goak(e)ses and the Gook(e)ses were originally Goateses, after all? The Goat(e) family had long been settled in Upton, which lies east of Norwich; the earliest relevant will – for James Goate of Upton, yeoman – was proved in the Norwich Consistory Court in 1625, but it is known that an earlier James Goate, son of John Goate of Upton, was apprenticed in Norwich to Edward Beavis, worsted weaver, in 1578/9. The earliest known Norfolk will for a Gooke, meanwhile – before we lose sight of that surname – is that of John Gooke of Snettisham, proved at the Archdeaconry Court of Norfolk in 1561.

What, then, have we achieved thanks to this fairly fundamental Goakes research? We now know that the surnames Goakes and Gooks would appear to have been interchangeable in both Wisbech and Doddington, with Goakes becoming the predominant version as time went by. There is evidence that individuals bearing the surname Gooks were living in Wisbech as early as the 1620s, and in the parish of Doddington by 1720. The deeper origins of these Goakes/Gooks may be represented by one or more of the following:

- A Lincolnshire family of **Gooke**s, living at Fishtoft from as early as the 1530s.

- A Cambridgeshire family of **Gootes**, settled in Ely as early as 1541.

- A Cambridgeshire family known variously as **Goat, Goats, Gotes** and **Gottes** in Littleport from 1558 onwards.

- A Norfolk family called **Gooke(s)**, known to be in Snettisham by 1561.

- A Norfolk family of **Goate(s)**, living in Upton as early as 1578/9.

- A Cambridgeshire family called **Goake**, in Tydd St Giles as early as 1604.

So now, although **Goakes** appears in no surname dictionary, we have collected what appear to be two alternative names, **Gooke(s)** and **Goat(e)s**, which do get a mention. Reaney and Wilson claim that **Gook** is derived from an Old Norse name for a cuckoo (*gaukr*), but the 13th and 15th century examples they quote are from Yorkshire, not East Anglia. However, they also list the surname **Gookey** (from the Old

Norse personal name *gauki*) with examples from Suffolk and Norfolk. Basil Cottle, in *The Penguin dictionary of surnames* (1967) picks up the *cuckoo* meaning, adding: *perhaps for promiscuity*. It should not surprise us, perhaps, to find a name denoting a cuckoo in East Anglia – a part of the country where surnames based on place-names are rather thin on the ground, but where animal and bird names are very much favoured, with plenty of **Pheasant**s and the like, and where **Sheldrake**s [a vain, flamboyant person] and **Peacock**s [a vain or fashion-conscious person] strut their stuff. So why not a cuckoo?

Suppose, after all, that Goakeses were originally Goates? More animal imagery? Well, yes, that is one possibility – a nickname for a person as stubborn as a goat, or one who kept goats – but it's just as likely to be used for someone who lived near a gate, or who guarded a gate as a watchman.

Once again, there are no definitive answers as to the original meaning of Goakes – but at least now we have an interesting range of possibilities in an area of study that often owes as much to intuition and to art as it does to intellect and science.

Two final sidelights on the Goakeses can round off our examination of the surname. A Goakes Family site on the Internet www.genealogy.com says that:

> The Goakes family is a small one when compared to the 'Jones', but we have a very colourful history and we're spread out on almost every continent…We share the same noses and dimpled chins.

This is a charming idea, though I'm not sure that I would wish to share my nose or chin with anyone else… And speaking of physical characteristics: lovers of unusual surnames will be delighted to hear that in 1747, in Leverington, Cambridgeshire, Gabriel Gokes married a lady by the name of Alice **Fleshbones**. No, don't even ask me what it could mean…

Case Study Three: WILDERSPIN of Cambridgeshire

Ezra Wilderspin…is our biggest man, and he pulls the smallest bell. He is our blacksmith, by the way…

(from *The nine tailors* by Dorothy L. Sayers, 1934)

Dorothy L. Sayers, known principally for her detective stories featuring Lord Peter Wimsey, was well acquainted with the fens, her father having taken over as Rector of Christchurch, near March in Cambridgeshire, in 1917. Her novel *The nine tailors*, one to gladden the hearts of all those who love or practise the grand old art of change-ringing, features the fictitious church of Fenchurch St Paul, which is modelled in part on St Wendreda's church in Town End, March, where Grammar School pupils and staff once met for assembly every Monday morning, seated beneath the glorious and famous double-hammerbeam roof with its carved angels.

In her foreword to *The nine tailors*, Dorothy L. Sayers says: *The surnames used in these books are all such as I have myself encountered among the people of East Anglia*, so it is no surprise to find a character in this novel called Ezra **Wilderspin**. As it happens, Sayers wasn't the first author to invent a character called Wilderspin for the purpose of writing fiction; she'd been beaten to the mark by the Scottish-born essayist and dramatist Andrew Halliday, who had written *The adventures of Mr Wilderspin in his journey through life* in 1860.

Now Wilderspin, a particularly distinctive Cambridgeshire surname, is something of an enigma. We can happily ignore at the outset the fanciful theory advanced by H.A. Long in *Personal and family names* (1883) that the name means *self-willed*, and consider instead what results can be obtained by taking a genealogical approach. Although a stray early reference to the name shows that Judeth **Welderspin** married John **Smith** at Standon, Hertfordshire, in 1676, it would be at Swavesey in Cambridgeshire that the family would establish its principal home base some decades later. There are still Wilderspins in this village in the 21st century, but over the years other family branches have made their home elsewhere in Cambridgeshire and in the former Isle of Ely, including the small town of Chatteris, where Wilderspin's Garage was once a familiar sight to inhabitants and passers-by alike.

When might the Wilderspins first have arrived in Swavesey? They do not appear in the 1662 Hearth Tax returns for Cambridgeshire, nor in any 17th-century records relating to the activities of the Bedford Level, for example. The first IGI reference to the surname anywhere in the British Isles dates from 24 October 1678, when William Wilderspin and his wife Ann took their daughter Jane for baptism at Swavesey parish church. Then there appears to be a gap until the year 1701, when Archibald, son of John and Mary Wilderspin, was baptised at Swavesey. Now so-called 'gaps' in records relating to a particular family are nothing new, but in this case I smelled a rat – and before long I discovered that there really was a rat to be smelled. The original parish registers for Swavesey do indeed feature a baptism on 24 October 1678 – but it's for Jane, daughter of William and Ann *Wilkinson*. Not a Wilderspin in sight. The Wilkinsons had long featured quite prominently in the Swavesey registers, which are extant from the 16th century onwards, and William and Ann had baptised an earlier daughter, Ann, at the parish church on 9 June 1676.

The challenge now is this: having undertaken a very general trawl of

---

1881 British Census

Dwelling: 39 Albion Rd
Census Place: Hackney, London, Middlesex, England
Source: FHL Film 1341064   PRO Ref RG11   Piece 0300   Folio 71   Page 67

	Marr	Age	Sex	Birthplace
Alfred WILDERSPOON	M	31	M	**Needingworth, Huntingdon, England**
Rel: Head				
Occ: Boot Salesman				
Mary WILDERSPIN	M	33	F	London, Middlesex, England
Rel: Wife				
Ernest A. WILDERSPOON		5	M	London, Middlesex, England
Rel: Son				
Occ: Scholar				
Arthur C. WILDERSPIN		2	M	London, Middlesex, England
Rel: Son				
T Gordon HUNT	U	18	M	London, Middlesex, England
Rel: Visitor				
Occ: Manager Of NEWSPAPER(AGENT)				
Harriet MOYIE		14	F	London, Middlesex, England
Rel: Serv				
Occ: Gen Servt				

Alfred and Mary Wilderspoon and Wilderspin and their children Ernest and Arthur Wilderspoon and Wilderspin. Surname instability in action, from the 1881 census. An entry like this lends credence to the theory that the English surname *Wilderspin* might be a variation on the Scottish name *Witherspoon*. [From the 1881 Census on CD-ROM, a joint venture by the Church of Jesus Christ of Latter-Day Saints and the Federation of Family History Societies. PRO RG11/0300. Reprinted by permission. Public Record Office. [©1998, by Intellectual Reserve, Inc].

genealogical information concerning the Wilderspins – no fine detail, just a preliminary overview – we seem to have hit a brick wall, stuck with the family in Cambridgeshire in the opening years of the 18th century, but no closer to determining either the place of origin of the Wilderspins, or the meaning of their surname. The chances of Wilderspin being derived from a place-name seem fairly slim, and we'd probably be well-advised not to try too hard to link it to *Wilderspool*, a small settlement near Warrington in Cheshire which gave its name to a brewery founded in the 18th century.

What can be done? If the family arrived at an inland location in Cambridgeshire in the early 1700s from elsewhere, they must have taken some established transport route to get there – be it by road or by river – so it would be worth looking at a map. Swavesey is a small village on the western edge of the county, lying between Huntingdon and Cambridge. A certain amount of background reading will help here. *The Drovers*, a book by K.J. Bonser, published in 1972, makes it clear that Swavesey's geographical position is significant in at least two ways. First, it lies very close to St Ives, just over the border in Huntingdonshire, a town on the

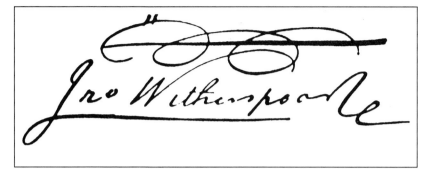

Signed on the Fourth of July. Scottish-born John Witherspoon was a signatory to the American Declaration of Independence on 4th.July 1776. Was there a family connection with the *Wilderspin*s of Cambridgeshire?

river Ouse famous since mediaeval times for its fairs, held at Whitsun and on 11 October for *cattle, sheep and general pleasure*. To such fairs, as Bonser says, ...*came the Scottish drovers with their cattle on their way to Barnet and Smithfield*. Secondly, Swavesey and St Ives lie very close to Alconbury Hill, near Huntingdon, where the Old North Road (now the A14 and A10) parts company from the Great North Road itself (now the A1). The importance of this area is underlined by the fact that immediately below Huntingdon lies the village of Buckden – now a charming and sleepy little place which has been by-passed by the A1, but which still contains the substantial remains of a palace built by the Bishops of Lincoln to allow them to enjoy a half-way break on their journey to London.

Drovers taking their cattle and other livestock south to London could have chosen either the Old North Road or the Great North Road route; indeed, the village of Standon, where Judeth Welderspin married in 1676, sits right beside the Old North Road (A10) at Puckeridge. In other words, the Wilderspin family can be found in 1676 and then again from 1701 onwards at locations which lie significantly close to two major roads which took travellers from the north into London and its markets.

At this stage, then, we could consider the possibility that the Wilderspins might have been cattle drovers from the north of England or from Scotland, who might have visited the fair at St Ives and decided to make their home at nearby Swavesey – with the marriage of a Welderspin lady in a Hertfordshire village just off the A10 thrown in for good measure. We are still within the realms of conjecture here, but I would suggest that this may well be exactly what happened.

The definitive dictionary of Scottish surnames – a wonderfully comprehensive work – is *The surnames of Scotland: their origin, meaning and history* by G.F. Black (1946), which includes references to many surnames not featured in the English-based works of Bardsley, Reaney and others. With Black's book as my guide, I was led to the conclusion ('Why didn't he think of this earlier?' I hear you exclaim) that Wilderspin may well be an anglicised version of the Scottish surname **Witherspoon**, with its wide range of varieties including **Weatherspoon**, **Wetherspoon**, **Widderspoon**, **Witherspoon**, **Widerspune**, **Wotherspoon**, and so on. The meaning is uncertain - *sheep pasture* has been suggested, *wether* being a name for a sheep and *spong* being an obsolete English word for a tongue-shaped piece of land – but the surname is known to have existed in Scotland since the 13th century, and will be familiar not only to fans of the legendary African-American blues singer and bassist, Jimmy *'Spoon'* Witherspoon (1923-1997) or to those who visit a *J.D. Wetherspoon* public house belonging to a chain founded in 1979 by a law student, Tim Martin, who named it after a former schoolteacher of his, but also to admirers of *America's new sweetheart*, Reese Witherspoon, star of the film *Legally Blond*, who is descended from the Scottish-born John Witherspoon, a signatory to the Declaration of Independence who was the first president of the College of New Jersey (later Princeton University).

It could well be the case, then, that it was a couple called John and Mary Witherspoon/Widerspune (or some such spelling) from Scotland who turned up at Swavesey parish church for the baptism of their baby son Archibald on 29 July 1701. It would seem likely that many if not most surnames were originally conferred (or imposed) upon individuals by others, not chosen by the bearers themselves – and no doubt the same process would often apply when it came to a change of surname. A couple arriving at the font of a Cambridgeshire parish church in 1701 for the baptism of their child and announcing in a broad Scots accent that their surname was Witherspoon or Widerspune might well have been met with blank stares. This is, after all, a curious name in anyone's terms, and those charged with writing it down in a register might well have merged Witherspoon with the familiar Swavesey surname of Wilkinson to produce a hybrid, 'Wilderspin' which is the name the family has used ever since, except in the case of a handful of family members in Cambridgeshire and in London in the late 18th and early 19th century who seem to have preferred the alternative Wilberspin – a variation which was short-lived.

From John and his wife Mary sprang several more generations of Swavesey Wilderspins, with a marked preference for the boys' names *Alexander* and *Archibald* – both Scottish Christian names with a vengeance! The first-name *Archibald*, as the genealogist Michael Gandy helpfully pointed out to me recently, would have been strongly associated at that period with the succession of Earls and Dukes of Argyll who were all called *Archibald Campbell*. Now if we consider parish and civil records for Glasgow, for example, we'll find a great number of *Alexander* and *Archibald Witherspoon*s, from the mid 17th century onwards – merchants, maltmen and tailors who were Burgesses and Guild Brothers of Glasgow. There is at least one early reference to a member of the family living in London: by a General Inquisition dated 21 November 1656, John Scot, Burgess of Glasgow, was served heir to his uncle, *John Witherspoone, tailyeor citizen in London.* The registers of St Martin in the Fields, a parish which lies in central London, though outside the Square Mile of the City itself, certainly feature the surname in the 17th century, and even contain a baptism record for *Archibald* son of *Alexander Wetherspoone*, dated 31 December 1637, whose sister Judith (baptised at St Martin's in 1632) could well be the Judeth Welderspin married at Standon, Hertfordshire, in 1676. And so on...

If at least one **Witherspoon** really did become a **Wilderspin** in the way I have outlined, he would not be the only Scot to make his home in Cambridgeshire from the 17th century onwards. Following Oliver Cromwell's victory at the Battle of Dunbar in 1650, ten thousand Scots were taken prisoner; many were quartered in towns in northern England, but one group of a hundred and sixteen men was marched to Earith in Cambridgeshire, where Scots and Dutch prisoners were set to work cutting the New Bedford River as it made its way north to King's Lynn. The Scots proved to be efficient at this task, and were eventually joined by a further two thousand of their fellow countrymen, force-marched to the Fens from York and Durham, some by way of Nottingham. Scots and Dutch prisoners, then, worked alongside free Huguenots and Walloons at drainage work that Fenmen were unable or unwilling to undertake. In more peaceful times many former Scots prisoners settled down in East Anglia and married local girls. Since Earith, the southernmost point of the New Bedford River, is close to Swavesey, I suppose I could even suggest that there may have been early Witherspoons who were Scottish prisoners-of-war – but for now, and for lack of firm evidence, I don't think I'll push my luck any further.

Probate matters for Swavesey were handled by the Archdeaconry Court of Ely, but the first Wilderspin reference we find in the archidiaconal calendars appears as late as 1752, when letters of administration were granted in respect of Elizabeth Wilderspin of Swavesey, deceased, wife of John Wilderspin, blacksmith.

The most famous Wilderspin of all was Samuel (1791-1866), joint-founder of the infant school system in England. The *Dictionary of National Biography* says that he was *...the son of Alexander Wilderspin, and was born at Hornsey, Middlesex, in or about 1792.* We can now be more precise than this: Samuel Wilderspin was born on 23 March 1791, and was baptised at the Great East Cheap Society of Swedenborgians in London on 10 April following, son of Alexander and Ann (née Vaughan), his parents having married at St Leonard's Shoreditch church on 20 February 1786. The Swedenborgians, followers of Immanuel Swedenborg, founded the *New Jerusalemite Church* in England, and it has been said that it was from *New Church* writings that Samuel developed the educational ideas he finally adopted.

In *Samuel Wilderspin and the Infant School Movement* (1982), Phillip McCann and Francis A. Young have this to say about Samuel's father, Alexander:

> *Alexander Wilderspin's forebears were said to have come to England from Holland in the seventeenth century to work on the drainage of the Lincolnshire fens and later to have settled in Cambridgeshire. Efforts to learn more about Alexander's ancestry, birth and early life have yielded little.*

It might be tempting to think of the Wilderspins as being one of a number of families of Dutch origin who helped drain the Lincolnshire Fens and subsequently moved to Cambridgeshire, but they appear in no relevant church records kept by Protestant refugees, and are as likely, for reasons I have outlined, to have come from Scotland as from the Netherlands. Furthermore, the origins of Alexander Wilderspin, father of Samuel, should perhaps not remain such a mystery to us, after all. *Alexander*, as we know, was a fine old Scottish Christian name much favoured by the Wilderspins of Swavesey in Cambridgshire, and Samuel's father was very probably the Alexander Wilderspin baptised in Swavesey on 22 January 1758, son of John and Mary.

I noticed recently that Samuel Wilderspin achieved the ultimate in celebrity by having a racehorse named after him, a beast described by one commentator as *mainly modest, seems best on heavy ground, but can't be discounted....* Now *there*'s fame for you!

Given the scarcity of the Wilderspin name, I was agreeably surprised a few years ago to stumble across a gravestone in the churchyard of the rather remote parish of St Thomas's in far-off Barbados which read:

> *Sacred/ To the memory of/ Mary F. Wilderspin/ Died 27th July 1891/ Aged 82 years/ And Martha J. Gibbs died 3rd Aug 1906/ Aged 72 years.*

However far they travelled and whatever fame they achieved, the Wilderspins have been an unequivocally Cambridgeshire family from the early 18th century onwards. It is probable that everyone of this surname shares a single ancestral line emanating from Swavesey, where gravestones in the parish churchyard bear witness to the fact that Wilderspins were being buried there as late as the mid 20th century.

It has not been my intention here to conduct a thoroughgoing genealogical investigation, simply to take a fairly generalised look at families with similar surnames, and to amass some corroborative evidence that Cambridgeshire Wilderspins might originally have been Witherspoons from Scotland. Whenever you find yourself proposing that such a change may have taken place, it is worth looking for examples of the surname in a state of flux, to locate hybrid forms that can help lend some credence to your theory. Thus it was that I was particularly gratified to discover that not only was there a Jane **Witherspin** getting married at Cathcart, Renfrew, Scotland, in 1848, but also that Alfred **Wilderspoon**, a boot salesman born in Needingworth in Huntingdon but living in Hackney in London in 1881, informed the census enumerator in that year that his wife was Mary **Wilderspin**, and that he had a daughter named Mary Wilderspin but a son named Ernest A. Wilderspoon. If the surname can wobble in this way in 1881, how much more likely that it had done so nearly two hundred years previously in Cambridgeshire?

I can now begin to draw the Wilderspin story to a close by offering a couple of pieces of corroborative evidence of an anecdotal kind. We have seen that it's always a good idea, if you're wondering about the origins or meaning of an unfamiliar surname, to ask family and friends. Thus it was that I asked my wife Heather whether she could make heads or tails of the name Wilderspin. Initially she could no more think what the name might mean than I could. Yet Heather's mother comes from Coatbridge, near Glasgow, where Witherspoon/ Wotherspoons seem to be more commonly met with than almost anywhere else in Scotland. When I finally tried out my Witherspoons/ Wilderspin theory on Heather, her reaction was simple: 'Well, to help prove your point,' she said, 'I must have mis-heard exactly what you were saying. I had thought you were asking me about the possible origin of the name Witherspoon all along – it's a name I know very well from visits to Glasgow.' Maybe it's not so surprising, then, that the Swavesey parish authorities heard what they wanted to hear and made of the surname what they wanted to make of it? I also tried out the theory I have just outlined on Cecil Humphery-Smith, a genealogist of international repute who is Principal of the Institute of Heraldic and Genealogical Studies in Canterbury. 'Can you make sense of the surname Wilderspin?' I asked, giving nothing away at that stage. 'Yes,' came the reply, 'it's probably a version of the Scottish name Witherspoon.' This was gob-smacking stuff, I must confess; it transpired that 'Humph' had had a teacher at school called Wotherspoon ('he always pronounced it *Witherspoon*') and that he'd investigated the name just for the fun of it over the years. 'Humph' even recalled seeing a London parish register entry in which the name was spelt **Wonderspon**. Clearly this is a surname which has changed shape not a few times during its life.

Now I have a confession to make. In this case, it turned out that there was a printed source which I hadn't consulted at the outset, but should have done. I'll own up freely to this oversight, not least because I hope that by doing so I'll be able to underline the fact that surname study should be an ongoing process. Even after you may think that you've laid a particular name to rest, it's always worth searching around for further information, or revisiting sources you thought you had already investigated thoroughly.

It's certainly the case that Wilderspin does not appear in any of what I might call the major surname dictionaries, but I discovered to my surprise, and very late in the day, that it does find a place in a very worthy publication called *Surnames of the United Kingdom: a concise etymological dictionary* by Henry Harrison (1918). There was a time when this book was not at all easy to find, though it has been reprinted in recent years. I bought my own two-volume set from a Hampstead bookshop in 1992, and soon afterwards I also came across an odd section in paper wrappers, described as 'Vol.II: Part 19'. Clearly the work was initially issued to subscribers in parts priced at one shilling each, to be bound up at some later stage.

Harrison is sometimes able to offer a fresh and original perspective on certain surnames, but it's not often that he has included a name which appears in no other similar work. Wilderspin is an exception. This is what he has to say:

> **Wilderspin**. *English. Dweller by the wild animals' enclosure [the genitive of Old English 'wilder', 'wildeor' (wild animal, deer) + 'pund', enclosure, pound].*

Perhaps most significantly of all, he then includes the annotation: *Compare* **Wetherspoon**. If we do just that, we read:

> **Wetherspoon**. *Anglo-Scottish. Dweller at the wether's pound [the genitive of Old English 'weth(e)r' + 'pund' (N.E. and Scots 'pun'), pound, enclosure].*

You will perhaps begin to understand, then, why I feel rather embarrassed at having to admit that I only decided to consult Harrison's book at the end of my investigation, rather than at the beginning? All I can say is that my theory about a possible connection between the surnames Wilderspin and Witherspoon/Wetherspoon was arrived at quite independently of any printed source. The fact that Harrison was clearly thinking along similar lines is a bonus, you might say, though his approach is slightly different from my own. What he is saying is that Wilderspin and Wetherspoon are different surnames, but that they bear comparison with each other. I have gone a step further, of course, by claiming that they are essentially the same surname, Wetherspoon being the original form as used in Scotland, leaving Wilderspin to be a corrupted form principally found in Cambridgeshire.

Whether the Wilderspins have Scottish origins or not – and that may well never be known for certain – it would be worth summarising what lessons can be learned from the approach I have adopted here:

- Speak a surname out loud and try it out on family and friends.

- If the meaning of a surname eludes you, carry out as much relevant genealogical research as you can, taking the name back further towards its place or places of origin. Make use of the *International Genealogical Index* by all means, but always treat it with a degree of caution if you plan to conduct anything approaching an in-depth study.

- Think carefully about how a surname might have changed over the years or in different places.

The essential point to bear in mind here, of course, is that it is precisely when a family moves to a different locality, particularly one where accents are very different, that a significant alteration in the surname may take place. When newcomers arrive in a place to make a new home there, they might have to accept the fact that their surname is altered for them, pronounced differently and written differently, whether they like it or not.

- Don't assume that all migrations involved only short distances.

A number of researchers have come to the conclusion that the population of the British Isles in centuries past moved from place to place more often than had previously been thought, but that most such migrations covered only a short distance – as far as the local market town or slightly beyond. Thus it is that you will hear researchers saying that they can find the marriage of an ancestor, but not his or her baptism, and that they are conducting a search in neighbouring parishes. This seems to make sense – but when Witherspoons can, conjecturally, move from Scotland to England and families can cross the Atlantic and other oceans, it's never safe to assume that all family migrations were local in nature. I once marked an examination script in which a candidate told me in all seriousness that the way to locate the place of origin of a person who arrived in London in the 18th century would be to work out steadily from London in ever-increasing circles, looking at parish registers and other records. The idea is preposterous! Anyone arriving in central London, in the present as in the past, is as likely to have made a journey of fifty – or five hundred – miles to get there as to have travelled a mere five miles from somewhere in Greater London or the Home Counties. People came to London for a variety of reasons, which we could all brainstorm: to be apprenticed, to find work, to sell goods, to buy goods, to obtain promotion, to find a husband or wife, to escape a husband or wife, to join family members or friends, to evade creditors, to be touched for the *King's Evil*, to go to law, to escape the law, to join the forces, to escape the forces, to rob and steal from rich people – or just for a bit of fun and a challenge. London, international metropolis as it has long been, is a special case here, but always bear in mind the possibility that migrants may have travelled long distances – and sometimes have put their surname at risk of change in the process.

- Look closely at possible migration routes, and consult a map.

Do bear in mind that people may have travelled by road, by track, by river or by sea; be aware that many places which seem to be situated far from the coast are, or have been, inland ports, and in more recent times think about those who built or who used canals and railways.

Case Study Four: PETTICOAT of Maryland, USA

We can now give some thought to the sort of migrational journey which makes a putative move by Witherspoons from Scotland to Cambridgeshire at the dawn of the 18th century seem no more than a casual afternoon stroll.

Thomas E. Rosensteel, a lawyer from Illinois in the USA, first wrote to me in February 1999 concerning the English origins of his ancestor William **Petticoat**, who had arrived in Maryland in the 1660s – possibly via Virginia.

I found myself unable to take on any new commissions at that stage, but carried out an initial search through some of the books in my library and reported what I was able to find. Yes, William Petticoat was featured in the *Bristol Servant Register* for 25 October 1665 as an emigrant bound for four years to Nicholas **Wyatt** of Virginia, though two years later Cornelius **Howard** would claim him as a so-called *headright* in Maryland. A certain John Petticoat (maybe a brother?) also arrived in Maryland a few years later, in 1674.

Virginia and Maryland were much of a geographical muchness at this period, as it happens, and although Lord Baltimore had wished to establish Maryland as a Roman Catholic enclave, he found to his regret that many people refused to recognise the fledgling state as being distinct from its infinitely larger neighbour, Virginia.

In the event I did end up doing some more work on the Petticoats, Thomas Rosensteel being very keen and persistent!

I could happily enough consider alternative spellings for the surname – it appears as **Petticoat(e)**, **Peticoat**, **Petticourte**, **Pethicourt**,

Peddicourte, **Peddicoarte**, **Peddicoat** and **Peddicord** in various records –
but whichever variant I looked for, I found myself in a cul-de-sac. The
IGI, naturally enough, was an early port of call. The story it was able to
tell was a starkly simple one: the surname and several of its variants
appears, predictably enough, in Maryland and elsewhere in America
from the early 18th century onwards, but as to any references before
that time, anywhere in America or Britain: nothing. There wasn't a
single solitary Petticoat to be found, not even the odd stray. This family
arrived on American shores in the late 17th century as if from nowhere.

This was worrying and initially perplexing. What might be the cause?
A few initial thoughts presented themselves:

- Fanciful speculation might suggest that the Petticoat family of
America appeared there by spontaneous combustion or were shipped
in from Mars aboard a UFO. Impossible or possible, depending upon
your views.

- The Petticoats originally might have been Pethicourts or some such
from France or elsewhere in mainland Europe. This is possible,
certainly, but no immediate evidence was to hand, and it would be a
very difficult line to pursue.

- The most likely explanation by far was that members of the family
changed their name once they arrived in America, or had it changed
for them by friends and neighbours.

This last possibility seemed to be the only one that might have legs, so I
gave it some serious consideration.

Assuming that the family was originally English and could access the
port of Bristol, what might the original surname have been? I was an
amateur dialectician before I was a genealogist, and although little of
this is an exact science and much of it is common sense, I decided
eventually that a surname such as **Pennicott** and its variants was the
most likely origin here.

It's easy enough to see how the final *-cott* element in Pennicott could
have become the *-coat* of Petticoat, since both English and English/
American speakers could well have pronounced the *o/oa* as an indistinct
vowel of the sort we find in a word like *collapse*.

But what of *Penn* and *Pett*? British speakers tend to make use of full
't' sounds where their American cousins (certainly at the present day)
do not. In America *Patty* is usually pronounced *Paddy* and *Letter* is
Ledder. After all, the only difference between the plosive sounds 't' and
'd' is that you give a 'd' some *voice* – that is, you engage your vocal
chords when you pronounce it. Taking all this into consideration, we
could well find that a *petticoat*, the garment, as pronounced by English
settlers in America in the 17th century, would be something like

peddycutt. Now comes the final stage. You pronounce a '*d*' sound by lodging your tongue behind the ridge of the top teeth, engaging the vocal chords in your neck, building up a quantity of air, and then letting it escape suddenly by opening your mouth. Quite a complicated process just to make one simple sound! Now with the tongue in precisely this position, and still using your vocal chords, if you try to push the air up your nose instead of spitting it out of your mouth, you make a nasal '*n*' sound instead of a '*d*'. In other words, with the slightest change in technique, you can say *Pennycut* rather than *Peddycut* – and will only just be able to distinguish between the two of them as you listen. Try it for yourself!

Here, then, is a stage-by-stage process whereby we can move from Pennicott to Petticoat. I hope I may have carried you with me on this one? I'll confess here, of course, that I appear to have joined the band of linguistically-minded surname scholars whom I have seemed to criticise elsewhere in this book for the narrowness of their perspective – but in cases like this, when all else fails, needs must.

I've had an ulterior motive in all this, of course. I've done what I needed to do when confronted with a brick wall: I've moved from the rootless English surname Petticoat to a surname which, thank goodness, has strong roots – that of **Pennicott**. So it was **Pennicott** or nothing.

The power of the written word is in evidence here: the letters '*n*', '*d*' and '*t*' look so different from each other on the page, that we can easily forget how similar the sounds they represent really are. We do need to be flexible in our thinking, even if it means speaking words aloud using a range of pronunciations and accents, in order to stand a chance of making progress on the more obscure surnames we might come across.

The surname Pennicott (also **Pennicod**, **Pennycod**, **Penicod**, **Pennicut**, **Pennicud**, **Penneycad** and the rest) is mainly encountered in the south of England, being especially prevalent in Sussex, Devon, Cornwall and Surrey. In Sussex it developed into (or was even derived from) the surname **Pentecost**. The name might have its origin in the place-name *Pennicott* in Devon or in one of the settlements called *Pencoed* or *Pencoyd* – possibilities which are discussed by Richard McKinley in *The surnames of Sussex* (1988), pages 403-404. There may even be a connection here – dare I add any more options? – with the Scottish surname **Pennycuick** (also spelt **Pennycook** and **Pennycock**), derived from a place called *Penycuik* or *Penicuik* near Edinburgh.

Interestingly enough, *The early settlers of Maryland* by Gust Skordas (1968), together with a supplement to the same by Carson Gibb (1997), not only feature **Petticoat** entries, but also include a John **Pennecoat/Pennycoake** (1671) and a James **Pentcoate/Penticoate** (1668–9), either or both of whom could well have belonged to the same family as William and John **Petticoat**.

So William Petticoat the emigrant to Maryland could, for example, be the same man as a William **Pennicott/Penycod** who was baptised on 21st October 1621 at Kidford in Sussex, but I've left this as a possibility to be investigated by other researchers. Let us suppose that such a man arrives in America in the 1660s and speaks his name aloud. A very distinctive and slightly unusual name, to be sure. Well, it sounds like *petticoat*, a term which has pleasant connotations and has the singular advantage of being a recognisable English word in its own right, easy to remember. William Pennicott might have insisted in vain that his name should neither be pronounced nor written (if he could read and write) as if it were a well-known garment, or he may well have bowed to the inevitable and modified his name very slightly. Thus, in my contention, the surname Petticoat was born.

At least two important issues which we have encountered before arise from the Petticoat story, whatever may be the final truth as to the surname's origins. Firstly, it is precisely when a family or an individual decides to migrate that a surname is most at risk of being altered – such would seem to have been the case, not only with Pennicott/Petticoat, but also with other examples we have already come across in this book, such as **Van Steenkolen (Stonhold)** and **Witherspoon (Wilderspin)**. Secondly, such alterations may bring an unusual name in line with something known and safe. Pennicott was obscure and meaningless, while Petticoat was cosily familiar.

Again, as with Witherspoon/Wilderspin, it was only after I had come up with the **Pennicott/Petticoat** theory that I found that another student of surnames had been thinking along not dissimilar lines. I was delighted to discover that R.S. Charnock, in the preface to his book *Ludus patronymicus; or, the etymology of curious surnames* (1868, page *xiv*) says:

> *Now, although some of the above surnames really mean what they appear to mean, very many of them...are gross corruptions, and the only way to account for their present form is that there is (as Mr Ferguson justly observes) a tendency to corrupt towards a meaning. Thus* **Pettycot** *will easily become* **Pettycoat**...

To *corrupt towards a meaning* is something that many of us do without thinking about it. The charismatic curate at one of our local Anglican churches in North London when I was a teenager was Ken **Habershon**; his parents were then living in Tunbridge Wells in Kent, and he'd had a good south-of-England education at Winchester and New College, Oxford, yet his surname, an unusual one derived either from a place called *Habergham Eaves*, near Burnley in Lancashire, or from a maker of coats of chain mail known as *habergeons* (opinions differ on this point), is mainly found in Lancashire and Yorkshire. Hanks and Hodges' *Dictionary of surnames* lists the name under the heading of **Haversham**, saying that: *After coats of mail became obsolete and the word [**habergeon**] fell out of use, the name was altered by folk etymology to assume the appearance of a habitation name.* Now I can attest to the truth of such folk etymology: I'd heard Ken's surname spoken aloud many times long before I ever saw it written down, and for months I assumed that it was something like **Havisham** – a name I knew from the character called Miss Havisham in Dickens' novel *Great Expectations*.

My dear friend Lucilla Good of San Francisco is perhaps the doyenne of such folk etymology; she was born and raised in Nicaragua, with Spanish as a first language, and she'll happily modify words in other languages until they conform to something she feels happy with. So, to her, President Gorbachev of Russia is *Garbage-koff*, and she is fond of saying with obvious disapproval that the late Princess Margaret, whose former husband was Lord Snowdon, 'never should have married that *snowman*'. I guess that we all cope with the unfamiliar as best we can...

The lesson here is this: find out, if you can, what general movements of people were taking place in particular localities at particular times past – be it Scottish drovers setting off for Cambridgeshire, German brewing families migrating to Brazil or to England, transported convicts being ferried to America or Australia, fortune-seekers leaving British shores for Virginia or the West Indies, Protestants or Jewish refugees fleeing persecution, and many more. Consider seriously the possibility that a family bearing a surname which interests you may have been swept up in such movements. Apart from the fun of the chase, you may be lucky enough to trace a surname further back towards its point of origin and – theoretically, at least – increase you chances of understanding its meaning and/or its origins.

And finally...

In conclusion, do let me encourage you to enjoy surnames, to respect them – even to stand in awe of them, since in most cases they are the oldest thing that we carry about with us every day of our lives, except for our genetic make-up. Because most surnames are so old, many of them have been subject to a fair bit of wear and tear over the years, as we've seen. So when you take a close look at a surname, don't be surprised to find that it has changed in some way or another during its long life. It might have been mis-spoken, mis-heard, mis-written, mis-spelt, mis-translated, mis-transcribed, misunderstood or misinterpreted – or deliberately or accidentally changed by listeners who wanted it to be a name they could understand or were already familiar with. Poor old battered surnames...

Here are a few final thoughts before we reach the end of the main part of this book:

Surnames might be shortened

Speakers being generally too lazy to get their tongues around a name of more than a couple of syllables, a fairly long surname like **Wolstenholme** is often stripped down to its bare essentials, becoming **Woosnam** or **Worsman**. These are Lancashire surnames in origin, so Kenneth Wolstenholme, formerly well-known as a football commentator and as the man who famously said at the end of the World Cup Final of 1966: *They think it's all over... It is now!*, fitted the mould, having been born in Worsley, near Manchester, though Ian Woosnam, the golfer, has parents who are both Welsh, and learned to play the game on his local course at Llanmynech.

Metathesis and double-letters

Letters may swap position in a name – a process known as *metathesis* – and consonants and vowels may be added to a name or subtracted from it. Double letters can become single, and singles can become double – giving us, in extreme cases, a surname like that of a Conservative Member of Parliament called Michael **Carttiss**, who was once unkindly described as *a walking spelling mistake*.

Vowels playing silly tricks

It shouldn't take us long to realise that vowels within a name may change or be unstable, and that even when the sound is the same, the

---

JOSEPH WOLSTENHOLME,
FILE AND STEEL MANUFACTURER,
No. 116, BROAD LANE, SHEFFIELD.

Too long for comfort. The surname *Wolstenholme* is often shortened to become *Woosnam* or *Worsman*. These are Lancashire surnames in origin, though in 1861 Joseph Wolstenholme, file and steel manufacturer, was in business in Sheffield, Yorkshire. [From Kelly's *Post Office Directory of the West Riding of Yorkshire* 1861].

spelling may vary, as in **Hurd, Herd** and **Heard**, for example. The genealogist Derek Palgrave has pointed out that the surname **Hether** can be spelt in many ways, including **Heether, Heather** and **Heither**, and that the first element in a name like **Eustace** can appear as *Eue, Ewa, Ew, Ewe, You, Yow, Eau, U, Ui, Yoi, Yu* and *Yui* (Federation of Family History Societies' *News and digest*, September 1992). We live in a house called *Yew Tree Farm*, but get letters addressed to *Ewe Tree Farm* and *U Tree Farm*, so I know what he means.

The letters '*i*' and '*y*', of course, were once interchanged almost at will in the written language, and an '*e*' may be present or absent at the end of a name, or be used after almost any syllable within it, in what may seem to be an arbitrary manner.

Consonants playing silly tricks

Consonants can also behave in ways that can be a real hindrance to the surname scholar.

Don't be fazed if a surname sometimes has a final '*s*' and sometimes doesn't, or if it appears both with an initial '*h*' and also without it; such minor variations are small beer in the world of surname study.

Voiced consonants (those which you create by using your vocal chords) and their unvoiced equivalents can often change places. This can affect the following matched pairs of letters: '*b*' and '*p*', '*d*' and '*t*', '*f*' and '*v*' and '*s*' and '*z*'. The fact that we know that the letter '*v*' is a voiced equivalent of an '*f*' will help to explain why it is that the personal name *Vivian* has given rise to surnames such as **Phythian** and **Fiddian**, which are pronounced with an initial unvoiced consonant and are spelled accordingly.

A letter '*g*', if it's pronounced in a soft manner (as in a word like *germ*), has the same sound value as a letter '*j*', and in such a case it can easily be mistaken for a *ch* sound. A hard '*g*' (as in *gone*) sounds ominously similar to hard '*c*' (as in *cash*), which itself is often represented by the letter '*k*' or by *ck* or *qu*. A soft '*c*' (as in *perceive*) has the same sound as an '*s*', and '*n*'s and '*m*'s, which are both nasal consonants, can easily be confused or change places.

The suffixes -*cott* and -*cock*, and -*ich* and -*idge*, can also sound all-too-similar, though the surnames **Aldrich** and **Aldridge**, however they are pronounced, will often be found to share a common origin, being derived either from a personal name or from a place-name.

The English language offers us two very different ways of representing the sound '*f*' in writing. We can either use the letter '*f*' itself, or we can choose the alternative *ph*, which means that **Filby** and **Philby** are essentially the same surname with slightly different spellings. Don't be too worried, or too impressed, if you come across surnames

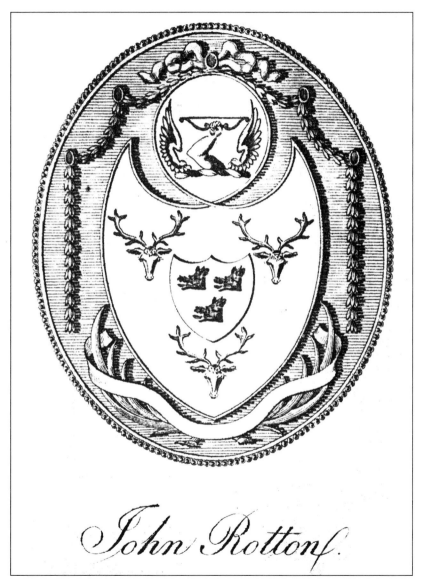

Rotton luck. The surname **Rotton** would appear to be derived from a place-name such as *Roughton* or *Rowton*. John Rotton, whose bookplate is shown here, might have been horrified to learn that he would one day have a namesake, *Johnny Rotten* (real name, *John Lydon*, born in Finsbury Park, North London, in 1956), who achieved notoriety as a punk musician with the Sex Pistols.

which begin with a double letter '*f*', as in **Ffrench**. This is a hangover from the days when this kind of doubling was simply a way of writing a capital '*F*', and strictly speaking, I suppose, it should be written as two lower-case '*f*'s. Above all, if you value your sanity and your dentures, don't attempt to pronounce two separate '*f*' sounds as you speak such a name aloud.

Since the English have always had a real problem with the initial guttural sound in Welsh surnames like **Llewelyn** or **Lloyd**, they have often resorted to using an '*f*' pronunciation instead, which has then been duly reflected in the spellings **Fluellin** and **Floyd**.

You should look out for '*v*'s and '*u*'s changing places, so that the Scottish surname **Methven** [from a place near Perth] can also be found as **Methuen**. Add to all this the possibility of transcription errors, including the representation of an old-style long '*s*' as an '*f*', which it closely resembles, or a name like **Davy** masquerading as **Dany**, and you have something of a minefield to pick your way through.

Most surnames have been around in one form or another for hundreds of years and – with a bit of luck – they will continue to flourish long after all of us have shuffled off this mortal coil. Let's salute such intrepid survivors!

Less exotic than it looks. The surname *Phethean* looks fairly exotic, but is simply a variation on the personal name, *Vivian*. [From Kelly's *Post Office Directory of Shropshire, Herefordshire, Gloucestershire and Bristol* 1879].

PART THREE:
Mainly For Fun

CHAPTER 11

Surnames Which Are
Not What They Seem

NOT AS DAFT AS THEY LOOK...

Some surnames are simply not what they appear to be; this may be because they have become corrupted and unrecognisable over the years, or because the language has moved on, introducing new words and meanings whilst abandoning the old, occasionally turning formerly innocent words into guilty ones or *vice versa*. There are no rules to follow when trying to understand names such as those in the following list; it's largely a matter of gleaning information from existing published material, include surname dictionaries, language dictionaries and the like.

For a truly breathtaking collection of charming and unusual surnames – some of which are explained, but many of which are not – you should take a look at *Suffolk surnames* by N.I. Bowditch, first published jointly in London and in Boston (USA) in 1857, followed by later expanded editions. This is based upon Suffolk in Massachusetts, you understand, not Suffolk in England, but any book featuring an index of over twenty thousand names must be worth more than a cursory glance. The following list of surnames-which-are-not-what-they-seem owes little to Bowditch, but has been taken from a variety of sources which I have come across over a number of years. Notice how often there is evidence of folk etymology at work here, whereby surnames have been corrupted to conform with familiar everyday words such as *hedgehog* or *rainbow*. A good many unfortunate names have been abandoned at some time in the distant or recent past, but the fact that a fair number were still in active use during the 20th century was brought home forcibly to James Pennethorne Hughes, author of a book entitled *Is thy name Wart?*, published in 1965. In a footnote he remarks rather wistfully: *I once said that **Drinkdregs** had disappeared, and one wrote to me...*

- **Alabaster**. *Alabaster* is a form of gypsum, but **Alabaster** as a surname represents the working of folk etymology on the occupational term *arblaster*, used for a person who made or who used crossbows.

- **Anger**. From a Germanic personal name, *Ansger*.

- **Arbuckle**. No connection with *buckles*, but a toponymic surname from a place in Lanarkshire, Scotland. The career of the 23-stone American film star *Roscoe ('Fatty') Arbuckle* (1887-1933) was brought to an abrupt end following a scandal during which he was accused of manslaughter.

- **Arlott**. From the Old French *(h)arlot*, but referring to a rascal, a travelling entertainer or a male servant, rather than to a lady of easy virtue, which is a later meaning.

- **Ashman**. Nothing to do with ash or ashes. Although this surname can be topographical in origin, there is a possibility that in certain cases it may be based on an occupational name for a seaman or pirate.

- **Badman**. *Batt*'s servant.

- **Bannister**. The use of the word *bannister* for a stair-rail dates only from the 17th century. Despite appearances, **Bannister** as a surname does not belong to the **Webster/Brewster** class of occupational names, frequently used for females, but refers to a basket weaver, a maker of what were known as *banastres*.

- **Batman**. Another member of *Batt*'s retinue.

- **Belcher**. Originally *bel chere* (fair face), and later confused with a form of address such as *bel sire* (fair sir). Although the usual pronunciation was once *Belsher* and not *Belcher*, a connection with the act of belching is still possible in certain cases since, as Leslie Dunkling puts it, *It would be surprising if someone's belching frequently was not commented on by his medieval contemporaries.* I might add that no one seems to have had any qualms in times past about conferring the surname **Petter** [nickname for a person suffering from flatulence] upon some of their fellow-men, and Hanks and Hodges make it clear that the Scottish surname **Smillie** or **Smellie** has

P. FRANKENSTEIN & SONS
[Manchester] Ltd.

Victoria Rubber Works
Newton Heath, Manchester 10

Phone : FAI 1166

The Frisson Factor. Thanks to the publication of Mary Shelley's novel of that name in 1818, the innocent-enough Germanic surname of *Frankenstein* would already have acquired a certain notoriety by the time Frankenstein's rubber works was established in Manchester in 1854. Perhaps the Frisson Factor was good for trade? [From *Culcheth Methodist Church and Sunday School 150th Anniversary (1813-1963) Souvenir Brochure*].

nothing euphemistic about it, either: *Nickname for someone notorious for giving off a smell that was obnoxious even by medieval standards, or for someone who made great use of perfumes and pomanders to counteract this tendency in an age when such measures were not generally considered necessary.*

● **Bigot**. Scholars have had fun with **Bigot** as a word and as a surname. It would seem to have its origins in an oath like *By God*; it was once an insulting term used by the French to describe the Normans, but was not applied to an intolerant and prejudiced individual until after the main period of surname formation. So not all men named Bigot were necessarily *bigoted*.

● **Blackadder**. A generation of television viewers will immediately think of Rowan Atkinson and his merry cast of actors who starred in *Blackadder* whenever this name is mentioned. It has nothing to do with poisonous snakes, but is a toponymic name derived from an estate and a river called *Blackadder* (presumed to be a corruption of *Blackwater*) in Berwickshire, Scotland.

● **Blackmonster**. Bardsley assures us that this is not merely an apocryphal surname and claims that it is derived from a place called *Blanchminster*

- **Blight**. From a Cornish name for a wolf.

- **Bloodworth**. This surname, which occurs variously as **Bloodworth**, **Bludworth**, **Blodworth**, **Bloudworth**, **Bleudworth**, **Bludsworth**, **Blardsworth**, **Bloodwork**, **Bloodwick**, **Bludwick**, or simply **Bludder**, has nothing to do with blood but is a toponymic surname derived from the village of *Blidworth* in Nottinghamshire – which itself is referred to locally even now as *Bliddeth*, though not as *Bloodworth*. There is talk of a missing fortune somewhere in the family, the *Bloodworth millions*, part of the unclaimed Angell estate which was worth 240 million pounds in the 1930s. The most famous person to bear this surname was Sir Thomas Bloodworth, alias Bludder, born in Heanor in Derbyshire, who was Lord Mayor of London at the time of the Great Fire of London in September 1666, and whom Pepys refers to in his diary as an utter nincompoop.

- **Bodkin**. This may in some cases be derived from the implement known as a *bodkin*, but its origins may also lie in a Cornish place-name, in the term *body-kin* (used for a little man), or in a diminutive form of the Old English word *boda* (a messenger).

- **Bonker**. *Bonkers*, meaning *mad* (as in *stark raving bonkers*), has only been in general use since the 1920s. The verb *to bonk*, meaning *to hit*, came into fashion just after the First World War, while its connection with sexual intercourse only dates from the mid-1970s. So whatever the surname **Bonker** might mean, it would appear to have nothing to do with insanity, pugilism or copulation. Parish register entries for **Bonkers**, **Beonkers**, **Bonckers**, **Bounkers**, **Bownkers** and **Bonckars** can be found in various English counties from the mid to late 16th century onwards, so it is not a surname which has arrived only recently. The precise meaning remains unclear; Bonker sounds for all the world like an occupational name, and/or it could be derived from words like *bank*, *bunk*, *bench*, or even *bunch* (which is known to have been used as a nickname for a hunchback). There are examples in mediaeval records of bynames such as *Del Bonk*, meaning *of the bank*, and in parts of the English Midlands and elsewhere, a bank associated with a coal-mine is still described dialectically as a *pit bonk*.

- **Boosey**. Nothing to do with heavy drinking, but a name used for someone who lived near a cattle stall, or was a cowherd. Scottish **Boosey**s may have come from *Balhousie* in Fife.

- **Bowell**. A Welsh patronymic (**ab Howell**) or a Norman name describing a person from *Bouelles*.

- **Brolly**. Long before the umbrella had been invented, and was referred to colloquially as a *brolly*, there were individuals bearing the surname **Brolly**, an anglicized form of the Irish *O'Brolaigh* (descendant of *Brolach*).

- **Buckthought**. A corruption of the place-name *Buckthorpe*, in the East Riding of Yorkshire. Indicating that the name is even found as far away from its place of origin as Cornwall, Bardsley says that *Having travelled in recent times to Land's End, it got corrupted 'by the way' into* **Buckthought**.

- **Cabbage**. I was once mildly surprised to find a reference of 1698 to a marriage between *Peter Griffin, vintner's servant, and Elizabeth* **Cabbage**, *spinster, in Queen Street in St Giles in the Fields* (Marriages, St James's, Duke's Place, London, 1691-1700). **Cabbage** as a surname can indeed refer to a head of cabbage (can it really mean that someone resembled such a thing?), but it can also have its origins in a fish called a *cabbage* – that is, a *bullhead*. Neither of these alternatives sounds very complimentary, do you think?

- **Cadger**. In modern terms, a person who is always looking for free hand-outs; originally a dealer in small wares.

- **Cash**. A box-maker.

- **Cattell**. From the female name *Catlin*, a surname chiefly found in the West Midlands.

- **Cockburn**. A Scottish and Northumbrian surname derived from a place in Berwickshire. The usual pronunciation is *Co-burn*, apparently adopted, in the immortal words of Hanks and Hodges, *to veil the imagined indelicacy of the first syllable*. Several people with the Cornish surname **Trebilcock** prefer to be known as *Trebilco*, presumably for the same reason.

- **Coffee**. An anglicised form of the Irish name **O'Cobhthaigh**.

- **Coffin**. An occupational name for a basket-maker. This is a surname well-known in Devon, where Rev John **Pine** of East Down assumed the additional surname and arms of **Coffin** by Royal Licence in 1797, thus establishing the well-known family of **Pine-Coffin**.

- **Colledge**. From *Colwich* in Staffordshire or *Colwick* in Nottinghamshire.

- **Cotton**. From one of a number of place-names.

- **Crank**. From a nickname for a cheerful or lively person – not a *cranky* one. I first came across this surname on a memorial inscription in a graveyard at Englesea Brook, Cheshire, where the

EX LIBRIS ⸱ JULIA DEXTER COFFIN

Cockburn, pronounced 'Co-burn'. The surname is derived from a place-name in Berwickshire, but the three cockerels on this armorial bookplate, together with the crest and the legend 'Rise with the morning', are used by way of a pun.

Coffin plate. *Coffin* was an occupational term for a basket-maker. Julia Dexter Coffin of Windsor Locks, Connecticut, used this plate for books in her music library. [From *American book-plates* by E.N.Hewins, 1895].

neighbouring chapel now acts as the museum of the former Primitive Methodist Connection.

- **Croaker**. From one of a number of places in Normandy called *Crèvecoeur*.

- **Cushion**. A cousin, relation.

- **Custard**. The derivation here is from a *costard* apple, though *Costard* is known to have been used as a personal name before it became a surname.

- **Daft**. **Daft** was once a not-uncommon name in the counties of Leicestershire and Nottinghamshire, where examples of it can be found as early as the 13th century. Long before the word meant *crazy*

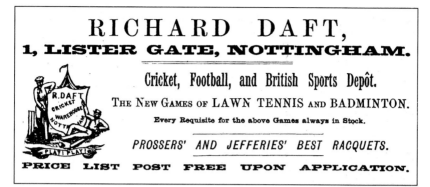

RICHARD DAFT,
1, LISTER GATE, NOTTINGHAM.

Cricket, Football, and British Sports Depôt.

THE NEW GAMES OF LAWN TENNIS AND BADMINTON.

Every Requisite for the above Games always in Stock.

PROSSERS' AND JEFFERIES' BEST RACQUETS.

PRICE LIST POST FREE UPON APPLICATION.

Not so daft after all. Richard Daft, dealer in sports equipment in Nottingham in 1876, is living in one of the Midland counties where his surname is most commonly found. *Daft* was originally a term applied to a person who was humble and meek, not one who was unintelligent. [From Kelly's *Post Office Directory of Derbyshire* 1876].

or *foolish*, it was applied to a person who was humble and meek; these once being regarded as principally female qualities, some men may have been called **Daft** because they were considered to be effeminate.

- **Dag**. A man named **Dag(g)** could have been a maker of daggers, or could have been known to carry one. Charnock maintains that the surname may have its origin in the Teutonic word *dæg* (day), or in the Cornish *dag* (someone of importance). None of this is likely to be of much consolation to anyone called **Dag** in Australia where (as in England) the word literally means *a lump of matted wool and excreta hanging from about the tail of a sheep* but where it is also used in everyday speech for an adolescent who is something of *an awkward social cripple* (Ramson, W.S., *The Australian national dictionary*, 1988).

- **Damson**. Son of a *dame* (a lady, possibly a widow).

- **Dandy**. From a pet-form of Andrew.

- **Deadman**. From *Debenham* in Suffolk.

- **Death**. This surname could mean what it says, though several alternative origins have been suggested: that it was once **D'Eath**, referring to a place-name in Flanders; that, as **Deeth** or **Deth**, it meant a maker of tinder, or that it referred to a person playing the character of *Death* in a pageant. All straws worth grasping at?

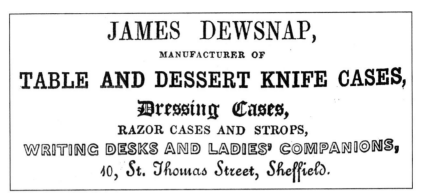

JAMES DEWSNAP,

MANUFACTURER OF

TABLE AND DESSERT KNIFE CASES,

𝔇𝔯𝔢𝔰𝔰𝔦𝔫𝔤 𝔠𝔞𝔰𝔢𝔰,

RAZOR CASES AND STROPS,

WRITING DESKS AND LADIES' COMPANIONS,

10, St. Thomas Street, Sheffield.

Not what it might seem... The origin of the surname *Dewsnap* is a place-name in Derbyshire. [From White's *Directory of Sheffield* 1852].

- **Dewsnap**. Nothing to do with *snap* in any modern sense, but a toponymic surname from *Dewsnaps* (meaning wet, poor pasturage) in Chinley, Derbyshire.

- **Diaper**. *D'Ypres*; from *Ypres* in Belgium.

- **Early**. From places called *Earley* or *Earnley*, or from an Old English word for a noble individual.

- **Eatwell**. From *Etwall*, Derbyshire.

- **Entwistle**. Does this sound as if it has something to do with a whistle? It doesn't. *Entwistle* is a place in Lancashire, composed of one Old English element meaning *hen/duck*, followed by another meaning *a tongue of land*. *Oswaldtwistle* is also in Lancashire, while *Tintwistle* is (these days) in Derbyshire.

- **Fake**. This is a variation on **Faulkes**, being derived from a Norman personal name, *Fau(l)ques* (from a Germanic byname meaning *falcon*). Distribution maps for the **Fake** surname and others asociated with it, compiled from data provided by Gerald **Feakes**, appear in *Atlas of British surnames* by G.W. Lasker and C.G.N. Mascie-Taylor (1990).

- **Fidget**. A diminutive of the name **Fitch**, the meaning of which is uncertain. A polecat? Someone who worked with an iron-pointed implement?.

- **Flower**. This name can be derived from a flower or blossom, but also from a miller, a flour merchant, or a person who made arrows.

- **Fog**. Derived from a dialectal term for long grass.

- **Flux**. From an Old Norse personal name, *Floki*. Alternatives include **Flook** – and **Fluck**, which was the original surname of the actress Diana **Dors**, who came from Swindon.

- **Freak**. A topographical surname from the word *frith*, referring to woodland or scrub.

- **Fridge**. A surname which long pre-dates the invention of the refrigerator. Cornish, from *fry*, *fridge*, meaning a promontory – literally a *nose*.

- **Funnell**. Someone who grew or sold the herb *fennel*.

- **Gammon**. A diminutive of the Norman French *gamb* (a leg; Modern French *jambe*).

- **Garment**. From an Old English personal name, *Garmund*.

- **Giddy**. From an Old English word meaning mad, insane.

- **Godless**. Having no goods, poor.

- **Goosey**. From *Goosey* in Berkshire.

- **Grumble**. From a Norman personal name, *Grimbald*.

- **Gum**. A Cornish surname, from *guimp* or *gump*, meaning *downhill*.

- **Gumboil**. Not as painful as it seems, but a corruption of the personal name *Grimbold*.

- **Haggis**. Based upon a place, not a savoury dish. Various places in the Scottish lowlands are called *Haggis*. One of the earliest known references to the surname, dating from the 14th century, spells it **Haggehouse**.

- **Hardman**. From the Old English personal name *Heardmann*, or an occupational surname used to describe a *herdsman*. The relationship between the sounds *er* and *ar* as used in surnames has already been discussed earlier in this book.

- **Headache**. This surname is surprisingly prolific. It is perhaps as likely to be a variation on what would seem to be the topographical or toponymic surname **Hedditch**, as to refer to a painful medical condition. Some scholars even associate it with the surname **Haddock**, which itself is of uncertain origin.

- **Hedgehog**. **Hedgehog**s are conspicuous by their scarcity on the genealogical scene. In 1745 Aaron Hedgehog and his wife Susan took their son Joseph for baptism at the parish church of Bromyard in Herefordshire, and in 1850 Charity **Langley**, née Hedgehog, is known

Not so hard. The surname *Hardman* can be derived from the Old English personal name *Heardmann*, or can be an occupational surname used to describe a *herdsman*. [From Wrightson's *New Triennial Directory of Birmingham* 1818].

to have died in Lee, Virginia, USA. Bardsley says *I have only once met with this curious name*, and then quotes the example in question, that of a licence being issued by the Bishop of London in respect of a forthcoming marriage between Dominick **Vanoutwick** and Barbara **Hedghogg**, widow of John Hedghogg in 1618/9. The marriage was due to be solemnised at All Hallows Barking, which is one of the very few London City churches not to have deposited its registers in Guildhall Library for safe keeping, so there could be a little nest of hedgehogs waiting to be uncovered by any interested researcher who would choose to spend some time consulting the original parish registers in the vestry of this charming church. Bardsley is happy enough to assume that Hedgehog as a surname is simply a nickname based upon the little bristly animal – a quite extraordinary proposition, I would have thought. Although the IGI offers us only the two Hedgehog references given above, it does include eight 18th-century **Hedg(e)hook** references; seven of these are in Birmingham, and the remaining one is also in Warwickshire. There is also a substantial list of people called **Hedgecock/Hedgecox**, some of whom were also living in Warwickshire. As early as 1608 a man described as *George Hedghogge, gent.*, of Warwickshire was a co-defendant in a case proceeding through the Court of Star Chamber.

> Mar. 2 Dominick Vanoutwick, of St Catherine Cree Church, London, Cord-
> wainer, & Barbara Hedghogg, widow of John Hedghogg; at All
> Hallows Barking, London.

Hedgehogs: scarce on the ground. In March 1618/9 Dominic Vanoutwick applied to the Bishop of London for a licence to marry a widow by the name of Barbara Hedghogg. *Hedg(e)hog(g)*, not the commonest of surnames, is probably derived by folk etymology from *Hitchcock*, which itself has its origins in the personal name *Richard*. [From *Allegations for marriage licences issued by the Bishop of London, 1611 to 1828*, edited by G.J.Armytage (from extracts made by Col J.L.Chester) for the Harleian Society in 1887].

I've got nothing against hedgehogs, flea-ridden as many of them may be, but I think it might be wise to assume that the very few people who are known to have carried the Hedgehog surname may have acquired it, not from the animal, but from the workings of folk etymology on a name like **Hitchcock** [diminutive of *Richard*], via **Hedgecock** and then **Hedgehook**. This is speculation, admittedly, but it's just the kind of process we are likely to encounter time and time again as we look at surnames.

● **Henn.** From the personal name Henry – or applied to someone who fussed around like a hen.

● **Hollyhock.** Some years ago my cousin Sue Weston married Max **Hollyhock**, and acquired a charming new surname in the process. This variation on the name **Holyoak** is no doubt a result of folk etymology whereby a plant name has been substituted for one meaning *holy oak* – that is, an oak tree with religious significance.

● **Hooker.** There might have been many *Happy Hookers* in times past – but they wouldn't have been ladies of easy virtue, simply makers or sellers of *hooks*, or people who lived near a *hook* of land.

● **Horrible.** Not the kind of surname you'd happily carry around with you. There are twelve references to this name in the British section of the IGI; half of these are repeat entries of one sort or another, and only one (for a marriage in Rotherham, Yorkshire, in 1794) is spelt **Horrible**, the rest appearing as **Harrowble**, **Horbill**, **Horribell**, **Horrobel**, **Horable** and **Horibill**. It could be that all these people were *horrible* by name and by nature, but the nearest I can come to a comparable surname which might have appeared in a corrupted form as Horrible is that of **Horobin**, which Bardsley would like to trace back to a small settlement near Taxal, Derbyshire (did such a place ever exist?), but which Reaney claims to be a name meaning *Grey Rabin or Robin* (ie, Robert). The Horribles remain a mystery for now.

- **Hoseason**. I seem to recall that when I first saw a travel company called *Hoseasons*, I thought that it was some kind of invented name intended to make would-be customers think of the *travel season* or some such. We live and learn. **Hoseason** is an old Shetland surname with an Old Norse origin, a corruption of *Aassieson* (son of *Aassi*, a form of *Oswald*). The pronunciation of the name in Scotland often reflects its original spelling (*Aassiesen*), with *Osison* or *Hosison* (hence Hoseason) as alternatives. You wouldn't want to book your holidays with a company called **Aassieson**, I feel sure, but at least such a name would be an ad-man's dream in that it would come almost at the very front of any alphabetical list such as that found in a telephone directory – immediately after *Aardvark*, perhaps?

- **Huntchback**. *Mrs Huntchback* of Featherstone, Staffordshire, relict of Peter **Huntchback**, Esq, was one hundred years old when she died in 1782. This surname may not have its origins in a physical affliction, but could be a variation on **Huntbach**, derived from a unknown place, the last syllable of which is identical with that found in Cheshire place-names such as *Sandbach* or *Comberbach*.

- **Inkpen**. From *Inkpen*, Berkshire, which in turn probably means *hill enclosure*.

- **Irons**. Folk etymology has turned the place-name *Airaines*, Somme, into **Irons**, the surname of Jeremy Irons the actor, amongst others.

- **Kingdom**. This is a common alternative spelling for **Kingdon**, derived from one of two places of this name in Devon. Both these varieties of the surname, together with **Kindon**, have been historically very closely associated with their county of origin.

- **Kiss/Kisser**. A maker of leg armour.

- **Kitcat**. Not an advertisement for a chocolate-and-biscuit bar, but a surname of unknown origin. The *-cat* suffix may be a corruption of *-cot(t)*, as found in a place-name surname such as **Westcot(t)**.

- **Kneebone**. It looks as if folk etymology might have been at work on this one. It would seem to come from a Cornish place-name, *Carnebone* or from *carnebol* (colt corral).

- **Lavender**. A washer of wool, from Anglo-Norman French (compare the Modern French verb *laver*, to wash).

- **Ledger**. From a Norman personal name of Germanic origin, *Legier*,

Not an owl in sight. *Lightowler* is a toponymic surname with its origins in a place called *Lightollers* in Lancashire.

or a modified version of the surname **Letcher** [dweller by a boggy stream], which could all too easily be mistaken for *Lecher*.

- **Leech**. A physician, or (as with **Letcher** above), someone who lived near a boggy stream. Alternative spellings include **Leach** and **Leitch**.

- **Linkletter**. Not some kind of a chain letter, but from one of two places in the Orkney Islands called *Linklater*. Peter **Linkletter** was one of the quartermasters of the ship *Bounty* in 1789, and stood by Captain Bligh during the famous mutiny.

- **Liquorish**. Lecherous, greedy, or liking fine food. Also found with the spellings **Lickorish**, **Lickrish** and **Licrece**.

- **Lightowler**. No connection with owls. This is a toponymic surname from *Lightollers* (*bright alders*) in Lancashire, though it is now more commonly found in Yorkshire.

- **Maggot**. A diminutive of *Margaret*.

- **Mapowder**. Nothing to do with powder, but a toponymic name which has its origins in *Maypowder*, Dorset, according to Bardsley. **Ma(y)powder**s are found mainly in Devon and Cornwall, while the alternative **Mapother** is in evidence in County Roscommon, Ireland, as early as the seventeenth century. This is a surname which seems not to have pleased Thomas Cruise **Mapother** IV (born in Syracuse, New York, in 1962), who has been known throughout his film-acting career simply as Tom **Cruise**.

- **Meanwell**. Not necessarily applied to a person of good intentions, but a Cornish name derived from the words *mean-wheal* or *mean-uhal*, relating to stones.

Sane Nutters. *Nutter* would have referred originally to a scribe or to a keeper of oxen. This is Henry Nutter who was both treasurer and secretary of Keighley Baptist Church in Yorkshire in the 1870s. [From *A century of Keighley Baptist history* by J. Rhodes (1910).]

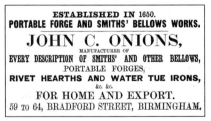

Knows his onions. The surname *Onions* can be a corruption of the Welsh personal name *Einion*. John Onions of Birmingham would like us to believe that his business was established in the year 1650. [From Kelly's *Post Office Directory of London*, 1854].

- **Missing**. Presumably a toponymic surname with its origin in place-names such as *Messing* (Essex), *Misson* (Nottinghamshire) or *Messines* (Belgium). Chris **Missing**, an antiquarian bookdealer living in Essex, has put his surname to good effect by using the delightful trade name of *Missing books*.

- **Nutter**. In modern slang a *nutter* is someone who is *nuts*, meaning *crazy*. The surname **Nutter** has an altogether different origin: it could refer to a scribe (compare the word *notary*) or to a keeper of oxen.

- **Oddie**. There is nothing necessarily strange or peculiar about people with the surname **Oddie** or **Oddy**, which comes from a Scandinavian personal name, *Oddi*. The surname's origins would appear to lie firmly in the West Riding of Yorkshire, though the well-known actor, writer and ornithologist Bill Oddie hails from Rochdale in Lancashire.

- **Onions**. This can be a name applied to a grower or seller of onions, but it can equally be a Welsh surname, a corruption of the personal name *Einion*.

- **Pertwee**. There's nothing *twee* about **Pertwees**. Jon Pertwee (1914-1996) was the third actor to play *Doctor Who* in the television series of that name, but wasn't the only member of his family to have made a mark in show business. Both his father Roland Pertwee and his brother Michael were writers in the film industry, and his son Sean and his cousin Bill Pertwee are actors. Jon Pertwee's biography, *Moon boots and dinner suits* (1984), is a highly amusing read, and has something to say about the Pertwee surname right at the start:

Pertwee is of French Huguenot extraction. According to our family tree, researched by a French priest, one Abbé Jean Perthuis de Laillevault and my cousin the late Captain Guy Pertwee RN, the original family of Perthuis de Laillevault were directly descended from the Emperor Charlemagne... The head of the family is Comte Bernard de Perthuis de Laillevault who fought with the RAF during the last war and is now a celebrated painter of murals. After the Huguenot purge of 1685, the refugees fled to many countries including England where they settled mainly in Suffolk and Essex... Due to the inability of the English to pronounce Perthuis any other way than Pertwiss, it was subsequently changed to Pertwee.

Being a true enthusiast for such things, Jon Pertwee carefully filed away genuine examples of the way in which his name has been interpreted over the years, including: *Tom Peetweet*; *Jon Peterwee*; *Jon Peartree*; *Mr Twee*; *Mr Pardney*; *Mr Bert Wee*; *John Peewee*; *Mr Pickwick*; *Miss Jane Partwee*; *Master J. Peewit*; *Mr Pertweek*; *Joan Pestwick*; *J. Pertinee*; *John Between*; *J. Parpertwuwe* – and even, in New York – *Jan Putrid*.

- **Pharaoh**. Thus the surname **Farrar** (occupational term for a smith) has been elevated to the giddy heights of ancient Egyptian civilisation, thanks to the workings of folk etymology.

- **Phoenix**. This is the surname **Fenwick** (from one of a number of place-names in England and Scotland) dressed up in unfamilar garb. Fenwick is usually pronounced *Fennick*, and **Phoenix** looks for all the world as if it has been created by the process of folk etymology, rather in the manner of **Pharaoh**.

- **Physick**. Some students of Cornish surnames would argue that this surname, like **Visick**, comes from a place-name, *Lefisick* (St Austell).

- **Pillock**. A mere twenty-one **Pillock(e)s/ Pileocks/ Pillaks/ Pilicks/ Pellieakes/ Pelakes/ Pillecks** appear in the IGI for the British Isles, though a Leicestershire Subsidy Roll reveals that in 1327 the village of Aylestone was home not only to a *John Pillokes* but also to a *John le Fartere*. A place to steer well clear of at that time, maybe? The word *pillock*, which in modern slang refers to an utter idiot, is a shortened form of *pillicock*, which was used from the 14th century onwards as a vulgarism for *penis* and from the late 16th century as a term for a young lad. It's a moot point as to whether the rare surname

Pillock might have had an innocuous meaning in some cases, or whether it might always have been as vulgar as it appears to be.

- **Pillow**. A name with a French origin, from *Piédeloup*, meaning *wolf-foot*.

- **Pinch**. From a Middle English word for a chaffinch; so, like the surname **Pink**, it refers to a chirpy person.

- **Plonker**. There are thirty-four **Plonker**s in the British section of the IGI, if I may put it that way without sounding offensive. Thirty of these were from Surrey, and the remaining seven from Hampshire, the overall covering dates being 1568 to 1704. This is clearly a surname which bloomed briefly and then died out – or was changed in some way. There are plenty of surnames which seem to have arrived from nowhere in fairly recent times; now here is one which used to exist but is with us no longer. The IGI also includes a number of **Plunker**s, **Planker**s and **Planner**s and, significantly, a wider look at relevant records reveals that the surnames Plonker, Planker and Planner can all be found recorded in the town of Godalming in Surrey and in the village of Bentley in Hampshire. It would seem likely, then, that these could be alternative spellings for the same surname. *Planker* as an occupational term for someone who hardened hats by felting is first known to have existed only as late as 1874. Maybe the word *planker* was once used to describe a carpenter who made planks? There is no firm evidence to back up such a theory, though it would seem to make at least some sense, and both the noun *plank* and the verb *to plank* date back to the Middle English period. The use of the words *planer* (a person who planes material to level it down) and *planner* (someone who lays a plan) are first recorded only in the late 16th and early 18th centuries respectively, though, as usual, each could have been used in everyday speech at an earlier date. But then could Plonker be a variation on the surname **Plunkett** [from *Ploquenet* in Brittany, or a maker or seller of blankets]? One thing here is certain amidst all the uncertainty: that the use of the word *plonker* to mean a *hopeless idiot* is a very recent arrival on the linguistic scene. There may have been plenty of *plonkers* around in former times, but none, it would seem, acquired Plonker as a surname because of his mental incapacity.

- **Ponder**. Not a deep thinker, but someone who lived near a pond.

- **Power**. Either derived from a place-name, *Pois* in Picardy, or used literally of a poor man or ironically of a miser. This is a surname often associated with Ireland, where it is particularly common in Munster

All Power... The surname *Power*, long associated with Ireland in general and with a brand of whiskey in particular, can be derived from *Pois* in Picardy, or can refer to a poor man or a miser. This is the bookplate of James Power of King William County, Virginia. [From *American book-plates* by E.N.Hewins, 1895].

and is well-known as the name of a brand of Irish whiskey.

● **Pratt**. **Pratt** seems never to have been the most complimentary of surnames, though it has suffered in recent times from an unjustified association with the use of the word *prat* to mean a *stupid or foolish person*. *Prat* was a term used for the buttocks from as early as the 15th century, but the surname Pratt would seem to be derived from an Old English word meaning *a trick*, and was apparently applied to a person who was known to have played tricks – or to have been what we would call a *trickster*, even. The founder of the well-known firm of *Christopher Pratt and Sons* of Bradford in Yorkshire began his professional life as an apprentice with *Joseph Nutter*. **Pratt** and **Nutter** – what a pair they must have made!

- **Pudding**. Could be a nickname for a podgy man, or one who made meat *puddings* rather in the style of present-day black puddings.

- **Purseglove**. Folk etymology would seem to have worked on the place-name *Purslow* in Shropshire to create two recognisable words joined together.

- **Quarrell**. A maker of crossbow bolts – or a nickname for a short man.

- **Rabbitt**. Pet-form of Robert, or from a Norman personal name, *Radbode/Rabbode*.

- **Raffle(s)**. Nothing to do with prize draws, but either a diminutive of the personal name *Ralph* or from a place called *Raffles* in Dumfries, Scotland.

- **Rainbird**. From an Old French personal name, *Rainbert*. Brought into line with the name for a plover.

- **Rainbow**. From an Old French personal name, *Rainbaut*.

- **Ramsbottom**. Mercifully, a place-name in Lancashire – the *valley where wild garlic grows* – is the origin here, though friends of mine in Derbyshire who named their folk-band *Ram's Bottom* and used a ram or a *tup* as a logo, had another meaning in mind.

- **Randy**. A pet form of *Randolph*. *Randy* can commonly be found as a personal name in the USA, though not in Britain, where *randy* in everyday speech refers to someone who is sexually promiscuous.

- **Raper**. A northern form of **Roper**, a maker or seller of rope.

- **Riddle**. From the Norman personal name *Ridel*, or from *Ryedale* in North Yorkshire.

- **Shitler**. A maker of shuttles, or possibly a seller of crockery.

- **Shufflebottom**. From *Shipperbottom* in Lancashire. For families called **Shufflebottom** to have opted for an alternative such as **Shovelbottom**, as some are known to have done, might perhaps be a case of escaping the frying-pan only to end up in the fire?

MARY: SHIFILBOTTOM: 1702

No shuffling of bottoms. Mary *Shifilbottom*'s name appears on a piece of pottery dated 1702. The surname has its origins in the Lancashire place-name, *Shipperbottom*.

- **Silly**. A variant of **Sealey**, used for a cheerful person (from the Middle English *seely*, meaning happy). *Silly* in its modern sense of *stupid* only dates back to the 15th century.

- **Sneezum**. Nothing to do with *sneezing*, but derived from a local pronunciation of *Snettisham* in Norfolk.

- **Spurgeon**. There would appear to be no connection with either *surgeons* or *sturgeons* here. Bardsley offers the following explanation: *Son of Spurgin... an old and long-forgotten Scandinavian personal name... the spelling is imitative, a copy of 'surgeon',* and says that the surname can be found in Norfolk as early as 1273. The *Dictionary of*

Neither surgeons nor sturgeons. The surname of Rev C.H.Spurgeon, the famous Baptist preacher, would appear to be derived from a Scandinavian personal name, *Spurgin*, though the jury is still out on this one.

No Swett. The surname *Swett* has its origins in the Middle English word *swete* (sweet), used of a pleasant person. This is the bookplate of John Barnard Swett of Newburyport, Massachusetts. [From *American book-plates* by E.N.Hewins, 1895].

National Biography entry for the great Baptist preacher, Charles Haddon **Spurgeon** (1834-1892), son of John and Eliza (née Parker), who was born in Kelvedon, Essex, on 19 June 1834 and baptised two months later at Stambourne in the same county, tells a different story, saying that he *came of a family of Dutch origin which sought refuge in England during the prosecution of the Duke of Alva.* Fernando, Duke of Alva (1508-1582), the despotic Governor of the Netherlands, had certainly killed many thousands of Dutch men and women, and driven others into exile, and Walter Rye has this to say in his book *Norfolk families* (1912/1913): *The late Judge Willis, when lecturing in 1903 on the 'great' Spurgeon, said he came out of Essex from a Boer family, but on my asking him for his authority he was unable to find it. Still it is not impossible, and Mr Willis may have been right, for the first time I find the name in East Anglia is when John Spurgeon was party to a fine in Carbrooke [Norfolk], Michaelmas 6 Elizabeth 1564, and the Dutch had been ariving in Norwich in 1563 and 1579.* IGI entries for the surname Spurgeon date from as early as 1558 in Suffolk, 1562 in Norfolk and 1572 in Essex.

- **Stammers**. There's no connection here with any speech defect; **Stammers** is derived from the Old English personal name *Stanmoer*.

- **Swett**. This sounds ominously like *sweat*, but actually comes from the Middle English word *swete* (sweet), used of a pleasant person. Those with the surname **Swett** (or variants like **Sweatman**) may feel that they have the option of keeping the good old original spelling, even if it could be taken to imply sweatiness, or changing it to **Sweet** (or **Sweetman**), which has more pleasant associations and is, after all, what the name really means.

- **Swindell**. Provided that it's pronounced carefully enough, with the stress on the second syllable, this surname shouldn't remind listeners of the word *swindle*. The origin here is uncertain; *Swindale* in North Yorkshire has been suggested, though the surname is commonly found in Lancashire.

- **Tadpole**. The really remarkable thing about the surname **Tadpole** is not that there seem to have been so few examples of its use over the years, but that it was ever used as a surname at all. Yet there they are – no fewer than thirty of them in the British Isles on the IGI, including a most charmingly named male child, *Faithfull **Tadpole***, who was baptised at St John the Evangelist, Dublin, on 11 November 1665.

  Those who are prepared to believe that the surname Hedgehog was first used of a man who resembled the animal of this name might have no problem in assuming that the first Mr Tadpole was a puny kind of a man or one who was always squirming around, like a diminutive tadpole. I'm no great fan of such theories myself, but I must confess in this instance that I have little else to offer – unless it be that folk etymology might have been at work on a word like *todpool* (a pool frequented by foxes), which itself might have been used to describe a topographical feature or even have acquired the status of a now-lost place-name. The jury is still out on this one.

- **Tallboys**. Nothing to do with height, but originally a nickname for a woodcutter, from the French, *taille(r) bois* (to cut wood).

- **Tickle**. From the Old English personal name *Tica*, or from *Tickhill* in Yorkshire. My attention was once drawn to a most unfortunate entry in a telephone directory: two ladies, each called *Miss Tickle* and living at the same address, appeared, quite correctly in an alphabetical listing, as: *Tickle the Misses*.

- **Tipple**. Not referring to a boozer, but a surname derived from the personal name *Theobald*.

Results: International Genealogical Index/British Isles (30 matches)

Select records to download - (50 maximum)

  ☐ **1.** Abell TADPOLE - International Genealogical Index
      Gender: M Christening: 17 Dec 1663 Saint John The Evangelist,
      Dublin, Dublin, Ireland

  ☐ **2.** Anne TADPOLE - International Genealogical Index
      Gender: F Birth: Abt. 1662 Dublin, Dublin, Ireland

  ☐ **3.** Anne TADPOLE - International Genealogical Index
      Gender: F Birth: Abt. 1662 Dublin, Dublin, Ireland

  ☐ **4.** Anne TADPOLE - International Genealogical Index
      Gender: F Marriage: 17 Jul 1682 Dublin, Dublin, Ireland

  ☐ **5.** Anne TODPOLE - International Genealogical Index
      Gender: F Marriage: 13 Jun 1750 West Wycombe, Buckingham,
      England

  ☐ **6.** Daniel TADPOLE - International Genealogical Index
      Gender: M Christening: 7 Feb 1655 Saint John The Evangelist, Dublin,
      Dublin, Ireland

  ☐ **7.** Daniel TADPULL - International Genealogical Index
      Gender: M Marriage: 5 Apr 1685 Saint Katherine By The Tower,
      London, London, England

  ☐ **8.** Deborah TADPOLE - International Genealogical Index
      Gender: F Christening: 11 May 1654 Saint John The Evangelist,
      Dublin, Dublin, Ireland

  ☐ **9.** Deborah TADPOLE - International Genealogical Index
      Gender: F Christening: 20 Feb 1655 Saint John The Evangelist,
      Dublin, Dublin, Ireland

  ☐ **10.** Faithfull TADPOLE - International Genealogical Index
      Gender: M Christening: 11 Nov 1665 Saint John The Evangelist,
      Dublin, Dublin, Ireland

Always a tadpole, never a frog. As if the surname *Tadpole* were not distinctive enough in its own right, it does seem particularly heartless of the Tadpoles of Dublin to christen one of their sons *Faithfull*. But then, what's the use of a tadpole, you might say, if he isn't faithful? [From the on-line version of the Church of Jesus Christ of Latter-Day Saints' *International Genealogical Index*, at: www.familysearch.org. Reprinted by permission. [©1980,1999, by Intellectual Reserve, Inc.]

● **Tortoiseshell**. It's difficult to avoid the conclusion that a name such as Tortoiseshell must be the result of folk etymology. It can be found with the spellings **Tortoiseshell, Tortoishel(l), Tortishell, Tortirshell, Tortershel(l), Tortoishal, Tortyshell, Tortoiceshell, Tortorshall, Tortoischell, Dortishell, Tartershell, Tortoishall** and **Tortorsell**, and IGI evidence alone would suggest that it is strongly concentrated in Staffordshire, but only appears there during the 18th and 19th centuries. We can observe the surname changing before our eyes in the case of Joseph **Tawtershell**, who married Anne Wakefield at St Werburgh's church in Derby in 1799, but who is described as Joseph **Tartershell** and then **Tortershell** at the baptism of two of his children. I'm going to suggest that *Tattershall* in Lincolnshire is the probable point of origin here; the surname **Tattersall** itself is quite thick on the ground in Lancashire and Yorkshire, while **Tortoiseshell**s only appear in Staffordshire for a limited period of time. I would contend that it's very likely that the two surnames share the same origin.

- **Totty**. These days this is a rather tasteless term referring to a desirable young lady (originally used of a high-class prostitute). The surname **Totty** is quite different, being a pet form of the Old English name *Tota* or *Totta*.

- **Tremble**. From an Old English personal name *Trumbeald*, with variants **Trumble**, **Trumbull** and **Trimble** (Northern Ireland). There may also be a connection with the surname **Turnbull**, and also possibly a Cornish origin (with variants **Trebell/Treble**) from places called *Trebell* in Lanivet or *Trebila* near Boscastle.

- **Trollope**. The novelist Anthony **Trollope** and his collateral descendant, the present-day writer Joanna Trollope, had ancestors who came from *Troughburn* in Northumberland, formally known as *Trollope*. The first known example of the word *trollop* being used for a slattern or a slut dates from as recently as 1615.

- **Truebody**. A Cornish surname, from *Tre-bude* (dwelling near a haven) or from *Tre-body* (the town of *Body*).

- **Trunchion**. Nickname for a short fat man. The French word *tronchon*, meaning a *stump*, which is the origin here, also gave rise to the word *truncheon* (a stump-like object), which has been used in English since the 16th century.

- **Tubb**. From the Middle English personal name *Tubbe*.

- **Turtledove**. It's possible to witness a brief infestation of **Turtledove**s at Folkestone in Kent in the early 18th century. They seem to have flown in during the 1720s and to have departed some twenty or so years later. John Turtledove or **Truteldove** and his wife Jane had three children baptised at Folkestone from 1721/2 onwards, and in 1746 a licence was issued to allow John **Grimes**, *a marine in Pawlett's Regiment, bachelor* to marry Mary Turtledove *of All Saints, Canterbury, spinster*. And that is more or less the end of the Turtledoves, except for a brief appearance at St Marylebone in London in 1769. I would assume that folk etymology has been at work on such a surname – but would welcome any suggestions...

- **Twatt**. A toponymic Scottish surname; the **Twatt**s of Orkney may derive their surname from *Twatt* in Birsay, and the Twatt family of Shetland from *Twatt* in the parish of Aithsting.

- **Ugly**. From *Ugley* in Essex or *Ughill* in Yorkshire.

- **Vague**. Theories as to the origin of this Cornish surname are also rather vague. It could be from the place-name, *Trevague*.

- **Virgin**. A surprising number of **Virgin**s have become parents over the years, as a glance at the IGI will indicate. As a surname, Virgin could have been used originally of someone who had taken the part of the Blessed Virgin Mary in a play.

- **Wedlock**. A Cornish surname, possibly a variant on **Vallack** [from *vallack*, *vallick*, meaning walled or fenced].

- **Wheel**. From the Cornish *wheal* or *huel*, terms used for a *work* (ie, a *mine*).

- **Whisker**. A variant on the Scottish name **Wishart**, derived ultimately from the Old French personal name *Guiscard*.

- **Wildsmith**. Not all **Wildsmith**s were wild in character; they were originally wheel-makers.

- **Winter**. This can be a toponymic Cornish name, from a place called *Gwinter* in St Keverne.

NOT AS FOREIGN AS THEY SOUND...

Our own instinct and experience usually will be a reliable guide as to whether a surname has its origins within the British Isles or not, but on occasions our expectations may be confounded.

Not French

It's an oddity of Anglo-French relations that when the French want to insert a touch of class into their language, they borrow an English word or phrase, whereas the English feel that there is something *chic* about the French language in general and French names in particular. So it is that while some French surnames have become anglicised (**D'Angerville** giving way to **Dangerfield**, for example), others have acquired a French flavour that they never started out with. A classic example of this process has been at work in Cornwall, where a place originally named *Pridias* gave rise to a surname spelt in an identical or very similar way. As time went by, both the place-name and the surname were modified by folk etymology into what appeared to be a French name, **Prideaux** (*près d'eaux* [near water] or *pré d'eaux* [meadow of waters]). An in-depth study of a family of this name, starting with Richard **Pridyas** of

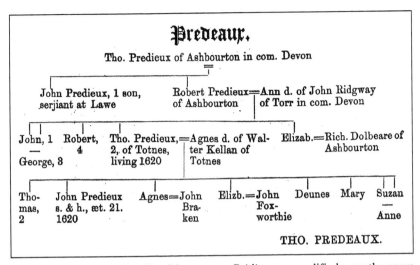

Cornish, not French. The Cornish surname *Pridias* was modified over the years until it became the French-looking *Predeaux* or *Prideaux*. This pedigree features a Devon branch of the *Predeaux/Predieux* family. [From *The Visitation of the County of Devon in the year 1620*, edited by F.T.Colby for the Harleian Society, 1872].

Orcharton, Sheriff of Devon in the 1270s, was written by Roy Prideaux and published in 1989 under the title *Prideaux: a West Country clan*. We know that a number of Cornish surnames sound 'foreign' when they are not; now, with Prideaux, we have a name which began life as the unusual-sounding Pridyas, but then became more like a fully-fledged European surname as time went by.

This process of what we may call *Frenchification* might also have been at work on two surnames which are principally found in Yorkshire, but I could be doing those who still bear such names a disservice by daring to suggest that this might be the case. **Cordeaux** sounds French enough, though the fact that it is also commonly spelt **Cordukes** (or **Curdox(e)**, **Curdix**, **Curdex**, **Cordeux**, **Cordox** and **Curdax**) would indicate either that English speakers have been spelling a French name as they heard it, or that it had an English origin in the first place, only acquiring a touch of French gloss later in its life. **Mallalieu** may indeed be a French name, as it appears to be, and it has been claimed that it is derived from the French town of *Malleloy*, though it will most often be encountered in the Saddleworth area of Yorkshire and may have originated there and been Frenchified later.

Two French words joined together have given us the place-name *Beaumont* [*beautiful mountain*] but as a surname, **Beaumont** can be also purely English in origin. David Hey makes the telling point that although there are various places called *Beaumont* in Normandy and elsewhere in France, the same name was also used for settlements in Cumberland, Essex and Lancashire. Similarly, a patronymic surname like **Martin** can as easily be English as French, and only careful genealogical research is likely to establish the true facts in any individual case.

The fact that a surname has a French origin might well escape us, of course, if one or more families which bore it were immigrants to Britain and opted to change or to translate their name in the process. A number of Huguenots, like Jews and other immigrant groups, sometimes went in for a straight translation, turning **Le Blanc** into **White** and **La Croix** into **Cross**.

Not German

The following surnames may appear to be German, but are usually English in origin:

Akerman [an *acreman* who was employed as a ploughman on a manor]; **Boorman** [variation on the surname **Bower**, used for someone who lived in a modest cottage, was a house servant, or came from a place called *Bower(s)*]; **Bedingfeld** [from *Bedingfield* in Suffolk]. The word *feld* is certainly used for a *field* in modern German, but the place in Suffolk now called *Bedingfield* was known as *Bedingefeld* from the 11th century onwards, and this forms the basis for the modern spelling of the name. There is a village, also in Suffolk, known as *Stansfield* (formerly *Stanefeld*), but it would seem that another *Stansfield* (formerly *Stanesfeld*) in the West Riding of Yorkshire is the place of origin of the surname **Stansfeld**, which follows a similar pattern to Bedingfeld.

The First World War was one period in history when to possess a German surname within Britain itself was a distinct disadvantage. At a time when even members of the Royal Family were to abandon their German names in favour of safer alternatives like **Windsor** or **Mountbatten**, it should come as no surprise to find that a man of lesser social status with a name like *George Frederick* **Feldman** would put his name through the laundry and emerge as *Mr George, Mr Frederick* or *Mr Field*.

Not Eastern European

We grow so used to expecting surnames which end in *-ska*, *-ski*, *-sky*, *-skis*, *-ov* or *-ow* to be of Eastern European origin, that it can come of something of a surprise to find that **Carminow** [from a place of this name in the parish of St Mawgan in Meneage] is a Cornish name, as is **Trevaskis**. In the latter case we would do well to focus less upon the *-skis* ending than upon the *Tre-* prefix, which is very characteristic of Cornish place-names and of the surnames which are derived from them. **Horisky** also has an Eastern European feel about it, but it's an Irish name, a corruption of **O'hUarghuis**. The place-name *Skalderskew* in Cumberland is referred to locally as *Skoderska*. As far as I know, this has not given rise to a corresponding surname, but if there were to be a family of **Skoderskas** around anywhere, they might have all their neighbours convinced that they came from Poland or Russia.

Not Italian or Spanish

A number of Cornish surnames like **Bevetto**, **Lansallos** and **Treganza** sound as if they might come from Spain or Italy, but the use of a final letter '*o*', at least, can be easily explained in such cases, being simply a Cornish plural or adjectival ending.

Frenchified? The surname *Cordeaux* sounds French, but with its variants such as *Cordukes* and *Curdax*, it could be an English name which has been 'Frenchified' for reasons of social prestige. Major Edward Kyme Cordeaux was a Justice of the Peace for parts of Lindsey in Lincolnshire, and this photographic portrait of him is featured in *Lincolnshire at the opening of the Twentieth Century: Contemporary biographies* by W.T.Pike (1908).

Not Jewish

It was in the early 19th century that a series of Imperial decrees throughout mainland Europe insisted that Jews, who had been in the habit of using a single non-hereditary Hebrew name within the family, should adopt fixed first and second names in order to make life easier for bureaucrats. This was an indignity that had to be endured: some Jews chose occupational names or place-names, or opted for one of a number of pleasant-sounding *ornamental* names based upon natural features,

Battenburg alias Mountbatten. A bookplate designed in 1923 for Lord Louis Mountbatten, whose father, Prince Louis Alexander of Battenburg (1854-1921) had modified his family's Germanic name during the First World War.

plants or minerals, such as **Blum** [flower], **Rosenthal** [rose valley] or **Garfunkel** [with variations **Gorfinkel**, etc: from Yiddish and German words (originally from Latin) for a jewel or diamond – but also meaning a *carbuncle*]. Others merely converted an unstable patronymic into a surname, giving **Abrahams** or **Isaac**.

Not all surnames based upon an Old Testament personal name are Jewish in origin, however, and there are Gentile families called **Solomon**, **Jacobs** and **Emmanuel**. **Coen**, meanwhile, is sometimes favoured by Jews as a shortened form of **Cohen**, but it can also be Irish, an anglicised version of **O'Cadhain** or of **O'Comhdhain**.

Many Ashkenazic Jews who found refuge in the British Isles during the last two centuries adopted an English surname which was a translation of, or similar to, their own. **Lewis** and **Lawson** were favoured as substitutes for **Levi**, **Moses** could become **Moss** and **Hirsch** could be translated into English, giving **Hart**. An ironic consequence of this is that British names like **Lewis** and **Hart** have themselves developed something of a 'foreign' feel to them in certain cases. It was a man called *Lemon Hart*, a Jewish wine and spirit merchant working in Penzance in the late 18th century, who first sold spirits under his own full name – and *Lemon Hart* rum still adorns the shelves of off-licences and supermarkets to the present day.

The 17th century had seen the arrival in England of a number of wealthy Sephardic Jews who were fleeing from persecution in Spain and Portugal; foremost among these were the families of **Mendes** and **da Costa**, who had intermarried so often that they were referred to as the **Mendes da Costa**s. This portfolio surname has become so strongly associated with English Jewry that it is easy to forget that it is composed simply of two Portuguese surnames which are only Jewish by association.

Not Chinese

Several British names which sound as if they might have come from China or from south-east Asia are nevertheless quintessentially English. Examples include **Spong** [dweller by the narrow strip of land], **Chin** [nickname for someone with a prominent chin, or known to be clean-shaven] and **Ching** [dweller by a *chine* or crevice]. G.W. Lasker and C.G.N. Mascie-Taylor make the further point that the surname **Lee** may be either English or Chinese in origin (*Atlas of British surnames* [1990]).

Genuinely Asian surnames like **Ng** or the even more minimalist Burmese name **U** or the Korean **O**, can be startling to an unprepared English listener, and it was fascinating recently to see that the director of the highly-acclaimed television series about the Normandy landings, *Band of Brothers*, was named Tony **To**.

Trenerry Edgar W,Glenview..........	**Perranporth**	21
Trengrouse Mrs. J,Trevenen.............	**Helston**	205
Trenoweth Valley Flower Farm Ltd....	**St. Keverne**	30
Trerise B,Frmr,Trenarth Barton.....	**Mawnan Smith**	48
Trerise J. C,Frmr,Trugo St. Columb........	**Fraddon**	22
Tresawna H,Lamellyn Probus.....	**Grampound Rd.**	41
Trescowe Call Office,PO..............	**Germoe**	9
Treseder & Co,Nurseries...................	**Truro**	26
Tresidder S. Lewis,Dntl Srgn,		
Lloyds Bank chmbs................	**Falmouth**	98
Tresidder W. J,Engr,The Island...........	**St. Ives**	131
Tresise & Son,Bldrs, Grcrs,Mylor bridge....	**Flushing**	33
Trespen Call Office......................	**Mitchell**	35
Tressider H. E,12 Lansdowne rd..........	**Falmouth**	288
Trethewey J. & Sons,Fish Mchts,East st...	**Newquay**	70
Trethewey L. R,Frtr,		
Tredinnick St Issey	**Rumford**	42
Trethewey's Garage......................	**Roche**	19
Trethowan C,Bldr,Hghr Brill..........	**Constantine**	17
Trethowan J,Cattle Dlr,Dudman...........	**Truro**	179
Trethowan J,Frmr,TregamennaVeryan Truro.	**Veryan**	23
Trevail C,City Monumental Wks,		
Boscawen bdge......................	**Truro**	462
Trevail C. T, J.P,		
Bodigo Luxulian Bodmin...........	**Stenalees**	76
Trevail J. H,Vlr,Higher Menadue Bugle...	**Stenalees**	74
Trevail W. & Son,Outftrs,95 Market Jew st	**Penzance**	539
Trevanion Private Hotel,Edgcumbe av....	**Newquay**	158
Trevarthen H. C,Hlr,Chestnut fm		
Ponsanooth Perranwell stn...	**Perran-Ar-Wrthl**	56
Trevaskis F,"Godolphin Arms,"		
Godolphin	**Germoe**	43
Trevaskis F,Grcr,PO...................	**St. Erth**	1
Trevaskis J,Tregilliowe Ludgvan........	**Cockwells**	21
Trevaskis J. H,Trescow.................	**Germoe**	89
Trevaskis Norman,Chyraise Milpool.......	**Germoe**	85
Trevaskis Stanley,		
Penhale Jakes Ashton nr Helston.....	**Germoe**	55
Trevaskis W,Haulage Contr,		
Hayle Causeway garage..............	**Hayle**	134
Trevaskis William,Frmr,		
Trenear Godolphin Breage.........	**Leedstown**	235
Treveighan Call Office...................	**St Tudy**	59
Trevellas Call Office,PO................	**St. Agnes**	012
Trevelmond Call Office.................	**Dobwalls**	14
Trevena S,Bldr,Contr,11 Bay View ter....	**Newquay**	517
Trevena W. S,Stanley vls...............	**Redruth**	87
Trevennen W.Frmr,		
Higher Colenso St. Hilary............	**Germoe**	75
Trevennen W,Frmr,Stable Hobba........	**Penzance**	441
Trevernue Tin Stream Co,Tuckingmill....	**Camborne**	157
Treverva Call Office,PO Penryn........	**Constantine**	29
Trevessa Hotel	**St. Ives**	43
Trevethan T,Btchr,Perranporth........	**Perranporth**	88
Treviscoe Call Office,PO................	**Nanpean**	22
Trevithick Alfred E,Nanjivey cottage.......	**St. Ives**	155

Cornwall, not Poland. A bygone age (1936) when it was possible to have a telephone number such as 'St.Erith 1'. The names here are unmistakably Cornish, though we might be forgiven for thinking that a surname such as *Trevaskis* sounds as if it would not be out of place in Eastern Europe.

Not Welsh or Irish

Names like **Richards**, **Edwards**, **Phillips**, **Hughes**, **Davis/Davies** (and even **Jones**), whilst they are commonly found in Wales, are not exclusively used in the Principality, and although it's usually safe to assume that a person called **Kelly** will have Irish ancestry, the surname can also be found in Scotland, where it is toponymic, and in England, where its origin is a place in Devon called *Kelly*.

Not 'foreign'

Some surnames which might sound oddly foreign or exotic to our ears – though we could hardly pin them down to a specific country or region overseas – turn out to be thoroughly British after all. Here are a few examples:

Docwra. I remember Dr Geoff Swinfield, a genealogist based in Kent, saying to me that he had once been asked to do some research on a family called **Docwra**, and thought of it as being an impossible kind of name until one day he found himself speeding past a van on the motorway with 'Docwra' printed on the side. It does indeed seem like a surname beyond human comprehension, but it has been happily borne by many people over the years, including Sir Thomas Docwra (died 1527), prior of the knights of St John at Clerkenwell, and William Dockwra or **Dockwray** (died 1716), who established a system of penny postage in London as early as 1680. **Dockray** is a more manageable alternative, and all surnames of this sort come from one of several places called *Dockray*, three of which, in Cumberland, are known to have been spelt *Docwra* or *Dokwra* in 13th century assize records. The origin of the name can also sometimes lie in the Irish **O'Dochraidh**.

Hakluyt is a another surname which looks for all the world like some foreign import, but is not. Famously the surname of the geographer Richard **Hakluyt** (?1552-1616), its origin is markedly unromantic: it means a lazy woodcutter, one who will *hack little* during a day's work.

Kekewich. Doesn't this sound vaguely foreign in a British context? Nothing of the sort: it's the surname of a family long settled in Cornwall and Devon, though it originates in *Kekwick*, Cheshire.

SCARCELY BELIEVABLE: OR, 'YOU CANNOT BE SERIOUS...'

There will always be some surnames which seem to defy belief. Every collector of unusual names will have a collection of oddities, and I'll content myself with listing just a small sample selection here.

- Private William **Tellogram** was awarded the Naval General Service Medal, having served at battles in Martinique (1809) and Guadaloupe (1810).

- Captain William **Chatterbox** of the Twenty-Seventh Foot regiment married Miss Gilman at Limerick in Ireland in November 1798.

- The poll tax returns for Tilney, Norfolk, in 1381 includes Marg' **Doredraught**.

- Mr Thomas Garrard of the parish of Clyffe Pypard, Wiltshire, married Katherine **Masculine** of Wootton Bassett at Clyffe Pypard on 1st June 1686. (Let's hope that Katherine wasn't *too* masculine ...)

- The parish registers of Kington St Michael, Wiltshire, include the following marriages, which look as if they might have benefited from the services of a computer spell-checker:

  Humphrey **Sturptup** and Frizey **Otridg**, 25th January 1723/4.
  Richard **Squce** and Eliner Poole, 24th June 1717.
  John **Bajsch**, weaver of Wilton, and Ann Horden, widow, 28th March 1768.

- The will of Isabella Morice of Ottryden, Kent, widow, proved on 20th June 1531, leaves a legacy of 20d to Ann **Pancak**.

- An entry in the parish register for Beby, Leicestershire, should give us pause for thought:

  1559, Aug 29. John and John **Sicke***, the children of Christopher and Anne* **Sicke***, were baptized. Item: 31 Aug. The same John and John were buried.*

We may assume that these were twins? Notice the habit, by no means unknown in earlier centuries, of giving two siblings the same Christian name.

- Amazing as it might seem, the well-known frozen food company *Birds Eye* took its name from the surname of its founder, Clarence (*Bob*) **Birdseye** (1886-1956) of Brooklyn, New York. Birdseye claimed that his unusual name (which was originally written as two words, not one) came from an English ancestor, a page in the Royal Court, who was nicknamed *Bird's Eye* by the Queen after having shot a diving hawk through the eye with an arrow (see Room, A., *Dictionary of trade name origins*, revised edition, 1982). Where *do* they get this kind of thing from? Not that anyone seems to be certain just where the name comes from, mind you, though early examples of its use may be found in Bedfordshire in particular. Bardsley says:

Clarence Birdseye: fact, not fiction. The well-known frozen food company *Birds Eye* was named after its founder, Clarence (Bob) *Birdseye* (1886-1956) of Brooklyn, New York. The surname probably has its origin in an English place-name.

Local, of Birdsey, I cannot find the place...But the meaning seems clear: the 'Birdseye', ie, the islet or eyot in the stream frequented by birds. Alternative spellings include **Birdsey, Budsey, Berdsay, Birdesey, Birdsaie** and **Birdsay(e)**.

CHAPTER 12

The Game of the Name

EPONYMS: SURNAMES REPAYING A DEBT

Every so often some word or other that has been part of the English language for a very long time is suddenly dragged kicking and screaming into the spotlight of public attention, and before you know where you are it's the flavour of the month or of the year.

The word *ubiquitous* had a brief spell in the number one spot a while ago, and so did *eponymous*; everyone, it seemed, was bursting to tell you that the character called *Oliver Twist* was the *eponymous* hero of the novel of that name by Charles Dickens. The use of the adjective *eponymous* causes few enough problems, but the related noun, *eponym*, is a bit odd, really. It sounds as if it ought to refer to a name, but in fact it refers to a person – someone who gives his or her name to a country, a geographical feature of the landscape, a city or town, a street, an institution, or almost anything else, whether it moves or is static.

We can think of this process as surnames repaying a debt to the language which gave rise to them in the first place; having taken something out, they are then in a position to put something back. A wood or a clearing called a *rod* in Old English gave rise to the surname borne by Cecil **Rhodes**, the African entrepreneur, and in due course his name was commemorated in the establishment of a country called *Rhodesia*; the street in which you live might commemorate a named person in a similar way, as might the school attended by your children, the park in which they play, the hospital where they were born, the library from which they borrow their books or the locomotive which pulls the train that takes you on holiday. The names of companies which manufacture the goods you buy in the shops may have become almost as familiar as the products themselves: you might like to eat cornflakes made by **Kelloggs** [from a pork butcher, one who *killed hogs*] or use a mouth-wash called *Listerine*, which was developed in the 1870s and named – against his will – after Sir Joseph Lister (1827-1921), the

Quaker surgeon who first made extensive use of antiseptics. **Lister** was an occupational name for a dyer. If you arrive home from the shops with a new **Kenwood** food mixer, it may not have struck you that the brand name was adopted by *Kenneth Wood*, who first began to manufacture electric mixers in Britain in the 1940s.

The eponymic process can be more complex than this, however. Nick Vine-Hall, an Australian genealogist with whom I regularly chat about such things, is a great collector of eponyms, and takes a particular interest in surnames which have returned to the language, not as the names given to roads, buildings or products, but as words in their own right. Nick might start off by talking about *wellington boots* or *sandwiches* – though we both know that the Duke of **Wellington** did not invent the boot named after him, and that the Romans were eating meat served between slices of bread long before the Earl of **Sandwich** ate similar snacks at the gaming tables and gave them his name. Nick is also fond of referring to Jean **Nicot**, after whom nicotine was named, or to the Earl of **Cardigan**, who no doubt liked to wear cardigans, or L. **Biro**, the Hungarian inventor after whom the *biro* was named, or Candido **Jacuzzi**, an Italian immigrant living in California, who developed a swirling water cure to make life more comfortable for his young son who was suffering from rheumatoid arthritis.

This has just scraped the eponymic surface. The truth is that it is not always possible to make a clear distinction between what we think of as a *name* and what we choose to call a *word*; names and words have been fraternising intimately with each other since time immemorial. *Caesarian* births owe their name to Julius **Caesar**, who entered the world in this way, the *saxophone* takes its name from Adolphe **Sax**, who invented it and introduced it into the French army bands during the 1840s, and J.B. **Stetson** [son of *Stedda* or *Stith*], who died in 1906, gave his name to the generous-sized hats which he made. Then there are words like *guillotine* [named after a French physician called **Guillotin**] or *silhouette* [Etienne **de Silhouette** was an author and politician]. Literary examples include the verse-form known as a *clerihew* [invented by E. *Clerihew* Bentley] or the *spoonerism*, an interchange of the initial letters of adjoining words said to have first been perpetrated on a regular basis by Rev W.A. **Spooner** [someone who made spoons, or who covered roofs with shingles], who is said (apocryphally?) to have upbraided a student in the following terms: *Sir, you have* **tasted** *two whole* **worms**, *you have* **hissed** *all my* **mystery** *lectures, you have been caught* **fighting** *a* **liar** *in the quad; you will leave Oxford by the next* **town drain**.

Certain names throughout history have become common currency, recognisable far and wide. The process here seems to work like this: if you achieve a degree of fame or infamy, your first name (or initials) and

A pair of plimsolls. The Huguenot surname of Samuel *Plimsoll* (1824-1898), formerly M.P. for Derby, has entered the language in two ways: the *Plimsoll Line* on ships is named after him, and in some parts of the country *plimsolls* is a word used to describe a pair of rubber-soled gym shoes.

your second name become well-known (*Amy **Johnson**, Dick **Turpin**, T.S. **Eliot**, J.K. **Rowley***); if you become more famous still, especially in the world of art, music literature, you are referred to by your last name alone (**Machiavelli, Shakespeare, Mozart, Picasso**); move on a stage further and your surname achieves the distinction of being used as an adjective (*Dickensian, Kafkaesque, Hitchcockian*). You'd need to belong to a very exclusive minority for your initials alone to be universally recognisable, as is the case with **JFK** (John Fitzgerald **Kennedy**), **GBS** (George Bernard **Shaw**) or **RLS** (Robert Louis **Stevenson** – though his full baptismal name was *Robert Lewis Balfour **Stevenson***). Our old friend Sir Arthur **Quiller-Couch**, however, must be one of the few people ever to have been referred to simply by the first letter of the first component of his double-barrelled surname: '**Q**'.

That being said, you might take the view that your surname has only really hit the big time when it enters the language neither as a noun, nor as an adjective, but as a verb. The name of the French chemist Louis **Pasteur** lives on in the verb *to pasteurize*, and it was an Austrian physician, F.A. **Mesmer**, who first perfected the art of *mesmerising* his patients. Captain W. **Lynch** [someone who lived on a hillside or in a place called *Lynch* or *Linch*; can also be an anglicization of more than one Irish name] of Virginia was once infamous for operating *Lynch's Law*, which gives us the modern verb *to lynch*. Then there is the verb *to tarmac*, which is derived indirectly from the surname of John Loudon **Macadam** [son of Adam] (1756-1836), who improved roads in England by making them of crushed stone. The Tarmacadam Company was formed in 1903. Captain C.C. **Boycott**, an Irish land agent, could little have thought that when he prompted an outraged reaction by tenants in the 1880s, his name would thereafter be perpetuated both as a noun and as a verb.

Then, of course, there is the famous case of an eponym which isn't an eponym at all. There is a long-standing story – what we might refer to nowadays as an *urban myth* – that it was the surname of Thomas **Crapper** (1836-1910) [a variation of **Cropper**, a person who cropped or reaped], a famous English sanitary engineer, which gave the English language its associated vulgarisms of *crap* (noun, faeces), *to crap* (verb, to defecate) and *crapper* (noun, referring to a person who craps, or the place where such crapping takes place).

This might sound oh-so-convincing, but, sad to relate, it's a myth which only has a modicum of truth about it. There was certainly a man called Thomas Crapper, son of Charles Crapper, a steamboat captain, and his wife Sarah, who was born in the Yorkshire hamlet of Waterside and was taken for baptism at the parish church of Thorne on 28 September 1836. When he was fourteen years of age, young Thomas was sent to London to be apprenticed to a plumber; before long he had his own business, and Crapper and Co. was eventually granted a number of Royal Warrants for the quality and reliability of its products. Following Thomas's death in 1910, the company which bore his name went through as many bad times as good, but in recent years the present owner, Simon Kirby, and his team have dedicated themselves to returning, Thomas Crapper & Co. now based in Stratford-on-Avon, to its former glory.

So much for the story of Thomas Crapper. Now we can lay to rest what remains of the Crapper myth. Firstly, Thomas Crapper, innovative as he was, never actually invented the water closet, though he had enough of them boldly on display at his showrooms in King's Road, Chelsea, to shock passers-by of a delicate disposition. Secondly, the word *crap* had been used in the English language for many centuries before Thomas Crapper was even a twinkle in his father's eye. *Crap*

The eponymous Mr Crapper. The pleasant-looking Yorkshire-born sanitary engineer Thomas Crapper (1836-1910), whose surname, a variation of *Cropper*, referred originally to a person who cropped or reaped. [Photograph courtesy of Simon Kirby of Thomas Crapper & Co., Stratford-on-Avon].

originally had a number of meanings, but the first known written use of the word as a singular or plural noun meaning *residues* (as of fat), or *dregs*, dates back to the late 15th century. It is possible that early settlers in America continued to make regular use of the word in this sense (or perhaps as a word for *rubbish* in general), while their English counterparts abandoned it in common parlance. The Americans, in any case, were playing a dice game known (from the 1840s onwards) as *craps*, and when American servicemen stationed in England during the First World War saw Thomas Crapper's name emblazoned on his cisterns and WC bowls, a broad smile crossed their faces – much to the bewilderment of their English contemporaries. The Americans promptly christened the WC itself *The Crapper* – and both American and British speakers have used *crap* as both a noun and as a verb ever since.

Thus the story goes, though elements of it are still hotly debated. We have, here, to accept a coincidence: Thomas Crapper was famous for his water closets, which are designed as receptacles for human effluent – yet Crapper's surname itself has a strong similarity to a word once used in English, and more commonly used in American English, to mean *rubbish* or *dregs*.

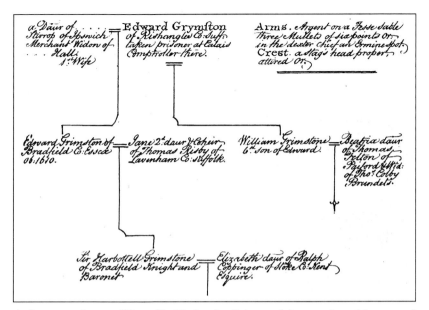

A forename in a million. Sir Harbottle Grimston(e) was given his unusual forename in honour of one of his great-grandfathers, John *Harbottle*. [From *Pedigrees of Essex families* by William Berry, 1838].

Many people named Crapper seem to have found little problem in sticking with this potentially-embarrassing surname, while others have abandoned it. At least bearers of the not-dissimilar surname of **Lillicrap**, chiefly found in Devon, have the option of choosing **Lillicrop** as an alternative – which seems reasonable enough, considering that the original meaning is *a man with a **crop** of very fair hair*.

SURNAMES USED AS FORENAMES

Another instance of a debt (or a compliment) being repaid, where the tide can be seen running in reverse, as it were, is when a surname becomes used as a forename, rather than *vice-versa*. During the reign of Elizabeth I, Edward **Grimston** of Bradfield, Essex, Member of Parliament for the Borough of Eye, married Jane or Joan **Risby**, whose maternal grandfather was named John **Harbottle**. Keen to perpetuate grandfather's surname, Edward and Jane/Joan promptly called one of their sons *Harbottle Grimston* – later to become *Sir Harbottle Grimston*, Knight and First Baronet.

This use of Harbottle as a forename was clearly a one-off

phenomenon which was specific to one family only, but other surnames, particularly those with illustrious associations such as **Cecil**, **Howard**, **Neville**, **Percy**, **Clifford**, **Douglas**, **Dudley**, **Graham**, **Keith**, **Leslie**, **Russell** and **Stanley**, were widely adopted as first-names across the social spectrum. In more recent times, the practice of using former surnames such as *Kyle*, *Kelly*, *Kimberley*, *Grant* and *Scott* as first-names has become associated with a certain socio-economic class, with the result that those of a more traditional frame of mind have generally given them a wide berth.

Shirley, which was originally a place-name, was then adopted as a surname and became by turns a first-name for boys and then for girls though the real name of the indisputably male Yorkshire wrestler *Big Daddy* is *Shirley Crabtree*. **Sidney**, taken from a minor place-name in Surrey, also made the move from surname to first-name; used mainly for males, it is also known to have been favoured as a girl's name on occasions, perhaps at times being confused with the female name *Sidony*. A short while ago a group of us paid a visit to Locko Park near Derby, long-time home of the **Drury-Lowe** family, and I couldn't help noticing that a pedigree chart on display included the marriage of John **Lowe** of Denby and Locko Park (1704-1771) to *Sydney* **Marriott** (d.1789), daughter and heir of Richard **Mariott** of Alscot, Bucks. My father's first name was *Sidney*, and he was never overly fond of it; maybe a lingering folk-memory associated it with the female of the species, rather than the male?

Further Reading

The subject of names in general and of surnames in particular has generated a vast amount of related literature, written in a wide variety of languages. The list which follows, it must be said, exhibits a wide variation in quality and reliability. Why, then, have I compiled a feature entitled *Further reading* which is something of a curate's egg, only good in parts? For two reasons: firstly, because some readers may enjoy the entertainment value of some of the lighter-weight titles featured here, even if some of the explanations they contain seem to be highly dubious. My second reason for spreading the net wide is that some of the more modest books listed here may contain a name, or a particular interpretation of a name, which may appear nowhere else in print; the information or the theory provided may be accurate, half-accurate or inaccurate, but it might at least spark off a line of investigation which may bear fruit in the long run.

Addison, Sir William. *Understanding English surnames.* 1978.
Anderson, W. *Genealogy and surnames.* 1865.
Ashley, L.R.N. *What's in a name?* 1989.
Bahlow, H. *Deutsches namenlexikon.* 1967.
Barber, H. *British family names.* 2nd edition, 1903.
Bardsley, A. *First Name variants.* 2nd edition, 1996.
Bardsley, C.W. *A dictionary of English and Welsh surnames.* Originally published in 1901. Reprinted several times since.
Bardsley, C.W. *English surnames, their sources and significations.* Originally published in 1873, reprinted 1969.
Bardsley, C.W. *Romance of the London Directory.* Originally published in 1879, reprinted 1971. Great fun – but not indexed.
Baring-Gould, S. *Family names and their story.* 1910.
Beider, A. *A dictionary of Jewish names from the Kingdom of Poland.* 1996.
Beider, A. *A dictionary of Jewish names from the Russian Empire.* 1993.
Bell, R. *The book of Ulster surnames.* 1988.
Black, G. F. *The surnames of Scotland.* Originally published in 1946. Reprinted several times since.
Bowditch, N.I. *Suffolk surnames.* 1857. (Suffolk, Massachusetts)
Bowman, W.D. *What is your surname?* 1932.
Brechenmacher, J.K. *Etymologisches worterbuch der Deutschen familiennamen.* 1994.

Charnock, R.S. *Ludus patronymicus; or, the etymology of curious surnames.* 1868.

Charnock, R.S. *Patronymica Cornu-Britannica.* Originally published in 1870, reprinted 2000.

Cole, J. and Titford, J. *Tracing your family tree: the comprehensive guide to discovering your family history.* 3rd edition, 2000.

Cottle, Basil. *The Penguin dictionary of surnames.* 1967 and later editions.

Currie, J. *Mull family names,* 1998.

Dauzat, A. *Dictionnaire étymologique des noms de famille et prénoms de France.* 1951.

Debrabandere, F. *Woordenboek van de familienamen in Belgie en Noord-Frankrijk.* Brussels, 1993. Revised edition planned for 2003.

Dolan, J.R. et al. *English ancestral names.* 1972. Deals in particular with occupational names.

Dorward, D. *Scottish surnames.* 1995.

Dunkling, L. *Dictionary of surnames.* 1998. The writer faithfully follows his own maxim that *a dictionary should be a collection of stories, each one briefly told and interesting in its own right.*

Dunkling, L. *The Guinness Book of Names* (1974).

Dyson, T. *Place names and surnames, their origin and meaning, with special reference to the West Riding of Yorkshire.* 1944.

Ewen, C.L'Estrange. *A guide to the origin of British surnames.* 1938.

Ewen, C.L'Estrange. *A history of surnames of the British Isles.* 1931.

Ferguson, R. *Surnames as a science.* 2nd edition, 1884.

Freeman, J.W. *Discovering surnames: their origins and meanings.* 2nd edition, 1973.

Fucilla, J.G. *Our Italian surnames.* 1949 (1998).

Gandhi, M. *The complete book of Muslim and Parsi names.* 1998.

Gourvil, F. *Noms de famille de Basse-Bretagne.* 1966. Simply an alphabetical listing, but useful for localising any given surname to this area of France.

Guppy, H.B. *The homes of family names in Great Britain.* 1890.

Hanks, P. and Hodges, F. *A dictionary of first names.* 1990.

Hanks, P. and Hodges, F. *A dictionary of surnames.* 1988. Includes many European and Jewish surnames as well as British ones.

Harrison, H. *Surnames of the United Kingdom: a concise etymological dictionary.* 1912-18, reprinted 1992.

Hoffman, W.F. *Polish surnames.* 2nd edition, 1998.

Hook, J.N. *Family names: how our surnames came to America.* 1982.

Hughes, J.P. *How you got your name.* Revised edition, 1961.

Hughes, J.P. *Is thy name Wart?* 1965.

Ingraham, E.D. *Singular surnames.* Philadelphia, USA. 1873.

Johnston, J.B. *The Scottish Macs: their derivation and origin.* 1922.

Jones, G.F. *German-American names*. 1990.

Kelly, A.C.M. *Names, names & more names: locating your Dutch ancestors in colonial America*. 1999.

Kelly, P. *Irish family names*. 1976.

Kneen, J.J. *The personal names of the Isle of Man*. 1937.

Lasker, G.W. and Mascie-Taylor, C.G.N. *Atlas of British surnames*. Wayne University Press, Detroit, for the Guild of One-Name Studies. 1990.

Linnartz, K. *Unsere familiennamen*. 1958.

Long, H. *Personal and family names*. 1883, reprinted 1968.

Lower, M.A. *English surnames: essays on family nomenclature*. First published in 1842.

Lower, M.A. *Patronymica Britannica*. 1860.

McKinley, R.A. *A history of British surnames*. 1990.

McLaughlin, Eve. *Surnames and their origins*. 1997. Contains, *inter alia*, some very enjoyable lists of names.

MacLysaght, E. *The surnames of Ireland*. 6th edition, 1985.

Matthews, C.M. *English surnames*. 1966.

Miller, G.M. *BBC pronouncing dictionary of British names*. 1971. Features family names and place-names.

Mills, Halford Lupton. *The family names of the Weald of Kent*. 1901.

Morgan, T.J. and P. *Welsh surnames*. 1985

Morlet, M-T. *Dictionnaire étymologique des noms de famille*. 1991.

[No author named]. *The Norman People and their existing descendants in the British Dominions and the United States of America*. 1874, reprinted 1975, 1989.

O'Murchadha, D. Family names of County Cork. 1985.

Orrye, B. *Dictionnaire des noms de famille du pays Creusois*. 1998. Surnames from this area of central France.

Payton, G. [revised by J. Paxton]. *The Penguin dictionary of proper names*. 1991.

Pine, L.G. *The story of surnames*. 1965.

Platt, L.D. *Hispanic surnames and family history*. 1996.

Quilliam, L. *Surnames of the Manks*. 1989.

Reaney, P.H. and R.M.Wilson. *A dictionary of English surnames*. 3rd edition, 1995.

Reaney, P.H. *The origin of English surnames*. 1967.

Redmonds, G. *Surnames and genealogy: a new approach*. 1997, new edition 2002.

Redmonds, G. *Yorkshire surnames series*. Part one: Bradford (1990); Part two: Huddersfield (1992).

Rogers, C.D. *The surname detective*. 1995.

Rogers. K.H. *Vikings and surnames*. 1991.

Room, A. *Dictionary of proper names*. 1994.

Room, A. *Dictionary of trade name origins*. Revised edition, 1982.

Room, A. *Naming names: a book of pseudonyms and name changes with a 'Who's who'*. 1981.

Rosenthal, E. *South African surnames*. 1965.

Rowlands, J. and S. *The surnames of Wales*. 1996.

Schimmel, A. *Islamic names*. 1995.

Seary, E.R. *Family names of the island of Newfoundland*. St John's, Newfoundland. 1977. A detailed and scholarly alphabetical listing, particularly strong on British surnames.

Smith, E.C. *American surnames*. 1969 (1986).

Smith, E.C. *New dictionary of American family names*. 1956, 1973.

Smith, E.C. *The story of our names*. 1950, reprinted 1970.

Swaen, A.E.H. *Nederlandse familienamen*. Zutphen. 1942.

Titford, D.G. *Moonrakers in my family*. 1995.

Titford, J.S. *Succeeding in family history: helpful hints and time-saving tips*. 2001.

Titford, J.S. *The Titford family 1547-1947*. 1989.

Titford, J.S. *Writing and publishing your family history*. 1996.

Unbegaun, B.O. *Russian surnames*. 1872.

Verstappen, P. *The book of surnames: origins and oddities of popular names*. 1980.

Weekley, E. *The romance of names*. 1914.

Weekley, E. *Surnames*, 1916.

Weekley, E. *Words and names*. 1932.

White, G.P. *A handbook of Cornish surnames*. 3rd edition, 1999.

Wilson, S. *The means of naming*. 1998.

Woulfe, Rev P. *Irish names and surnames*. 1923. Reprinted several times.

Various scholarly volumes in the *English surnames series*, the result of work carried out as part of the English Surnames Survey at the University of Leicester, were published in the period 1973-1998. The counties covered are: *Yorkshire, West Riding; Norfolk and Suffolk (Middle Ages); Oxfordshire; Lancashire; Sussex; Devon; Leicestershire and Rutland.*

Not all printed literature on surname studies has appeared in book-form. Material on Scottish surnames compiled by Alasdair Steven has appeared in *The Scotsman*, complementing the published work by G. F. Black, and the Society for Name Studies in Britain and Ireland, which concerns itself with the study of place-name, personal names and surnames, has published its prestigious journal, *Nomina*, since 1977.

Index

Surnames

*Look also at alphabetical
lists on pages 75-9
(occupational surnames)
and 210-32 ('Not as daft...').
Names will also be found in
the appropriate chapter - eg
Hill under Topographical
surnames; Knight under
names from 'Official
status'.*